For the Good of the Church

Unity, Theology and Women

Gabrielle Thomas

scm press

© Gabrielle Thomas 2021

Published in 2021 by SCM Press
Editorial office
3rd Floor, Invicta House,
108–114 Golden Lane,
London EC1Y 0TG, UK
www.scmpress.co.uk

SCM Press is an imprint of Hymns Ancient & Modern Ltd
(a registered charity)

Hymns Ancient & Modern® is a registered trademark of
Hymns Ancient & Modern Ltd
13A Hellesdon Park Road, Norwich,
Norfolk NR6 5DR, UK

British Library Cataloguing in Publication data

A catalogue record for this book is available
from the British Library

978 0 334 06060 4

Typeset by Regent Typesetting
Printed and bound by
CPI Group (UK) Ltd

Contents

Acknowledgements

Because of confidentiality agreements I cannot name the women who participated in the research, but you know who you are. I enjoyed every minute of journeying with you all and I am thankful for your willingness to share personal thoughts and experiences. Each and every one of you is a gift to the Church. This book emerged from post-doctoral work at the Centre for Catholic Studies in the Department of Theology and Religion, Durham University, UK. As an Anglican, I treasured the experience of working closely with my colleagues in the Centre for Catholic Studies: Paul Murray, Greg Ryan, Carmody Grey, Anna Rowlands, Gerard Loughlin and Rik Van Nieuwenhove contributed to this research and to my faith and academic formation. Karen Kilby deserves a special mention. During our numerous conversations, she could not have done more to sharpen and develop my thinking with respect to this research and to my work on historical theology. I benefited from many conversation partners in Durham, especially Simon Oliver, Lewis Ayres, Mike Higton, Mathew Guest, Walter Moberly, Alec Ryrie and Pete Ward. I was also blessed by sharing in the life of Durham Cathedral, where I flourished alongside friends and colleagues, both lay and ordained. I owe a special 'thank you' to the Cathedral vergers: Jeffrey, Neil, Brian, Trevor, Rebekah and John. This wonderful team made sure that one way or another I always ended up in the right place, even in the most complex processions.

After a transatlantic move the book was completed at Yale University, Connecticut, where my students and colleagues have continued to shape my work. A special thanks goes to Rona Johnston Gordon, Chloe Starr, Melanie Ross and Laura

Nasrallah for encouraging me to keep writing while adjusting to teaching new courses.

I am also thankful for insightful cheerleaders, some of whom also commented on draft chapters: Jenny Leith, Julie Gittoes, Sanjee Perera, Jo Cundy, Avril Baigent, Mary Cunningham, Theresa Philips, Andrea Murray, Alex Williams, Clare Watkins, Al Barrett, Liz Clutterbuck, Anna Alls, Rebecca Ogus, Clive Marsh, Nick Adams and Natalie Collins. I am also thankful for all those involved in the editorial process: Terry J. Wright, Linda Carroll, Rachel Geddes and David Shervington. Each responded generously to my various requests and gave excellent advice. And, a huge thank you to Ally Barrett for designing the illustration on the cover of the book.

My family employs endless patience with respect to my work – my sister and father underwent many calls in which we discussed nothing other than this book. Added to this, they read and commented on drafts. My mother died long before I began this project; nevertheless, she has contributed to it by raising me to believe that the Spirit calls women to participate in the work of the church in all kinds of ways. My husband, Matthew, yet again has journeyed with me through research on a subject that is so very different from his own work. I dare say he knows far more than any man really needs to know about women's experiences of working in churches! I am thankful.

Lastly, Jacqueline Stuyt left a generous legacy which found its way to the Centre for Catholic Studies via the National Board of Catholic Women and contributed to funding the first two years of research. I did not have the privilege of meeting Mrs Stuyt before she died, but many people have told me how she loved to see women flourish. I hope that this book goes some way to honouring her and the members of the National Board of Catholic Women. I spent many happy hours praying, eating, chatting, and laughing with these women, while testing ideas and receiving candid feedback. I am especially thankful for Janet Ward, Freda Lambert, Janet Wiltshire, Cathy Wattebot, Siobhan Canham, Sister Brigid Collins, Jane Lavery, Helen Mayles, Janet Evers, Mary McHugh, and Patricia Stoat. These generous women are dedicated to the good of the church and in turn I dedicate this book to them.

Introduction

During the early phase of Covid-19, presidents of Churches Together in England called for a National Day of Prayer and Action on Sunday 22 March 2020. This was timely amid the confusion and uncertainty, resulting in tens of thousands of Christians lighting a candle in the windows of their homes as a visible symbol of the light of life, Jesus Christ, 'the source and hope in prayer'. To support their call to prayer, the presidents representing Pentecostal, Catholic, Anglican, Coptic Orthodox and the Free churches released a series of videos with a unified message, apposite for an ecumenical collaboration: 'to keep praying prayers of hope, because prayer makes a difference'.[1] I watched these exhortations, encouraged to see a group of church leaders, ethnically and denominationally diverse, gathering together to highlight the central place of prayer in the pandemic. And yet these videos conveyed a further, implicit message: ecumenical leadership and exhortation to prayer is the work of men.

For the Good of the Church tells a different story, one that shines a spotlight on the ecumenical practice of women who work in diverse traditions across England, and whose commitment to Christian unity has led them to pray and work for the good of the church, often behind the scenes. Despite being from radically different backgrounds and contexts and possessing distinct approaches to ecclesiology, the women share a common passion: the church. Having drawn women together from churches as ecumenically diverse as those mentioned above, the book explores themes arising from their exchanges, bringing these into conversation with theologians who span centuries, and who represent diverse theological approaches and methods, such as Thomas Aquinas, Luke Bretherton, Elaine Crawford, Gregory of Nazianzus, Mercy Amba Oduyoye, Letty Russell and John Wesley. At first glance, these theologians may appear to have little in common, but in doing theology at different times and from within distinctive traditions, each aims to contribute to the good of the church. Through engaging with their work, my hope is that this book will foster Christian unity and ecumenical imagination.

The women's exchanges took place during research that draws on receptive ecumenism to explore women's experiences of working in churches in England. Simply put, receptive ecumenism asks: 'What do we need to learn from another Christian tradition to help us address some of the difficulties in our own?' One way of thinking about this would be to imagine an English afternoon tea.[2] This tradition involves the hosts bringing out the finest bone china covered with delicate sandwiches, scones and a selection of sweet delights. On these occasions, the convention is to use only the very best china and crockery, preferably a matching set. If the host owns broken or chipped cups, then these must be kept hidden at the back of a cupboard, well out of the sight of any guests.

Sometimes when churches come together ecumenically, it can be a little like an English afternoon tea in which we share only the best of ourselves. We do very well at hosting the tea party and at admiring our own bright and shiny crockery. We are so often ready to share our gifts with other churches and to explain to them how to 'do church properly' (if only everyone else could be like us!). Meanwhile, we keep hidden any aspects of church life that are not fully functioning. Just like those old, chipped cups in the back of the cupboard, when we meet together ecumenically our dysfunctions and sins are kept firmly out of sight. Doubtless, every church has within its possession a cupboard with some old, chipped crockery hidden at the back which would benefit from being sifted through. In light of this, receptive ecumenism calls for churches to change their typical way of engaging, since churches are invited to lay out broken and chipped crockery for the other(s) to examine. With its brokenness in sight, one tradition asks another whether God has given to them any gifts that could help heal the brokenness. In this instance, brokenness refers to those aspects of our traditions where destructive practices or dysfunctions are at work. Anyone who has participated in receptive ecumenism will be aware that it is demanding, since it asks for honesty, integrity and humility from those involved.

Why use receptive ecumenism to explore women's experiences of working in churches in England? Since this ecumenical practice has been formalized by men, is it not simply the case that, as Grace Jantzen observes, 'in order to speak, women must use men's language, play by men's rules, find themselves in a foreign country with an alien tongue'?[3] Through the course of this book, I hope to persuade readers not only that there are good reasons for women to practise receptive ecumenism, but that women's participation contributes constructively to this form of ecumenical engagement.[4] Women have been working ecumenically for decades, most often at grass roots, and have much experience and insight to contribute. Their involvement in formal ecumenism is not immediately obvious, since men do much of the public ecumenical work in England. This applies to ecumenical dialogues also. For example, among the 29 participants of the current Anglican–Roman Catholic International Commission (ARCIC), only four are women, and even fewer participate in the Anglican–Oriental Orthodox International Commission (AOOIC).[5] There can be no doubt that formal ecumenical conversations are poorer for lack of engagement with women's voices.

Returning to the question, 'Why would we use receptive ecumenism to explore women's experiences of working in churches?', with its focus on both healing wounds and receiving gifts, receptive ecumenism creates a space for women's voices to be heard, which is not only for the good of women but for the good of the church. A further response to the question comes from one of the youngest participants in the research, an Anglican in her twenties who works in a lay role in the Church of England. During her feedback, she described her experience of practising receptive ecumenism for the first time with an ecumenical group of women who work in churches:[6]

Receptive ecumenism transforms ecumenism. I believe that talking to and learning from each other is vital, particularly within the various Christian churches. The most surprising thing I learnt from participating in this research was that the issues which women face within my church are almost exactly the same as faced by women in other churches and, I suspect, will be very similar to the experiences of women within other faiths as well. To me this suggests that the issues women face within faith organizations are not to do with one particular organization but to do with how faith groups view women in general. This is important because it highlights once again how far behind society at large (at least in this country) faith groups are, particularly in the matter of equality and viewing all individuals as valuable. As a result, I think others would value this experience because it allows people to see that the problems they face within their own church are not unique to them; they are part of a far wider issue. By listening to and learning from one another, we have a hope of beginning to address these wider problems.

The sentiment of this woman's comment reverberates throughout the book. As much as we are accustomed to thinking that the 'grass is greener on the other side', no tradition is without its challenges. Similarly, each tradition has particular gifts to share with its ecumenical partners.

A note on reading the book

While the book draws on comments and insights from women, it is not written with only women in mind. Rather, it is for those who are committed to the unity of Christ's church and who want to reflect on new ways in which diverse traditions might engage positively with one another's differences, along with a range of theological interlocutors.

The book is divided into two parts in order to help readers locate with relative ease the aspects of the research in which they are most interested. Part 1 discusses the design, implementation and findings of the research, bringing to the fore the participants' voices. The first chapter begins by asking, 'What is receptive ecumenism?' I examine its inception and evolution, locating receptive ecumenism in the broader ecumenical movement, after which I analyse constructively the philosophical and biblical beliefs woven throughout. To depict this ecumenical practice, one might imagine a scenic route rather than a motorway, and just like any long journey those who choose to take the scenic route need to exercise patience and tenacity. For this reason, the chapter concludes by probing the virtues necessary for receptive ecumenism to flourish, establishing that this is a formational process as well as a path towards Christian unity. Readers might want to return to this chapter to think through in greater depth some of the related ecclesiological questions.

Chapter 2 outlines how I designed research that draws on receptive ecumenism to explore women's experiences of working in churches in England. I do not apply 'women' as a universal category of experience, but throughout the book I treat each person's experiences and views as unique while highlighting some experiences that are commonly identified, such as sexism. All too often, we do not speak the same language even in our own churches, but this can become even more complicated when we work across diverse traditions. In light of this, important questions arise, such as how to understand 'work' and 'church', whose voices are present and absent, and how the various 'groups' within the church communicate with one another. The chapter concludes with feedback from the participants, through which it becomes evident that receptive ecumenism can be used to create a space for candid conversation in which people feel able to share difficult experiences safely in addition to providing a new way of walking towards Christian unity.

The following chapter reports on the women's experiences arising through focus groups and research conversations. My aim in this chapter is to create a space for the reader to hear the women's voices themselves. I ask questions such as: What, if any, are the differences between the churches with respect to women's experiences? What can women who are based in radically different traditions learn from one another? Since women make up roughly 65 per cent of churches in England, we might expect to hear of women performing all kinds of roles and using their gifts and skills in a variety of ways, but is this always the case? Since receptive ecumenism encourages churches to be honest about their wounds, sins and dysfunctions, the chapter interrogates the most prevalent difficulties pertinent to the women's experiences of working in churches. These include systemic sexism and sexual harassment, singleness, motherhood and being women of colour. Womanist theologians have critiqued the supposed universality of 'women's experience', demonstrating how women of colour have been, and often still are, subsumed into white women's experience. This chapter will observe how the participants of colour testified to additional difficulties not only because they are women, but also because they are persons of colour. I close with recommendations from the women with respect to how the churches in England might attend to women's voices and move towards greater ecclesial unity.

Interrelated themes arise from the women's conversations: hospitality, vocation, leadership and power. These form the structure of Part 2, in which I draw on receptive ecumenism to construct four case studies, each engaging theologically with these core themes. As such, Part 2 stands apart from Part 1, and some readers might prefer to dive straight into this, returning later to the context from which these studies emerged. The chapters in Part 2 vary in focus and approach, bringing into conversation theologians who have written at different times and with different methods for the good of the church. Receptive ecumenism itself is not a prescriptive method; therefore, rather than constructing case studies that present the definitive approach to reflecting theologically with receptive ecumenism, I aim to engage creatively with the hope of sparking the imagination of the reader.

I close this section with a comment on my decision not to capitalize 'church' when speaking of the one church of Christ – I will return to this point in the following chapter. While I recognize that many authors choose to capitalize 'church' both for theological reasons and for clarity in any given text, two motivations lie behind my decision not to make this move. First, as I hope this book will demonstrate, my preference is not to capitalize 'church' to avoid the risk of hypostatizing it into a notion of a transcendent, pre-existent 'Church'; the kind of model that various contemporary ecclesiologists have challenged. I hope to bring into focus the messy reality of church, and the kind of church with which most readers will be familiar and to which many of us are firmly committed. Second, this book is an ecumenical endeavour and I recognize that not every Christian tradition capitalizes 'Church' when speaking of the whole church. For example, Catholic presses such as Liturgical Press specify that 'church' should not be capitalized when referring to 'the whole body of Christians, worldwide or throughout time'. I support this guidance and follow it throughout this book.

A note on the author

Before these pages became a book, extracts and chapters existed as conference papers; this is evident through the endnotes, which include my thanks to the many insightful people who have offered constructive feedback. The final chapter explores uses and abuses of power, and when I spoke to a group of academic theologians about this, one reflected back to me that she is always 'suspicious of people who work on power because they rarely recognize it in themselves'. This point relates to Elaine Graham's article on 'Power, Knowledge and Authority in Public Theology', in which she explores the power of the one who shapes theological discourse.[7] Graham calls on those involved in public theology to ask questions about 'whose voices, whose perspectives are incorporated into theology and by implication, whose voices and experiences are absent'.[8] In light of this, I want to attend to the particularity of my own context and perspective. For example, I am white. I have a good education and some letters that I can include in front of my name. I am ordained, and at the time of writing I work at a prestigious university in the United States. While far from being the most powerful person in the church or the academy, the list of privilege is extensive nonetheless. My aim is to shape the theological discourse of this book in the hope that it creates a greater space for women's voices to be heard in the ecumenical forum, as well as in their own traditions. I make this move, recognizing (a) the limits of my contribution, and (b) that this is only one conversation of the many in which theologians need to engage. With respect to this contribution, I hope that the stories and case studies in the book encourage readers to appreciate more fully the role women play as a vital stepping stone to a more flourishing ecumenical conversation, as well as inspiring creative ecumenical practice.

Notes

1 Churches Together in England, '"We Need to Keep on Praying: Prayer Makes a Difference" – Message from CTE Presidents', *Churches Together in England*, www.cte.org.uk/Articles/576014/Home/Corona virus/We_need_to.aspx.

2 This tradition dates back to the nineteenth century in England, although in India and China tea drinking began hundreds of years earlier. The metaphor of 'afternoon tea' expands on Paul D. Murray's description of receptive ecumenism in 'Introducing Receptive Ecumenism', *The Ecumenist* 51.2 (2014), pp. 1–7 (pp. 4–5). For Paul D. Murray's profile in the Department of Theology and Religion, see www.dur.ac.uk/theology.religion/staff/profile/?id=2007.

3 Grace M. Jantzen, *Becoming Divine: Towards a Feminist Philosophy of Religion* (Manchester: University of Manchester Press, 1998), p. 42.

4 Since women contribute to merely two of the 32 chapters of the foundational book on receptive ecumenism – Paul D. Murray (ed.), *Receptive Ecumenism and the Call to Catholic Learning: Exploring a Way for Contemporary Ecumenism* (Oxford: Oxford University Press, 2008) – my book aims to bring their contributions to the fore.

5 Receptive ecumenism was the chosen way of engagement for ARCIC: www.anglicancommunion.org/ecumenism/ecumenical-dialogues.aspx.

6 In the following chapters, I will outline how I use 'church' and 'work'.

7 Elaine Graham, 'Power, Knowledge and Authority in Public Theology', *International Journal of Public Theology* 1 (2007), pp. 42–62 (p. 44).

8 Graham, 'Power', p. 44.

PART I

I

What is Receptive Ecumenism?

At the heart of receptive ecumenism lies the belief that each Christian tradition has an ecumenical responsibility to ask: 'What do we need to learn from another tradition to help us address difficulties in our own?'[1] Ecclesial unity is a core concern of receptive ecumenism and therefore it focuses on the Christian faith, taking seriously the broken witness that the Christian churches 'give to the world by not being able to live consistently in full and visible structural, sacramental, and ministerial communion'.[2] Diverging from but not replacing other forms of ecumenism, receptive ecumenism begins by calling for ecclesial conversion akin to a prophet in the wilderness who cries out to the people of God, 'Repent.'[3] This chapter locates receptive ecumenism within the broader ecumenical movement before surveying the web of philosophical and biblical imagination woven through this way of ecumenical engagement. The receptive journey calls for long-term commitment and is not a quick fix to the challenges of ecclesial unity; therefore the chapter closes by asking, 'How important are virtues to receptive ecumenism?'

The Introduction described an English afternoon tea as a means of capturing the heart of receptive ecumenism. A further image is one of a church holding out its hands to receive a gift from another, hands that bear wounds. These wounds, weaknesses or sins may take a number of forms. They might be found in theological-doctrinal webs and the ways in which these are complicit in broken ways of being church. The webs will need scrutinizing and reconfiguring for the reception of desired learning. Added to this, churches might be struggling with aspects of organization, leadership, culture, or mission and evangelism.[4] Following the way of receptive ecumenism, a church will need to examine itself and ask the Holy Spirit to shine a light on the wounds, sins or dysfunctions within its doctrines and practices. Having done this, and recognizing that it is not yet imaging Christ as fully as it might, each church is called to repent and reach out to others for healing gifts.[5]

To engage in receptive ecumenism is to encourage churches to pause and to be honest with themselves. It creates the space to admit that our churches do not function perfectly; rather, there are wounds and difficulties in each of our traditions that await the Spirit's transformation. This takes courage. Churches engaging together in receptive ecumenism respond to the call to become transformed through ecclesial encounter, rather than expecting to be transformed before any ecclesial encounter takes place. In light of this, churches do not focus on their differences from one another, nor do they seek to find areas on which they can agree. Instead, each one examines itself and asks what it might learn and receive with integrity from the other traditions.[6] Integrity is crucial, since receptive ecumenism does not advocate the destruction of traditions. Each tradition should be more wholly itself or, put another way, each church should image Christ more fully.[7]

In an essay on 'Receiving Gifts in Ecumenical Dialogue', Margaret O'Gara offers a pertinent metaphor with respect to retaining the integrity of diverse traditions. She suggests that rather than imagining ecumenism as a melting pot of gifts, which seeks to eliminate all differences (and therefore potential gifts), instead a mosaic is an apposite image of ecumenical gift exchange.[8] A mosaic creates the space for different patterns and colours to come together; not at random, but in such a way as to create a vision of diversity in which each contribution is valued for its role in the overall picture. While O'Gara is speaking of ecumenical dialogue and not receptive ecumenism, this image fits well the aim of receptive ecumenism in which the integrity of each tradition is celebrated.

The image of a mosaic evokes a particular view of ecclesiology that lends itself to receptive ecumenism. This relates to Nicholas Healy's critique of 'blueprint' approaches to ecclesiology on the grounds that a blueprint ecclesiology offers an abstract and theoretical view of the church, which I will discuss later in the chapter.[9] To attempt an all-encompassing definition of the church would be foolhardy, since each church differs radically concerning sacraments, worship, and many other matters. Ecclesiologist Dan Hardy characterizes the church as 'a practice of commonality in faith and mission' on the grounds that 'the Church was not first an idea or a doctrine'.[10] He argues, quite rightly, that the church exists within history and within the story of God's ways with the world; it cannot be abstracted from the 'varying social embodiments of Christian life in the world'.[11] When I refer to the whole Christian church, I assume that this comprises 'churches', such as the Catholic Church,[12] Anglican churches, Pentecostal churches, etc., as well as local churches and congregations. Since the churches and denominations discussed throughout the book vary in their own self-understanding, I have followed as much as possible the descriptions that the churches and denominations apply to themselves.[13]

The broader ecumenical movement

As we turn to locate receptive ecumenism within the broader ecumenical movement, it is important to note that it does not aim to replace other forms of ecumenical engagement; rather, it contributes to the variety of ways that churches seek transformation and unity.

Receptive ecumenism joins an ecumenical movement on a rocky path towards Christian unity.[14] Since the formation of early Christian communities, groups and individuals have disputed Christian doctrine and practice. Mutual excommunication of churches began early in the history of the church, taking most effect in 1054 when the heads of the churches of Constantinople and Rome split from one another. Moving forward some 500 years, the splits were not confined to East and West but occurred within the Western churches also. One of the results of the Protestant Reformation was that ecclesial communities broke communion with one another; for example, the Lutheran and Reformed (Calvinist) churches of Germany and France, and the Church in England.[15]

A notable shift in the ecumenical landscape began with a series of movements focused upon world mission. It is commonly recognized that the Third Ecumenical Missionary Conference, convened in Edinburgh in 1910, played a prominent role in 'the initial shaping and endorsing of modern ecumenism'.[16] Important movements followed, known as Life and Work, and Faith and Order. Life and Work arises from an emphasis on churches working together, crossing ecumenical divides in order to focus on social justice by running winter shelters, foodbanks and gatherings for prayer.[17] Rather than focusing on the differences between faith traditions, this movement centres on the practical outworking of the gospel, taking its lead from the theme prevalent throughout Scripture, stated in the letter of James 2.14–17:

> What good is it, my brothers and sisters, if you say you have faith but do not have works? Can faith save you? If a brother or sister is naked and lacks daily food, and one of you says to them, 'Go in peace; keep warm and eat your fill,' and yet you do not supply their bodily needs, what is the good of that? So faith by itself, if it has no works, is dead.[18]

Along with the world missionary movement, Life and Work and Faith and Order are at the heart of the World Council of Churches, which began its journey in 1937 and 1938. Faith and Order has tended to focus on discussing issues that have divided churches historically, such as eucharistic sacrifice, *sola fide* and church structures.[19] The World Council of Churches Faith and Order Commission encourages churches to 'reflect on how they understand and claim their own ecclesial identity and how they regard the ecclesial status of other churches and other Christians'.[20] The aim of this kind of engagement is to find common ground on areas of doctrine, structure and practice. Great progress has been made with regards to churches growing in their understanding of one another; nevertheless, one weakness prevails. Due to the formal nature of this kind of ecumenism, Faith and Order involves necessarily those church members in positions of significant authority within their churches. The result of this is that the representation of minority groups in Christian leadership (for example, women) is low.

Ecumenical relations continued to flourish with the momentum of Second Vatican Council (1962–5). A strong theme emerges from Vatican II which paves the way for receptive ecumenism: God does not restrict God's gifts to one church or to a particular cluster of churches. Instead, God has given gifts across the diversity of the Christian tradition. Moreover, these gifts are of value to the whole Christian church and should not remain hidden within each tradition or denomination. In 1964, Pope Paul VI promulgated *Lumen Gentium* ('Light of the Nations') which states that 'gifts belonging to the church of Christ are forces impelling toward catholic unity'.[21] Put another way, the gifts that are spread across the churches each have a contribution to make towards Christian unity. This theme appears again in *Unitatis redintegratio* (Vatican II's Decree on Ecumenism) which speaks of the Spirit of Christ using the gifts given to the churches by God as means of salvation.[22] Two decades later in his encyclical *Ut Unum Sint* ('That They May be One: On Commitment to Ecumenism'), John Paul II speaks of ecumenical dialogue as an 'exchange of gifts'.[23] 'Exchange' is significant here, since the Pope does not believe that the Catholic Church is the only church to which God gives gifts. Likewise, in *Evangelii Gaudium* ('The Joy of the Gospel'), Pope Francis writes:

> If we really believe in the abundantly free working of the Holy Spirit, we can learn so much from one another! It is not just about being better informed about others, but rather about reaping what the Spirit has sown in them, which is also meant to be a gift for us.[24]

The effect of Vatican II upon ecumenism cannot be underestimated. In 1965, a momentous event occurred when Pope

Paul VI and Patriarch Athenagoras agreed to lift the excommunications that were in place. Although East and West are not yet in full eucharistic unity with one another, the Eastern Orthodox churches, for example, are now 'sister churches' to those in the West, whereas previously their discipleship went unrecognized.

Since the 1960s, dialogues across a plethora of denominations have taken place, both bilateral and multilateral. The Porvoo Declaration (1995) was signed by Anglican Churches in Britain and Ireland and the Lutheran Churches in the Nordic and Baltic countries of Europe. They agreed to interchangeable ministries and full eucharistic communion; at the time this was groundbreaking. According to the Porvoo Declaration,

> the signatory Churches regard baptized members of each other's Churches as members of their own; welcome overseas congregations into the life of the receiving Churches; welcome those who are ordained as bishops, pastors and deacons in any of the 10 Churches, to minister in accordance with the receiving Church's regulations; and consult on significant matters of faith and order, life and work.[25]

Why, then, in light of these productive dialogues, and against the backdrop of the ecumenical energy directed towards Life and Work, have ecumenists declared the mid-late twentieth century an 'ecumenical winter'?[26] In part, this is because Life and Work does not resolve the problem of sacramental unity, although shared work is important and moves churches towards greater understanding and friendship. This observation is not intended to undermine the importance of social justice, nor to devalue the work in which churches engage together in order to seek the common good; rather, I aim to highlight a further underlying tension that Life and Work does not resolve. Likewise, the Faith and Order dialogues take the churches towards unity only partially, since it is increasingly difficult to find common ground. Speaking about the place of receptive ecumenism alongside Life and Work and Faith and Order, the lay Catholic theologian Paul D. Murray puts it like this:

Going beyond all this, we also need grace-filled repentance met by grace-filled conversion: repentance of the deep sin of division into which God has given us up; repentance of our own tradition's complicity in this divided state of the church; repentance of our blindness to the dreadful significance of these divisions; and repentance too of our blindness to the particular character of our own tradition's sinful complicity in them.[27]

Murray developed receptive ecumenism as a means of continuing to inspire ecumenical imagination and to breathe life into the ecumenical status quo. Along with colleagues, he organized popular conferences dedicated to exploring and interrogating this fresh way of ecumenical engagement. Initially, the conferences were held in Durham, UK (2006, 2009), the first of which was devoted to Catholic learning, with the second focusing on ecclesial learning more broadly. These conferences received significant attention, leading to further gatherings in Fairfield, Connecticut, USA (2014), and Canberra, Australia (2017).[28] The international conferences probed receptive ecumenism, asking pertinent questions about practice and discernment. The most recent conference on receptive ecumenism was planned for June 2020 in Sigtuna, Sweden, until the disruption of Covid-19 led to its postponement. When it takes place, this conference will explore possibilities and implications for Scandinavian churches, also asking the important question, 'How are the Pentecostal churches receiving receptive ecumenism?' I shall turn to this question shortly.

The conferences in Durham were followed by a five-year collaborative research project between churches in the North East of England and Durham University. One aim of the research was to test the integrity of receptive ecumenism and engage it in such a way as to bring theory and practice into conversation with one another. The denominations taking part consisted of the United Reformed Church (Northern Synod); the Salvation Army (Northern Division); the Roman Catholic Diocese of Hexham and Newcastle; the Northern Baptist Association; the Methodist District of Newcastle; the

Methodist District of Darlington; the Anglican Diocese of Newcastle; and the Anglican Diocese of Durham. The churches worked in partnership with the staff of Durham University's Department of Theology and Religion, Durham University's Business School, and the former North of England Institute for Christian Education. The aim was that the churches should explore together and learn from one another in three areas, namely, Governance and Finance, Leadership and Ministry, and Learning and Formation.[29] The reports from this research are available on the Durham University website; they demonstrate that receptive ecumenism can be fruitful but demands tenacity, since the process of engaging receptively takes time.

Receptive ecumenism has moved beyond its initial home in Durham through its adoption by the third main phase of the Anglican–Roman Catholic International Commission (ARCIC III). ARCIC III's first 'Agreed Statement', *Walking Together on the Way*, demonstrates a shift in methodology for formal bilateral dialogues.[30] Rather than either exploring areas of commonality or seeking to resolve apparent differences, the document shows that it can be fruitful to consider how one tradition is different from the other, and how these differences can bring helpful challenges to each tradition, particularly with respect to difficulties being faced.

Part of the appeal of receptive ecumenism is that participation is possible in a variety of contexts, spanning from ARCIC, which includes academic theologians, through to practitioners, churches and congregations working at grass roots. Churches Together in England and the South Australian Council of Churches have each produced accessible pamphlets with ideas for practising receptive ecumenism in their respective contexts.[31] The documents were designed for Christians who want to come together ecumenically and engage in fresh ways with a view to learning and receiving from one another.

Sara Gehlin, a Swedish ecumenist, writes on a further example of receptive ecumenism in practice.[32] She and colleague Sven-Erik Fjellström led an ecumenical project initiated by the Workgroup for Mission Theology at the Christian Council of Sweden and the Swedish Mission Council. The project engaged members from the Orthodox, Catholic, Lutheran and Free Church families. The research took the form of a pilgrimage to the respective churches, with a view to learning from one another how each church approaches mission. The participants of this journey presented a workshop together at the Fourth International Conference on Receptive Ecumenism, held in Canberra, 2017.[33] Listening to them, it was clear to me that the participants had indeed deepened their understanding of one another's traditions which in turn increased trust and friendship, paving the way for collaboration in the future, as well as learning about how to shape their approaches to mission. Their presentation demonstrated that despite receptive ecumenism being grounded in a complex web of philosophical thought, it is possible to grasp and engage with it imaginatively. Added to this, the creativity and flexibility of receptive ecumenism means that it can be used to serve a number of aims, from ecclesial unity through to understanding one another's traditions more accurately.

Receptive ecumenism, like Faith and Order, has tended to attract traditional churches. In April 2018, I was invited to speak about receptive ecumenism at the gathering of the Global Christian Forum held in Bogotá, Colombia, where it was received with interest.[34] The Global Christian Forum gatherings provide a space for traditional and newly forming churches to learn from one another while developing relationships between Christian churches and traditions that have not been in conversation with one another previously. This movement of representatives from diverse Christian churches, organizations and traditions, who meet on an equal basis, aims to foster mutual respect and to address common challenges together. Since Christianity is growing in the majority world, the newer churches have notably different gifts to share, and those of us based in locations such as the UK have a great deal to learn and receive from them. Receptive ecumenism could prove an effective approach to ecumenical engagement for these kinds of conversations and learning.

My research outlined in the following chapters is the first to engage women from Pentecostal and Free Evangelical churches in receptive ecumenism. Bringing together Christians who are based in radically diverse ecclesial contexts was not without challenges, as I will discuss in Chapter 2. One challenge pertains to how we conceive Christian traditions and their relationship to one another. If we understand a church's liturgies and creeds, doctrines and practices as building blocks that lead to rigid structures, then Christians are going to struggle with receptive ecumenism since it requires flexibility. The most helpful image here is one of a web which can cope with the tension of movement and growth since a web is dynamic.[35]

The philosophical landscape of receptive ecumenism

A rigorous web of philosophical thought is woven through receptive ecumenism in order to provide a resilient context for the discernment of gift reception as churches grapple with an eschatological reality that 'refuses to be confined to a future that is of no relevance to the present'.[36] Taking seriously the witness of Scripture to the Spirit's transforming work at Pentecost, the churches lean into the Spirit, expectantly seeking transformation and renewal. This expectancy best flourishes within the philosophical landscape of pragmatism.

As he describes the philosophical environment in which receptive ecumenism thrives, Murray draws on philosopher Nicholas Rescher, a German-American philosopher at the University of Pittsburgh.[37] Rescher provides, contra Richard Rorty, a means of taking the question of truth seriously through his 'pragmatic idealism'.[38] Rescher's approach is that of a 'committed pluralist position' (this is Murray's description), combining elements of the European continental idealism with American pragmatism.[39] Murray argues for 'acknowledging the pluralist reality of the world' while making a claim 'precisely for the legitimacy and rationality of particular rooted commitment in this context and for the way in which this might be appropriately lived'.[40] The emphasis on human reasoning as that which begins 'in the middle of things' is pervasive through receptive ecumenism, which aims to start where churches are now rather than in an idealized position. This relates to Healy's rejection of the 'blueprint' ecclesiology to which I referred at the beginning of the chapter. The contemporary context is already shaped by assumptions, values and received knowledge, in all the messiness that comes from being embedded in particular contexts. Nicholas Rescher is helpful here because he takes seriously the 'situatedness' of human existence while asking continually what is revealed about one's situatedness when it is held up to the light of another's. Truth, therefore, is expressed, but only in part, since we journey towards truth rather than consider ourselves to have already arrived. A stance such as this allows 'differences' to be 'differences' instead of approaching differences as problems. Conflict is not inevitable where difference exists because the way one approaches difference is that it serves as a mirror which enables scrutiny of one's own position and beliefs.

Nicholas Adams, in an article comparing receptive ecumenism with scriptural reasoning, takes this further and expands on a feature of receptive ecumenism which allows it to engage in discourse positively.[41] He begins by explaining that discourse in ecumenical dialogue typically displays 'binary shapes', by which he means there are two elements: a variable and a value.[42] As Adams explains, many claims within theology operate, quite rightly, in a binary fashion. A claim is made ('the world is God's good creation' or 'Jesus is fully divine and fully human') and a value is assigned ('these claims are true'). Where there is disagreement, there is a straightforward opposition between the values assigned to a variable. For example, if I affirm the truth of X, and you deny the truth of X, there is a contradiction between the value assigned to the variable: X is true vs X is false. Disputes governed by binary shapes generate contradiction and these manifest as tensions in ecumenical dialogues. For example, trinitarian doctrine is disputed in ecumenical discussions. Catholic creeds affirm that the Spirit proceeds from the Father and the Son; Orthodox Christians deny it. Each sees the other as not merely confused but doctrinally errant. When the form of a judgement is binary (where there is variable and value), ecumenical difficulties ensue. Often the way of engaging these difficulties is anxiously to seek what is common to both faith traditions (finding identical values) while sitting uncomfortably with what is different (avoiding contrary values).

Receptive ecumenism, however, introduces triadic shapes. The dyad of variable and value is transformed by the addition of a third element: the condition for assigning values. Another way of putting this is to say that it pays attention to who is making the claim. For example, 'in Catholic doctrine, it is taken as true that the Spirit proceeds from the Father and the Son'. There is a variable (the procession of the Spirit), a value (it is taken as true) and a condition (in Catholic doctrine). The significance of a triadic shape is that if the condition is changed, one can expect the value may change. For example, 'in Orthodox doctrine, it is taken as false that the Spirit proceeds from the Father and the Son'. The variable is the same, but the condition is different, and so is the value (it is now false). In a triadic shape the contradiction of values is qualified (and added to) by the difference in conditions. For example, one faith tradition believes X, another believes Y (or even not-X), but this does not mean to say they both must affirm Z (finding common ground) in order to continue fruitful ecumenical discussion. Difference is preserved, as observed with respect to Rescher's pragmatism.

In response to Adams's insight, we might ask whether this inevitably ends in some kind of relativism in which I affirm that X is 'true for me' but 'false for you'. Adams argues that a triadic structure does not change the values (their truth or falsity); it changes how many elements there are (by adding the conditions for assigning value, by adding the 'who'). Questions of truth (the assigning of value) are preserved:

> A triadic claim describes *for whom* a value is assigned to a variable. The problematic claim assigns a value (indeed two contrary values) to a variable; it does not properly describe for whom (or how) a value is assigned to a variable. That is not the main problem, however. The deeper problem is that it [saying 'true for me'] misuses the word 'true'. X is either

true or not true. A triadic form does not modify the assigning of a value to a variable. Triadic forms do not adjudicate truth claims at all. A triadic form preserves that act of assigning [value] without modification. It adds a description: it specifies who assigns the value to the variable.[43]

Thus, following a triadic shape, receptive ecumenism avoids making claims about what is 'essential' and 'inessential'. Nor does it make use of undifferentiated 'we' claims. This is because in a triadic structure the 'we' is typically the third element. The 'we' (the condition for assigning value) becomes available to inquiry in addition to the truth of the claims (note that this is in addition to, not instead of). I can ask why you affirm something that I deny (a triadic matter) and not simply consider you wrong (a binary one). We may continue with good reasons to consider each other wrong after such an inquiry. Rather than seeking common ground or a resolution of difference into shared belief, the differences are beneficial to those engaging with one another: it is in the face of difference that we are able to gain fresh perspective on ourselves (for good or for ill). Receptive ecumenism provides a way of engaging differently because the goal for the long term is not simply 'agreement'. Instead, it is the transformation of churches.

The biblical imagination of receptive ecumenism

As well as philosophical thought, biblical imagination permeates receptive ecumenism. As far as I am aware, biblical scholars have not yet engaged in work on receptive ecumenism; therefore what follows is my own contribution as a place from which to begin. For the sake of brevity, I identify three themes: union with God, listening to the Spirit, and God as the giver of good gifts, all of which form threads running through Scripture.

At the very heart of receptive ecumenism is Christ's final prayer for his friends in John's Gospel (17.20–22):

I ask not only on behalf of these, but also on behalf of those who will believe in me through their word, that they may all be one. As you, Father, are in me and I in you, may they also be in us, so that the world may believe that you have sent me. The glory you have given me I have given them, so that they may be one, as we are one.

These verses are cited frequently in relation to the unity of the church in such a way that the mystery through which Christians are brought into union with God is too easily forgotten. While it is not my intention to undermine the importance of seeking the kind of Christian unity that demonstrates the love of Christ in the world, nevertheless these verses recall a vision greater than a plan for successful mission and evangelism.[44] Origen, interpreting John's Gospel in the third century, explains some of the implications of Christ's prayer. As the first theologian to develop a systematic hermeneutic for reading Scripture, he interprets Christ's prayer as speaking about nothing other than the complete restoration of humankind through union with God:

... so also from one beginning there are many differences and varieties, which, in turn, through the goodness of God, and by subjection to Christ and through the unity of the Holy Spirit, are recalled to an end which is like the beginning.[45]

Origen's interpretation is far removed from understanding Christ's words as concern for ecumenical relations. One century later, John Chrysostom explores this prayer, interpreting it differently from Origen, but still with an emphasis on God rather than the unity of believers. Chrysostom reminds his readers that Jesus, a few chapters earlier in John 13.34–35, commands believers to love one another because the world will know him if the disciples follow this command. Recalling these verses, Chrysostom writes:

This is similar to what he said earlier, 'By this shall all know that you are my disciples, if you love one another'. And how will they believe this? 'Because,' he says, 'you are a God of peace.' And, if therefore the [disciples] keep that same peace that they have learned [from me], their hearers will know the teacher by the disciples. But, if they quarrel, people will deny that they are disciples of a God of peace and will not allow that I, not being peaceable, have been sent from you. Do you see how he proves his unanimity with the Father to the very end?[46]

For John Chrysostom, this prayer reveals the truth about Christ's divinity and unity with the Father. God, therefore, is peace, and there is no competition between the Father and the Son. This in turn makes possible the peace of believers, because Godself is peace. Yet again, the focus is on God, and the way that believers treat one another is a natural consequence of the unity of God.

The communication of the Holy Spirit to the churches in the book of Revelation forms the second biblical theme woven through receptive ecumenism. Revelation repeats the phrase, 'Let the one who has an ear hear what the Spirit says to the churches.' By making this move, the author draws on a phrase that appears in the Synoptic Gospels (Matt. 11.15; 13.9; Mark 4.9, 23; Luke 8.8; 14.35; Rev. 2.7, 11, 17, 29; 3.6, 13, 22; 14.13; 19.10; 22.17). In the Gospels, when Jesus uses the phrase, it is for the purpose of encouraging a particular response to whatever he has urged his listeners to do.[47] In Revelation, the phrase is repeated at the close of each of the seven letters to the angel of the churches, and on each occasion they are called to repentance and transformation. This emphasis on repentance echoes the words of the prophets. As Richard Bauckham observes:

> In post-biblical Judaism, as is well known, the Spirit is especially the Spirit of prophecy, the Spirit who speaks through the prophets. In Revelation also the Spirit is almost exclusively the Spirit of prophecy.[48]

Bauckham explains the different ways in which the Spirit in Revelation speaks the word of Christ. The Spirit rebukes, encourages, promises and threatens, touches, and draws the hearts, minds and consciences of the Spirit's hearers while 'directing the lives and the prayers of the Christian communities towards the coming of Christ'.[49]

An important question relating to this concerns whether this Spirit is confined to the Christian prophets in Revelation; or, is it possible to make a case for the whole church having a prophetic vocation? Bauckham argues that the whole church has a prophetic relationship because 'the witness of Jesus' is the Spirit of prophecy. The Spirit speaks through the Christian prophets and brings 'the word of the exalted Christ to his people on earth, endorsing on earth the words of heavenly revelations, and directing the prayers of the churches to their heavenly Lord'.[50] Against this backdrop, those engaged in receptive ecumenism ask, 'In what ways is the Spirit calling our churches to repent?' As already observed, key to receptive ecumenism is the belief that none of the churches are perfectly serving the Kingdom of God. Therefore, we lean into the Spirit and ask for guidance regarding our denominational weaknesses. This requires courage and humility, since it can be painful to come face to face with our own transgressions and failings as churches. But we hope in the Spirit for transformation and renewal, because we trust that the Spirit longs to draw believers closer to God and one another.

The third scriptural theme that features prominently in receptive ecumenism recognizes that God is the giver of all good gifts. Christ by his own self-definition is gift. During John's narrative of his encounter with a woman at a well, Jesus says to the woman, 'If you knew the gift of God, and who it is that is saying to you, "Give me a drink," you would have asked him, and he would have given you living water' (John 4.10). The same theme appears in the Gospel of Matthew when Jesus commands his disciples to give freely because they have received freely (10.8). Likewise, in the book of Acts 2.38 and throughout the epistles, the Holy Spirit is described as gift.[51] Observe Matthew 7.7–11:

Ask, and it will be given you; search, and you will find; knock, and the door will be opened for you. For everyone who asks receives, and everyone who searches finds, and for everyone who knocks, the door will be opened. Is there anyone among you who, if your child asks for bread, will give a stone? Or if the child asks for a fish, will give a snake? If you then, who are evil, know how to give good gifts to your children, how much more will your Father in heaven give good things to those who ask him!

God's children are told 'ask and you will receive, seek and you will find'. In light of this, receptive ecumenism acknowledges that the Spirit gives gifts to each of the churches, equipping believers for worship, mission and ministry. Therefore, through prayer and conversation, we open ourselves to the possibilities of receiving gifts from other churches, particularly in relation to where we are weakest. Rather than assuming that whatever church to which I belong has been given all the gifts, receptive ecumenism calls each church to seek the gifts in another.

Receiving a gift

How we understand 'gift' is not straightforward.[52] In what follows, I will summarize, albeit very briefly, how I understand 'gift' in receptive ecumenism. Along with the biblical themes, this is the first conversation on the function of gift within receptive ecumenism. The definition in the online edition of the Oxford English Dictionary describes a gift as being 'transferred to another without the expectation or receipt of an equivalent'.[53] This indicates an understanding of gift as 'pure'. A pure gift implies the possibility of being free from obligation; and while this is often accepted in the modern West, elsewhere across the globe and throughout history gift is understood differently. For example, the fourth-century bishop Hilary of Poitiers describes 'gift' in such a way that reciprocity is essential. Writing on the Trinity, Hilary states, 'The donor, therefore, is greater, but at the same time He is not less to whom it is given to be one.'[54] Moreover, academics from diverse areas have demonstrated that reciprocity is a key feature of gift-giving; this applies whether the focus of research is anthropological, historical, sociological, philosophical or theological.[55]

Early-twentieth-century anthropologist Marcel Mauss in his 1923 publication of *The Gift* laid the foundation for an understanding of gift that presupposes some kind of reciprocity and his book then became the basis for all subsequent discussions on gift.[56] Since his overall thesis is beyond the scope of this chapter, I will focus only on the key theme in his argument, which is that pure gift is impossible. By pure gift, Mauss means the kind of gift that is not reciprocal. Drawing on decades of fieldwork he argues that gifts involve some kind of exchange and have meaning that goes beyond the gifts themselves. Mauss's theory is analogous to ancient beliefs about gift exchange, as John Barclay has argued recently. In a comprehensive review of ancient sources from the Greco-Roman world, Barclay argues that the sources demonstrate how 'the expectation and obligation of return' accompanies the gift that is given.[57] Barclay's argument does not stand alone with respect to Christian theology, since it is commonly held that pure gift is not possible when we account for the coherence of gift and reciprocity. Responding to this, Simon Oliver's account of creation establishes that the only pure gift is the gift of creation, which God gives as *creatio ex nihilo*. The implications of reciprocity mean that, as Oliver puts it, the gift is 'imbued with something of the giver's character or power'.[58] This follows what Mauss himself writes: 'to make a gift of something to someone is to make a present of some part of oneself'.[59] An example of a gift that bears meaning would be a child who paints a picture for their parents. The gift is treasured beyond its monetary value which, unless the child is an artistic genius, would most likely be very little. And yet most parents are compelled to give something back, whether this be in the form of gratitude or coupled with framing the picture and hanging it in a visible spot.

Gift, then, is not pure but incorporates some degree of exchange which is identifiable in the sharing of gifts in receptive ecumenism, as we shall see in the following chapters. One further point: Mauss observes that generosity is closely connected to power, which emerged as a prevalent theme during research on women's experiences of working in churches in England using receptive ecumenism. I will return to this in Chapter 3, where I report on the theme of power in the women's conversations; in Chapter 4, when I will explore the place and practice of hospitality within receptive ecumenism; and again in Chapter 7, when I discuss how the women themselves experienced abuses of power and how power is shared among those who lead churches. The themes of gift and power run implicitly and explicitly throughout this book.

Virtues necessary for receptive ecumenism

It should be evident by now that receptive ecumenism, like any other kind of ecumenical work, is not without challenges; and, as well as 'imagination, faithfulness, and perseverance', it takes patience.[60] It bears repeating that receptive ecumenism is not a quick fix nor a short-term project but a commitment made by churches to journeying together towards unity.[61] It 'requires *both* active trust that we are being resourced for this and led into it in the ways we require *and* patient recognition that any real receptive learning necessarily takes time to be realised'.[62] In short, receptive ecumenism is a journey of 'humble ecclesial learning'.[63]

Writing on this, Antonia Pizzey highlights the strong resonances between receptive ecumenism and Cardinal Kasper's spiritual ecumenism, added to which she explores the importance of virtues to receptive ecumenism.[64] She identifies the necessity of love, hospitality, humility and hope, where love is the 'primary motive behind all ecumenical activity'.[65] Murray also argues that 'we are changed by love not by anger and if we are in turn to effect creative ecclesial change then it must be through the sustained passion of love rather than frustration'.[66] Ecumenism therefore is a 'matter of the heart', of 'falling in love with the experienced presence and action of God in the people, practices and even structures of another tradition'.[67] Jesus's final prayer for his disciples in John's Gospel asks that they love one another. Loving is risky, however, and churches are called to trust that the Spirit will not lead them into harm when they seek to learn from and receive gifts from the other.[68] Love finds a practical outworking in hospitality, where 'responsible hospitality' is one of the 'core values' of receptive ecumenism.[69] This is motivated by the necessity of the host listening and learning from the guest, and aiming to be converted rather than to convert. In her work on hospitality, Christine Pohl highlights that 'hospitality is fragile because it is to be offered out of kindness only'.[70] Receptive ecumenism, like all other forms of ecumenical work, is not practised in abstraction from daily life and involves candid conversations between human persons in whose contexts gifts and doctrines are embodied, lived and shared. I shall return to this theme in Chapter 4 in which I explore how a group of women in the UK are practising hospitality and how their practices contribute to understanding the importance of hospitality within receptive ecumenism.

Pizzey observes that along with love and hospitality, humility is essential, since each of the churches must be willing to acknowledge their own wounds, confessing their brokenness before the other(s).[71] The New Testament witnesses to the importance of humility for discipleship and ecclesial unity. For example, Peter's first letter explains that humility is necessary for Christian communication: '... all of you must clothe yourselves with humility in your dealings with one another' (1 Peter 5.5). Clothed with humility, any work towards ecclesial transformation must be accompanied by hope, rooted in the belief that unity is the will of the Holy Spirit, and therefore Christians 'must seek to live courageously and imaginatively in hope'.[72]

According to Thomas Aquinas, hope, along with charity and faith, is one of the three 'theological virtues'.[73] As we shall discuss further in Chapter 6, Thomas explains that theological virtues are so called because their object is God. The virtues are infused in human persons by God alone and are made known by divine revelation, as revealed in Scripture. In his exposition of human hope, Thomas identifies four features. First, because hope is good, it only regards that which is likewise good; second, it is future-oriented; third, it is difficult to obtain; fourth, and most importantly, hope is possible to obtain.[74] As a theological virtue, hope unites believers with God, bringing them into 'full communion with the Persons of the blessed Trinity, a relationship made possible for us only by the saving work of Jesus Christ'.[75] This is precisely the kind of hope called for when engaging in receptive ecumenism. Listening, learning and receiving gifts from others is not easy to put into practice; but if we agree with Thomas in his analysis of hope, journeying towards ecclesial unity is possible.

Conclusion

The chapter began by locating receptive ecumenism within the broader ecumenical movement and identifying how receptive ecumenism overlaps with and differs from other forms of ecumenical engagement. Receptive ecumenism does not aim to replace other forms of ecumenism but to diversify the ways in which churches engage with one another. Recognizing the bleakness of the ecumenical winter, receptive ecumenism aims to provide a fresh way of walking towards spring asking, 'What do we need to learn from another tradition to help us address difficulties in our own?'

As well as pointing to its established features, this chapter has engaged constructively by examining how receptive ecumenism witnesses to biblical and philosophical imagination. Three threads that weave through Scripture which point to the commitments of receptive ecumenism are (a) Christ's prayer for unity, (b) the Spirit calling churches to account, and (c) God, who lavishes gifts on the Church – gifts that are for the good of the Church and for the good of the world. Christ by his own self-definition is gift, and we hear of this same Christ encouraging his followers to ask the Father for good gifts.

The Spirit's cry to the churches in Revelation also highlights

FOR THE GOOD OF THE CHURCH

core features of receptive ecumenism: the belief that God speaks today and that the Spirit continues to call our churches to repentance. Would that we take the time to listen amid our anxieties precipitated by the numbers attending services on Sundays, whether online or in a building. Added to this, engaging with the philosophical conversation on gift brings to the fore the way reciprocity features in the practice of receptive ecumenism. I will provide further evidence of this in the following chapters.

Receptive ecumenism offers hope not only for ecclesial unity but also for the transformation of churches, whether on a congregational level, on a national level, or within global ecumenism. That said, receptive ecumenism is a challenging task because it is not easy to admit that churches are functioning imperfectly or that they show signs of weakness. This is where the question of 'which virtues?' comes to the fore. While all virtues are important to ecumenical work, we saw that, as Antonia Pizzey has identified, love, hospitality, humility and hope each play a particularly significant role in the receptive encounter. We will return to the importance of virtues with respect to receptive ecumenism throughout the book.

How then does this relate to women? In the following chapter, I will discuss how I moved from theory to practice, adapting receptive ecumenism in order to research women's experiences of working in churches in England. By engaging in receptive ecumenism, women, who are often cast as the stumbling blocks to Christian unity (because of their desire to pursue all kinds of vocations), become the stepping stones to ecumenical learning and gift reception.

Notes

1 Receptive ecumenism resonates with Scriptural reasoning by drawing on post-liberal strategies that take 'seriously the particularity and plurality of traditioned commitment' (Paul D. Murray, 'Families of Receptive Theological Learning: Scriptural Reasoning, Comparative Theology, and Receptive Ecumenism', *Modern Theology* 29.4 (2013),

pp. 76–92 (p. 76)). Scriptural reasoning creates space for diverse religions to learn from one another through reading Scripture; see David F. Ford, *Christian Wisdom: Desiring God and Learning in Love* (Cambridge: Cambridge University Press, 2007), pp. 277–80.

2 Paul D. Murray, 'Introducing Receptive Ecumenism', *The Ecumenist* 51.2 (2014), pp. 1–7 (p. 2). For a brief video summary of receptive ecumenism see the 2018 Common Awards Symposium: www.dur.ac.uk/theology.religion/common.awards/themes/receptivity/.

3 For an extensive discussion of this metaphor, see William Rusch, 'Impressive Theological Agreement during the So-called "Ecumenical Winter"', *Ecclesiology* 6.2 (2010), pp. 201–6.

4 Paul D. Murray, 'Searching the Living Truth of the Church in Practice: On the Transformative Task of Systematic Ecclesiology', *Modern Theology* 29.4 (2013), pp. 251–81 (p. 278).

5 Thomas J. Reese, SJ, 'Organizational Factors Inhibiting Receptive Catholic Learning' in Paul D. Murray (ed.), *Receptive Ecumenism and the Call to Catholic Learning: Exploring a Way for Contemporary Ecumenism* (Oxford: Oxford University Press, 2008), pp. 346–58 (p. 354).

6 Murray, 'Searching the Living Truth', p. 278.

7 Paul D. Murray and Andrea L. Murray, 'The Roots, Range and Reach of Receptive Ecumenism' in Clive Barrett (ed.), *Unity in Process: Reflections on Ecumenism* (London: Darton, Longman and Todd, 2012), pp. 79–94 (p. 87).

8 Margaret O'Gara, *The Ecumenical Gift Exchange* (Collegeville, MN: Liturgical Press, 1998), p. viii.

9 Nicholas Healy, *Church, World, and the Christian Life: Practical–Prophetic Ecclesiology* (Cambridge: Cambridge University Press, 2000), p. 38.

10 Daniel W. Hardy, *Finding the Church: The Dynamic Truth of Anglicanism* (London: SCM Press, 2001), p. 29.

11 Daniel W. Hardy, 'Church' in Ed Hastings (ed.), *The Oxford Companion to Christian Thought* (Oxford: Oxford University Press, 2009), pp. 118–21 (p. 119). See also Daniel W. Hardy, *God's Ways with the World: Thinking and Practising the Christian Faith* (Edinburgh: T&T Clark, 1996).

12 I am indebted to my colleagues Gregory Ryan and Paul D. Murray for conversations on using 'Catholic' versus 'Roman Catholic'. For the most part, I use 'Catholic' since this is often the way the tradition describes itself, whereas in general 'Roman Catholic' appears in official documents when they are related to ecumenism. In dictionary entries, the two terms are often applied interchangeably with the entry designated as 'Catholicism'; see, for example, Richard P. McBrien (ed.), *The HarperCollins Encyclopedia of Catholicism* (San Francisco, CA: Harper, 1995). Vatican II uses 'Catholic', so also the 'Catechism of the Catholic Church' (1994): www.vatican.va/archive/ENG0015/_INDEX.

HTM. The web page of the Catholic Bishops Conference of England and Wales is entitled 'The Catholic Church': www.cbcew.org.uk.

13 For an exploration of the theology of 'denomination', see Barry A. Ensign-George, *Between Congregation and Church: Denomination and Christian Life Together* (London: Bloomsbury Publishing, 2017). Ensign-George argues for the retrieval of 'denomination' as a theological rather than a sociological term (p. 1).

14 A thorough treatment of the history of ecumenism until the 1950s can be found in Ruth Rouse and Stephen Charles Neill (eds), *The History of the Ecumenical Movement* (London: SPCK, 1954). A discussion of the most recent developments in ecumenism can be found in Samuel Kobia, 'Ecumenism in the 21st Century', *The Ecumenical Review* 70.1 (2018), pp. 21–9.

15 Alec Ryrie, 'The Reformation in Anglicanism' in Mark Chapman, Sathianathan Clarke and Martyn Percy (eds), *The Oxford Handbook of Anglican Studies* (Oxford: Oxford University Press, 2018), pp. 1–13.

16 Ola Tjørhom, 'The Early Stages: Pre-1910' in Geoffrey Wainwright and Paul McPartlan (eds), *The Oxford Handbook of Ecumenical Studies* (2017), pp. 1–12 (p. 9). This article summarizes the movement(s) towards modern ecumenism.

17 For an active example of Life and Work ecumenism in the twenty-first century, see the Churches Together in Boston website. Here, the organization describes the night shelter organized jointly by diverse Christian traditions: www.churchestogetherinboston.org.uk/nightshelter.

18 Scripture references are from the New Revised Standard Version.

19 For a critique of the tensions existing between Life and Work and Faith and Order, see Paul D. Murray, 'In Search of a Way' in Wainwright and McPartlan (eds), *The Oxford Handbook of Ecumenical Studies*, pp. 1–18 (pp. 3–5).

20 World Council of Churches, *The Nature and Mission of the Church: A Stage on the Way to a Common Statement*, Faith and Order Paper 198 (Geneva: World Council of Churches, 2005), p. 11.

21 §8; see www.vatican.va/archive/hist_councils/ii_vatican_council/documents/vat-ii_const_19641121_lumen-gentium_en.html. *Lumen Gentium* is a document of Vatican II promulgated by Paul VI. It is one of the four central Constitutions and not a papal document.

22 §3; see www.vatican.va/archive/hist_councils/ii_vatican_council/documents/vat-ii_decree_19641121_unitatis-redintegratio_en.html.

23 §28; see http://w2.vatican.va/content/john-paul-ii/en/encyclicals/documents/hf_jp-ii_enc_25051995_ut-unum-sint.html. I shall discuss gift exchange further in Chapter 4.

24 §246; see http://w2.vatican.va/content/francesco/en/apost_exhortations/documents/papa-francesco_esortazione-ap_20131124_evangelii-gaudium.html.

25 Anglican Communion, 'Porvoo signed', *Anglican Communion News Service*, 7 October 1996, www.anglicannews.org/news/1996/10/porvoo-signed.aspx.

26 Peter Phan, 'Interreligious and Ecumenical Dialogue at Vatican II: Some Rethinking Required' in *Conversations on Jesuit Higher Education* 42.1 (2012), art. 5, pp. 12–17 (p. 14).

27 Paul D. Murray, 'Formal Ecumenism, Receptive Ecumenism, and the Diverse Local Churches of the Global Catholic Communion' in William T. Cavanaugh (ed.), *Gathered in My Name: Ecumenism in the World Church* (Eugene, OR: Wipf and Stock, 2020), pp. 155–73 (p. 160).

28 Expanded papers from the conferences in Durham can be found in Murray (ed.), *Receptive Ecumenism and the Call to Catholic Learning*. For further work on receptive ecumenism, see Gregory A. Ryan, *Hermeneutics of Doctrine in a Learning Church: The Dynamics of Receptive Integrity* (Leiden and Boston: Brill, 2020).

29 For these reports and further documents relating to receptive ecumenism, see www.dur.ac.uk/theology.religion/ccs/projects/receptive ecumenism/projects/.

30 ARCIC III committed to employing receptive ecumenism at its first annual meeting in May 2011 at the monastery of Bose in northern Italy. This eventually culminated at its seventh meeting in Erfurt, Germany, 14–20 May 2017, with the finalization of *Walking Together on the Way: Learning to Be the Church – Local, Regional, Universal. An Agreed Statement of the Third Anglican–Roman Catholic International Commission* (ARCIC III) (Erfurt, Germany, 2017), www.vatican.va/roman_curia/pontifical_councils/chrstuni/angl-comm-docs/rc_pc_chrstuni_doc_20180521_walking-together-ontheway_en.pdf.

31 Churches Together in England resources: www.cte.org.uk/Groups/246101/Home/Resources/Theology/Receptive_Ecumenism/Receptive_Ecumenism.aspx. For the ideas from the South Australian Council of Churches, see www.sacc.asn.au/en/index.php?rubric=en_receptive+ecumenism.

32 Sara Gehlin, 'Receptive Ecumenism: A Pedagogical Process' in Vicky Balabanski and Geraldine Hawkes (eds), *Receptive Ecumenism: Listening, Learning and Loving in the Way of Christ. A Forum for Theology in the World*, 5.2 (Adelaide: ATF Press, 2018), pp. 111–22.

33 Australian Centre for Christianity and Culture, '4th International Conference on Receptive Ecumenism', *Australian Centre for Christianity and Culture*, https://about.csu.edu.au/community/accc/projects/2017-conference-receptive-ecumenism.

34 www.globalchristianforum.org/. Also see Gabrielle Thomas, 'Receptive Learning Between Churches' in Larry Miller (ed.), *Proceedings from the Global Christian Forum Gathering, April 2018, Bogotá, Colombia* (forthcoming).

35 This image belongs to Paul D. Murray. I am thankful for his lively descriptions of spiders' webs during our conversations! Paul D. Murray, 'Discerning the Call of the Spirit to Theological–Ecclesial Renewal: Notes on Being Reasonable and Responsible in Receptive Ecumenical Learning' in Virginia Miller, David Moxon and Stephen Pickard (eds), *Leaning into the Spirit: Ecumenical Perspectives on Discernment and Decision-making in the Church* (Cham, Switzerland: Palgrave Macmillan, 2019), pp. 217–34.

36 Paul D. Murray, 'Receptive Ecumenism and Ecclesial Learning: Receiving Gifts for Our Needs', *Louvain Studies* 33 (2008), pp. 30–45.

37 Nicholas Rescher, *A System of Pragmatic Idealism*, vols I–III (Princeton, NJ: Princeton University Press, 1992–4).

38 Paul D. Murray, *Reason, Truth and Theology in Pragmatist Perspective* (Leuven: Peeters, 2004).

39 Paul D. Murray, 'Receptive Ecumenism and Catholic Learning – Establishing the Agenda' in Murray (ed.), *Receptive Ecumenism and the Call to Catholic Learning*, pp. 5–25 (p. 8).

40 Murray, 'Receptive Ecumenism and Catholic Learning', p. 8.

41 Nicholas Adams, 'Long-Term Disagreement: Philosophical Models in Scriptural Reasoning and Receptive Ecumenism', *Modern Theology* 29.4 (2013), pp. 154–71.

42 Adams, 'Long-Term Disagreement', p. 162.

43 Adams, 'Long-Term Disagreement', p. 163, my emphasis.

44 For a discussion of this question, see Gert J. Malan, 'Does John 17:11b, 21–23 Refer to Church Unity?', *Theological Studies* 67.1 (2011), pp. 1–10.

45 Origen, *On First Principles* 1.6.2. Edited and translated by John Behr (Oxford: Oxford University Press, 2017), p. 107.

46 John Chrysostom, 'Homilies on the Gospel of John' 82.2 in Joel Elowsky (ed.), *Ancient Christian Commentary on Scripture: John 11–21* (Downers Grove, IL: Intervarsity Press, 2007), p. 257.

47 Brian K. Blount, *Revelation: A Commentary* (Louisville, KY: Westminster John Knox Press, 2009), p. 50.

48 Richard Bauckham, *The Climax of Prophecy: Studies on the Book of Revelation* (Edinburgh: T&T Clark, 1993), p. 160.

49 Bauckham, *The Climax of Prophecy*, p. 161.

50 Bauckham, *The Climax of Prophecy*, p. 160.

51 Romans 12.1; 2 Corinthians 8.5; Philippians 2.17.

52 Risto Saarinen approaches ecumenism through the notion of gift in *God and the Gift: An Ecumenical Theology of Giving* (Collegeville, MN: Liturgical Press, 2002).

53 www.oed.com/. For many years I have benefited greatly from Simon Oliver's work on 'gift'. This chapter draws on conversations with him and his published work; see *Creation: A Guide for the Per-*

plexed (London: T&T Clark, 2017). Any errors in interpreting his work are mine.

54 Saint Hilary of Poitiers, *The Trinity* 9.54. Translated by Stephen McKenna (Washington, DC: Catholic University of America Press, 2002), p. 377.

55 For example, Michael L. Satlow (ed.), *The Gift in Antiquity* (Oxford: Wiley-Blackwell, 2013); Mark Osteen (ed.), *The Question of the Gift: Essays Across Disciplines* (London: Routledge, 2002); Kathryn Tanner, *Economy of Grace* (Minneapolis, MN: Augsburg Fortress, 2005); John Milbank, 'The Gift of Ruling: Secularization and Political Authority', *New Blackfriars* 85 (March 2004), pp. 212–38; John Barclay, *Paul and the Gift* (Grand Rapids, MI: Eerdmans, 2017). For a practical analysis of gift-giving, see Nigel Rooms, 'Missional Gift-Giving: A Practical Theology Investigation into what Happens when Churches Give Away "Free" Gifts for the Sake of Mission', *Practical Theology* 8.2 (2015), pp. 99–111.

56 Marcel Mauss, *The Gift: The Form and Reason for Exchange in Archaic Societies*, translated by W. D. Halls (London: Routledge, 2007).

57 Barclay, *Paul and the Gift*, p. 63.

58 Oliver, *Creation*, p. 211.

59 Mauss, *The Gift*, p. 16.

60 Margaret O'Gara, 'Ecumenical Dialogue: The Next Generation' in Margaret O'Gara and Michael Vertin (eds), *No Turning Back: The Future of Ecumenism* (Collegeville, MN: Liturgical Press, 2014), pp. 206–31 (p. 217).

61 Walter Kasper, *That They May All Be One: The Call to Unity Today* (New York: Bloomsbury, 2004), pp. 155–72.

62 Murray, 'Families of Receptive Theological Learning', p. 87.

63 Murray, 'Receptive Ecumenism and Catholic Learning', p. 16.

64 This section draws on Antonia Pizzey's work on virtues in *Receptive Ecumenism and the Renewal of the Ecumenical Movement: The Path of Ecclesial Conversion* (Leiden: Brill, 2019). An edited collection of essays exploring the development of receptive ecumenism is in progress; see Paul D. Murray, Gregory A. Ryan and Paul Lakeland (eds), *Receptive Ecumenism as Transformative Ecclesial Learning: Walking the Way to a Church Re-formed* (forthcoming).

65 Pizzey, *Receptive Ecumenism*, p. 149.

66 Murray and Murray, 'Roots, Range and Reach', p. 89.

67 Murray, 'Receptive Ecumenism and Catholic Learning', p. 14.

68 I will explore in depth the theme of love and friendship in Chapter 6 in dialogue with Thomas Aquinas, who identifies charity as a theological virtue.

69 Murray, 'Receptive Ecumenism and Catholic Learning', p. 16.

70 Christine Pohl, *Making Room: Recovering Hospitality as a Christian Tradition* (Grand Rapids, MI: Eerdmans, 1999), p. 142.

71 On this, see also Antonia Pizzey, 'On the Maturation of Receptive Ecumenism: The Connection between Receptive Ecumenism and Spiritual Ecumenism', *Pacifica* 28.2 (2015), pp. 108–25.

72 Murray, 'Families of Receptive Theological Learning', p. 87.

73 *ST* II.I.62 *ad* 1. Citations of *Summa Theologiae* give Part, question, article, part of article. For example, *ST* I.1.10 *ad* 1 = *ST* Part One, question 1, article 10, the response to the first objection.

74 *ST* II.I.40.

75 Romanus Caesario, OP, 'The Theological Virtue of Hope (IIa IIae, qq. 17–22)' in Stephen J. Pope (ed.), *The Ethics of Aquinas* (Washington, DC: Georgetown University Press, 2002), pp. 232–43 (p. 233).

2

Designing the Research

I feel like I've been part of something really important for me personally and for the church, and I've learnt more than I imagined I would. I've been so very inspired by the godly women I've met through this research and the way that we formed as a group so quickly, especially since we were from such different church contexts. I have to say though – I can only just pronounce 'receptive ecumenism'. I do think that this ecumenical practice is a tough call for anyone who wants to bury their head in the sand about the issues we have in our churches. For this to take hold, we need to be humble and not afraid to show our 'cracks'. It requires a good deal of courage and a humble mindset. (Methodist, 42)[1]

This chapter identifies how I drew on the core commitments of receptive ecumenism to explore women's experiences of working in churches in England. I begin by introducing readers to the National Board of Catholic Women (NBCW), which is a body of women seeking 'to promote the presence, participation and responsibilities of Catholic Women in the Church and society, in order to enable them to fulfil their evangelical mission and to work for the common good'.[2] As described in the previous chapter, the global conferences on receptive ecumenism attracted the attention of a wide audience. Members of the NBCW were among those interested in exploring a different approach to ecumenism. They thought that it would be of great value to 'try receptive ecumenism with groups of women' since they were inspired by the emphasis that it places on receiving gifts. After much reflection and prayer in 2013, along with women from other churches they initiated small-scale, ecumenical conferences for women in the Midlands, UK, upon which Chapter 4 will shine a spotlight. After some successful gatherings, the NBCW designated funding for formal research that would explore women's experiences of working in churches through receptive ecumenism. This brief, alongside a two-year funding limit, formed the early parameters of my work. During the design phase, and through the following phases, I worked closely with the NBCW to craft research, which (a) was academically rigorous, (b) furthered ecumenical learning, and (c) created a space for women's voices to be heard in an ecumenical forum.

The chapter concludes with feedback from the participants, through which it becomes evident that receptive ecumenism can be used to create a space for candid conversation in which people feel able to share difficult experiences safely in addition to providing a fresh way of walking towards Christian unity.

Why women?

The Introduction identified that while women work ecumenically and creatively for the good of the church, this work is rarely brought to the fore on social media or in the popular Christian press. I pause here to recall that this research does not represent 'all women', nor do I apply 'women' as a universal category of experience.[3] The diverse views and experiences of the participants reflect the particularity of each person, as we shall see in the following chapter. Likewise, the research does not represent every Christian tradition in England. Rather, the aim is to create space for the voices of the participants themselves.

Why focus on women? In many respects the ecumenical movement reinforces 'a patriarchal status quo'[4] which excludes women's voices in formal ecumenical dialogues. All too often women are depicted as a 'stumbling block' to Christian unity especially when questions arise concerning leadership and vocation:

Many women in both Catholicism and Orthodoxy object to being treated as scapegoats and made to feel responsible for the growing difficulties of ecumenical dialogue. They also feel greatly concerned when the issue of women's ordination is used as a tool to hinder collaboration between the World Council of Churches (WCC), the Conference of European Churches (CEC) and the Bishops' Conference of Europe.[5]

By creating space for women to engage ecumenically, the ecumenical movement advances, disrupting the status quo. Rather than being presented as stumbling blocks to Christian unity, on the basis of this research women might better be described as stepping stones to a more flourishing ecumenical conversation.[6] Further to this, women are more inclined to speak freely in groups in which a critical mass of women is present.[7] Sharing personal experiences places them in a vulnerable position; thus it is important to create a space that is as safe as possible.[8]

A word on the researcher

It is beyond the purpose of this book to discuss the breadth of my own experiences of faith, ecumenism, and ministry; nevertheless, some degree of disclosure is necessary because my experiences have informed this research in a number of ways. My professional life as a historical theologian who is interested in retrieval will be evident in the following chapters, as will the fact that I have worked in the Church of England in both lay and ordained roles. While conducting this research, I was licensed as a Minor Canon in Durham Cathedral. This was a non-stipendiary role in addition to my full-time job at Durham University. I did not wear my clerical collar – or, indeed, any clothing indicative of a clerical role – while leading and participating in the research. However, some of the participants understood me as an 'institutional insider', whereas others identified with me because I am a woman who has also worked in a church as a lay person. I did not share my own experiences of working in churches, although I resonated with particular experiences shared by participants. This would have been evident through my facial expressions, since I do not always mask my reactions.

During the feedback, several participants noted that I facilitated a space where personal stories were shared openly, ranging from light-hearted and amusing tales through to narrating experiences of sexual assault for the very first time.[9] My own training as a pastor in addition to being a researcher will have undoubtedly contributed to creating a safe and productive space for research. I note this because on some occasions the women shared harrowing wounds which required a pastorally adept response. On this and on the role of the theologian, I resonate with Christian Scharen and Eileen Campbell-Reed who write:

> We intentionally inhabit the hybrid roles of theologians and researchers, for instance, beginning group interviews with prayer, and making explicit to our participants that we, too, are pastors who have heard a call to ministry and served congregations as well as other church-related roles. Among other things, this has heightened our respect for listening deeply, and allowed a crucial place for silence in the midst of our work as the space in which God holds us in love, and out of which God hears us into speech.[10]

Prayer became a core aspect of the receptive journey, to which I will return throughout the book. I prayed at the beginning and close of each focus group and research conversation, and also held a space for prayer open to all participants.[11]

Location and timing

The research was limited to women who work in churches in England since Scotland, Northern Ireland, and Wales each have their own cultural diversity and questions.[12] Five focus groups gathered across England during 2018, each consisting of between 8 and 16 women.[13] I learnt quickly that smaller groups were the most effective since participants were eager to share their stories. The groups met for five to eight hours in a variety of locations: three were held in church function rooms, one met in the function room of a café, and another gathered in the front room of a home. Women commented at every meeting on the importance of the location, whether they spoke about geography, parking, travel arrangements, or about the kind of building used. Important considerations related to wheelchair access and general accessibility. Since not all churches in England are properly accessible or equipped, location became a core consideration which I discuss further in Chapter 4.

The principal complication in gathering women together for the focus groups was finding a time that worked for everyone. Many participants worked full-time with working hours that revolved around various church commitments, including weekends. I conducted research conversations so that some of the women who were unable to attend focus groups could contribute to the research. These also took place during 2018 through pre-arranged private meetings lasting approximately one hour.[14]

Participants

Participants were invited initially from pre-existing networks, after which invitations were rolled out more widely.[15] I invited women who worked within member churches of either Churches Together in England[16] and/or the UK Evangelical Alliance.[17] These included Catholic,[18] Anglican,[19] Baptist,[20] Methodist,[21] Orthodox,[22] Assemblies of God,[23] Independent Evangelical, and Independent Pentecostal churches.[24] Women from other churches were approached to take part in the research but were unable to for a variety of reasons.[25] I mention this because women from traditions such as the Salvation Army, Quakers and Vineyard are not represented in this book. Some agreed to participate but withdrew at the last minute for personal reasons. Since ecumenism is at the heart of this research, when quoting participants I identify them only by the traditions in which they work, along with their ages. A list of participants' roles is included in Appendix 2, but I have not added any further information for the purpose of anonymity.

As noted in the previous chapter, this research is the first in England to draw together members of traditional churches with those of 'newer' churches for the purpose of practising receptive ecumenism. Engaging women from diverse traditions presents challenges. Some from evangelical and/or charismatic churches approached their church leaders and elders to ask for permission and were told that they should not take part. Others reported that they could not participate because the research involved Catholics, whom they did not regard as Christians. Still others thought that this research might be considered 'dangerous'. I include these responses to highlight some of the wider issues with respect to (a) the ecumenical landscape in England and (b) the restraints placed upon the freedom of women affiliated to a variety of Christian traditions.

Adapting the principles of receptive ecumenism

When inviting participants, I explained that the research would involve women from diverse Christian traditions who are working in churches in England in a lay or ordained capacity (paid or unpaid), and that the aim was to use receptive ecumenism to reflect together on the women's experiences of their respective work. Prior to meeting, I provided a brief explanation of receptive ecumenism, inviting each woman to think about some positive and negative experiences of working in her church that she would be willing to share with a group.[26]

We began with refreshments, followed by a welcome and introduction, and agreements on confidentiality. We committed to God our time together through reading John 17, followed by a period of silence, and through prayer. I asked, 'What might we need to learn from another Christian tradition to help us address some of the difficulties in our own?' Added to this, I used the two images described in the Introduction and in Chapter 1: the English afternoon tea and 'wounded hands, held open to receive healing gifts'. These images were vital for the women, who were unfamiliar with the terminology of receptive ecumenism. Participants responded differently to the concept and practice of receptive ecumenism, adopting it with varying degrees of ease and difficulty. I shall analyse in the following chapter possible reasons for their differing responses. When women shared their experiences, participants listened silently to the one who was speaking.[27] They were invited to respond or ask questions after women had finished speaking. This process lasted for the morning session after which conversations continued over lunch. When the group gathered back, participants wrote on sticky notes according to the following three themes:

1 Wounds according to my experiences of working in a church.
2 Gifts according to my experiences of working in a church.
3 Gifts in another's church, which would contribute to healing wounds in my tradition.

This resulted in many sticky notes – with varying degrees of legibility – stuck to three separate sheets of paper as a visual aid for discussion. The following chapter includes responses to these themes. Following this activity, the groups discussed the comments and explored together the viability of receiving particular gifts while also exploring common wounds. As we closed, I invited the women to pray for one another, after which they departed, promising to fill in feedback forms.

A word on 'work'

I made the decision in collaboration with women from a range of churches to use 'work' rather than 'ministry' or 'service'.[28] In some Christian traditions (for example, in Anglican and Baptist churches), one might describe women's work in a church as 'ministry'. This could relate to youth ministry, lay ministry, hospitality ministry, priestly ministry, etc. There are potential problems when we use 'ministry' in an ecumenical context, however, since those affiliated with the Catholic Church might assume 'ministry' aligns with the role of the priest which might exclude women from the conversation.[29] I then considered using 'service', but also decided against this because 'service' may also bear negative connotations when used in conjunction with women, where women have been subservient to men in leadership. For example, there may be women in a congregation with skills and gifts in leadership but who are restricted to serving tea and coffee after morning worship or Mass (by this, I do not intend to devalue hospitality; we will explore its importance in Chapter 4).

After much consultation I settled on 'work' as a means of describing women's activity in churches. I made this move in the hope that 'work' bears fewer denomination-specific exclusions than 'ministry' while recognizing that it bears some possibility of misunderstanding, since 'work' is often associated with payment, unless it is designated as 'voluntary work'. Defining 'work' is no simple task. Dorothy Sayers, author and Anglican theologian, emphasizes that work should be looked upon

> not as a necessary drudgery to be undergone for the purpose of making money, but as a way of life in which the nature of man should find its proper exercise and delight and so fulfill itself to the glory of God. That it should, in fact, be thought of as a creative activity undertaken for the love of the work itself; and that man, made in God's image, should make things, as God makes them, for the sake of doing well a thing that is well worth doing.[30]

This takes us some way towards understanding women's roles in churches as 'work', especially those who delight in the tasks they perform.[31] Miroslav Volf argues that what distinguishes pleasant work from a useful hobby is 'that work must either be necessary to satisfy needs other than the worker's need for activity itself or be not primarily done for its own sake'.[32] In light of the women's work in churches we might understand work as paid or unpaid and as that which contributes to the satisfying of others' needs. It is worth noting that participants receiving financial recompense for their work shared negative experiences as frequently as those in unpaid roles.

Feedback

I invited the women to provide feedback on the experience of engaging in receptive ecumenism after they had participated in a focus group or research conversation. The feedback was positive, indicating as much about the participants, and their willingness to engage with one another and the process, as about receptive ecumenism itself. The responses highlight:

(a) women's desire for unity among their churches;
(b) the positive experience of receiving from one another;
(c) the recognition that each tradition has something to learn with respect to women's flourishing; and
(d) receptive ecumenism as a way towards healing wounds.

Responses

I wanted to say how inspiring it was to sit around a table of female leaders and discuss the various challenges and issues raised of being a female in a predominately male world! The level of vulnerability was stunning, and it was almost 'healing' being able to talk about experiences and help one another overcome hurts and frustrations. I felt called to be a part of this research because it's so important that we recognize where we have come from and how, if at all, our workplace is changing. I love God's kingdom and want to see it grow, so to be able to be unified was very special. If you want to meet new people from differing denominations and cultures, this day is for you; and if you feel you can talk about your experiences it will only help us further break down barriers that need to be dismantled! (AoG, 48)

It was an inspired way of getting us together so that we don't have to compete about whose church is 'best'. I think that it took our group a while to grasp that, but when we did it was spiritually transformative because in that sense it was unifying. (Anglican, 39)

I've always wanted to preach the gospel. After taking part in this day, one of the other participants invited me to preach in their church. It was awesome, in spite of the fact that I was very, very nervous. I received so much positive feedback and I'm going to do it again. I don't want to leave my church, I want to change it, and this means that I can have support from outside as well as inside. (Catholic, 26)

We are not on our own and were encouraged by each other. I would like to do further gatherings which use receptive ecumenism because I can see how, if we were to hone down a particular question, this would be to the benefit of all kinds of churches. (Methodist, 37)

I listened in awe to women who never gave up, who are blessed and strong; women who faced the challenges of life with confidence, humility, wisdom, and a strong sense of purpose. Thank you! What a privilege just to be there. I learnt that our churches have common 'wounds' despite being very different theologically. (Independent Pentecostal, 53)

I came along thinking, 'Oh no, not another women's group full of women moaning.' I went away thinking what a wonderful and unique gift is given through receptive ecumenism. We were brought to a place of recognizing brokenness without judgement and were able to receive one another's gifts, even gifts of women which had been rejected elsewhere. It was precious and powerful. (Anglican, 53)

What have I received through all this? So many things. As a student, I studied and lived with Methodists and found myself fascinated by the cell-group model of church. I remember attending a total immersion baptism for the first time, in a Baptist church, and realizing just how minimal Catholic sacramental symbols often were. In ecumenical student activism, I saw how powerful Christian witness can be when it is ecumenical; perhaps the biggest gift has been simply to witness and receive from women in ordained ministry in other traditions. (Catholic, 62)

Change happens at grass roots. Let's continue to use our gifts even though it challenges our churches – that way eventually things will change. (Baptist, 58)

I think one of the things I've learnt about participating in this is that the challenges for women are not limited to one denomination, so it can't be put down to varying theology or doctrine. So many of the stories could have been interchanged with 'Anglican' written in place of 'Baptist', etc., and still be wholly believable. That tells me it is about patriarchal structures, not about doctrine. (Anglican, 39)

I was able to share for the very first time that I was sexually abused by my priest when I was younger. I could not quite believe that I was saying it out loud and was overwhelmed by the responses of the other women. Receptive ecumenism is important for all churches everywhere, but I believe that it is especially a gift to women, since so many of us have been wounded and abused in so many emotional, physical, and spiritual ways. I was able to go on and get some support and help to work through a burden I've been carrying all my life. I cannot endorse this enough! (Catholic, 66)

As identified in the previous chapter, the current literature that focuses on receptive ecumenism has not brought to the fore the way in which reciprocity functions when churches – or indeed the women who work in them – receive gifts from one another. The comments above demonstrate reciprocity moving like an undercurrent through the women's engagement with one another through receptive ecumenism. This theme will continue in the following chapters.

The feedback also indicates that participants experienced the process as 'spiritually transformative'. A number noted that their experience of the time together was 'extremely powerful', and that praying together was an 'important part of the research experience' for them. As the researcher, I identified with this.[33] Towards the close of one of the focus groups, the women prayed for one another at some length according to their own traditions and in ways in which they felt comfortable. These women were radically different from one another in their approaches to their work, faith and church, and yet through engaging receptively with one another they began to understand one another's traditions and perspectives. This led to their decision to pray for God's blessings on one another and to pray for Christian unity.

The prayer below was prayed by a woman who works in an Independent Pentecostal context. It indicates the close fellowship experienced among the group and serves as an example of what women hope for through their work and through gathering for receptive ecumenism.

Dear Lord, we thank you for every woman here. We thank you for the uniqueness of their stories and that your Holy Spirit has been working in the lives of each and every one of us. Lord, we thank you and we praise you and we honour you, Lord God, as women: women that you have called, women that you have chosen, Lord God, and planted in your vineyard. Lord, we thank you. We feel so inadequate at times, but we thank you for your Holy Spirit who guides us, enables us, and empowers us to be the mighty women that you have called us to be.

There are many challenges that we may face, but we know that you're with us and guide and direct us. We thank you for all the wonderful things that you have implanted within us, the zeal for your kingdom, to see your will be done on earth as it is in heaven.

And Lord, as we have talked and laughed and shared and cried together today, we thank you for your healing Spirit that heals broken hearts and brings people back together; the united kingdom of your work. Not our work, but your work, that we may be one as you and your Father are one. So help us to continue to do your will.

Help us in the midst of all this to be able to embrace our full communities as we reach out. Not only just looking in, with our busy lives and busy schedules, help us to never lose focus of you and what you require us to do so that your name may be magnified and glorified because it's all about you, Lord God, and not about us. And we thank you for vision and inspiration in moving forward.

Empower us, we pray, to be effective in this generation.

We thank you in Jesus' name. Amen.

Through prayer and the practice of virtues, we observe the overlap between spiritual ecumenism and receptive ecumenism, discussed in the previous chapter. Before turning to explore the principal themes emerging from the women's stories and conversations, I will identify two areas from the feedback upon which further engagement in receptive ecumenism would prove fruitful.

Further research

1 Working in a church as a woman of colour[34]

I found myself brought to a standstill by one piece of feedback, shaking my head and wiping back tears while reading the words below:

I am a theologically educated black woman who is often excluded from even being 'at the table', let alone being taken seriously when I'm there. This was the first time I have ever felt properly heard and respected in a room full of white people who work in churches. You all took me seriously as a leader. I think that receptive ecumenism could be a viable way forward for bringing churches together, although I recognize that it would be tough. I'd like to see the day where a white church comes to a black church and actually wants to learn from us. We've made a start today, though, and for that I give thanks to the Lord. (Independent Pentecostal, 52)

As it happened, this participant was the only woman of colour in the focus group she attended, due to unforeseen circumstances. Her reason for participating was 'to be involved in theological reflection with other women and to be able to inhabit a space where I can tell some of my stories because the Lord has been present in them all and has been faithful to me'. I was thankful for her presence, for her candid contributions, and for her generosity in helping me see a little more clearly. As A. D. A. France-Williams puts it: 'Women of colour can have their particularity shoved off the end of the bench on a regular basis. They cannot trust the unconsidered white feminist narrative to represent or even recognise their own realities.'[35] I did not design this research in order to explore race as the sole consideration, or sins relating to racialized abuse; however, this theme arose consistently, as the following chapter identifies. Every minority ethnic participant referred to their experience as a woman of colour, highlighting the dysfunctional behaviours and systemic sins of racialized abuse in white majority churches in England. Women of colour who are in leadership positions shared harrowing stories, and two women suggested that further research using receptive ecumenism might work as a way forward in addressing the sins relating to whiteness in English churches. That said, the churches in England which consist of predominantly white people will need to recognize that we have much to repent of and even more to learn in order for transformation to be possible.[36]

2 Lay vocation

For a woman who thinks of herself as a leader and teacher but who cannot be ordained, this was a great opportunity to reflect on important issues intelligently with women from other churches. The cakes were superb (thanks to those who brought the refreshments!), but it was so much more than 'tea and scones', to quote a woman in our group. One of the problems with ordination overall is that people like me are often excluded from leaders' networks. This is a great shame as I have theological contributions to make and I want to make them in the church rather than the academy. Receptive ecumenism worked today as a leveller. I don't think it would do that necessarily, but it is possible. I'd like to see more of this done across the board with all the laity. (Catholic, 63)

During the course of the research, conversation often arose with respect to women in leadership and the related difficulties. Since the groups consisted of women who work in lay and ordained roles, reflections frequently touched on the challenges resulting from the ordination (or not) of women. As we shall see in the following chapter, lay vocation is an area that requires further theological reflection and transformation across all traditions, even those whose theology of leadership is such that priesthood is not a core feature. Different kinds of receptive learning would have taken place if no ordained women were present. While this research intentionally brought lay and ordained together, it became clear through the process of the research that lay voices would benefit from further attention, and that further work on lay vocations is vital.

Notes

1 See Appendix 2 for participants' responses to the phrase 'receptive ecumenism'.

2 Angela Perkins and Verena Wright (eds), *Healing Priesthood: Women's Voices Worldwide* (London: Darton, Longman and Todd, 2003), p. ix. For further details, see www.nbcw.co.uk.

3 As Rosemary Radford Ruether argued, the uniqueness of theologically reflecting on women's experiences 'makes the sociology of theological knowledge visible, no longer hidden behind mystifications of objectified divine and universal authority'; see her *Sexism and God Talk* (Boston, MA: Beacon Press, 1993), p. 13. For an excellent exploration of the methodological questions involved in researching female faith, see Nicola Slee, Fran Porter and Anne Phillips (eds),

Researching Female Faith: Qualitative Research Methods (Abingdon: Routledge, 2018).

4 Margaret O'Gara, *The Ecumenical Gift Exchange* (Collegeville, MN: Liturgical Press, 1998), p. 135.

5 Catherine Gyarmathy-Amherd, 'The Ordination of Women in the Roman Catholic Church', in Ian Jones and Kirsty Thorp (eds), *Women and Ordination in the Christian Churches: International Perspectives* (London: T&T Clark, 2008), pp. 40–53 (pp. 48–9). For an overview of the historical conversation, see the WCC website: www. oikoumene.org/en/resources/documents/wcc-programmes/ecumenical-movement-in-the-21st-century/member-churches/special-commission-on-participation-of-orthodox-churches/sub-committee-ii-style-ethos-of-our-life-together/faith-and-order-on-womens-ordination.

6 The most recent and public example of women's ordination being perpetuated as the means of disunity involves the consecration of the Revd Susan Bunton Haynes as a bishop in The Episcopal Church. Due to lack of building space, a nearby Catholic priest had offered space for the consecration on 1 February 2020. A petition from Catholic parishioners ensued. In her letter to Bishop Knestout, bishop of the Catholic Diocese of Richmond, and Monsignor Lehman, pastor of St Bede, Bishop-elect Haynes wrote: 'I am writing to withdraw from our contract to use the lovely, holy space of St Bede for my upcoming consecration as the 11th bishop of the Episcopal Diocese of Southern Virginia. We have so appreciated and admired your grace and courage in extending this hospitality abiding by your invitation even under fire from those within your own flocks' (http://images.acswebnetworks. com/1/2279/ConsecrationRelocationrelease2020.pdf).

7 Gloria Bonder, *The New Information Technologies and Women: Essential Reflections* (Santiago, Chile: United Nations Publications, 2003), p. 30; Sue Jackson, *Differently Academic? Developing Lifelong Learning for Women in Higher Education* (UK: Springer Publications, 2004), p. 68.

8 For earlier examples of women's negative experiences of being in churches, see Dorothy McEwan (ed.), *Women Experiencing Church: A Documentation of Alienation* (Hereford, UK: Fowler Wright Books, 1991).

9 In a foundational article, Finch observes the dynamics at play when women are researching women: 'However effective a male interviewer might be at getting women interviewees to talk, there is still necessarily an additional dimension when the interviewer is also a woman, because both parties share a subordinate structural position by virtue of their gender. This creates the possibility that a particular kind of identification will develop.' See Janet Finch, '"It's Great to Have Someone to Talk To": The Ethics of Interviewing Women – Social Researching' in Colin Bell and Helen Roberts (eds), *Social Research-*

ing: Politics, Problems, Practice (London: Routledge, 1984), pp. 70–87 (p. 76).

10 Christian Scharen and Eileen Campbell-Reed, *Learning Pastoral Imagination: A Five-Year Report on How New Ministers Learn Practice* (New York: Auburn Studies 2016), p. 11.

11 I draw on work by Karen McCarthy Brown when referring to the 'research conversation' as preferable to 'interview': 'Writing About "the Other" Revisited' in James V. Spickard, J. Shawn Landres and Meredith B. McGuire (eds), *Personal Knowledge and Beyond: Reshaping the Ethnography of Religion* (New York and London: New York University Press, 2002), pp. 130–3.

12 See, for example, a report on ecumenical research on women in ministry by lay-Catholic theologian Dr Anne Francis: *'Called': Women in Ministry in Ireland 2017*, available online at www.irishchurches. org/cmsfiles/REPORT-Women-in-Ministry-in-Ireland-Final.pdf. Francis occasionally tweets work on Twitter: @abfrancis1. She comments on the need to restrict research to a particular location due to the increase in the cultural and spiritual diversity of Christianity across countries.

13 Each group was recorded and later transcribed; once transcribed, the recordings were deleted.

14 The research conversations explored the same themes as the focus groups. They were recorded, transcribed, and later deleted. I did not meet women from churches other than those involved in the focus groups.

15 Before I contacted participants, the Ethics Committee of the Faculty of Arts and Humanities at Durham University approved the research plan and literature that I sent to participants.

16 Churches Together in England is the 'national ecumenical instrument supporting and encouraging churches from a wide range of traditions to work together in unity'. For a list of member churches, see www.cte.org.uk/Groups/234690/Home/About/Membership_of_CTE/Member_Churches_of/Member_Churches_of.aspx.

17 The Evangelical Alliance is 'the oldest and largest evangelical unity moment in the UK', to which thousands of churches belong: www.eauk.org.

18 Catholic churches are designated by the Catholic Bishops' Conference of England and Wales: www.cbcew.org.uk.

19 The Church of England: www.churchofengland.org/.

20 Baptist churches are those belonging to the Baptist Union of Great Britain: www.baptist.org.uk.

21 The Methodist Church: www.methodist.org.uk.

22 Women came from two Orthodox traditions: the Archdiocese of Thyateira and Great Britain (Ecumenical Patriarchate in Constantinople): https://thyateira-deanery.uk/; the Russian Orthodox Church in Great Britain and Ireland, Diocese of Sourozh (Moscow Patriarchate): www.sourozh.org.

23 Assemblies of God: www.aog.org.uk.

24 'Independent Evangelical' and 'Independent Pentecostal' do not appear as named traditions on the websites of Churches Together in England and the Evangelical Alliance. I have chosen these names at the request and suggestion of participants, who did not want to name their churches in the book.

25 Note that each church has its own system for counting members and they vary in reliability, accessibility and utility in research terms. For a discussion of the challenges, see Mathew Guest, Elizabeth Olson and John Wolffe, 'Christianity: Loss of Monopoly' in Linda Woodhead and Rebecca Catto (eds), *Religion and Change in Modern Britain* (London: Routledge, 2012), pp. 57–78. The data in this article is now out of date, although the challenges remain the same. For up-to-date sources (church-based and social-survey-based), see the British Religion in Numbers website: www.brin.ac.uk/.

26 Appendix 1 outlines possible approaches to engaging groups in receptive ecumenism.

27 On my approach to listening, see Appendix 2.

28 For further comment on 'work' in a religious context, see Abby Day, 'Understanding the Work of Women in Religion' in Nicola Slee, Fran Porter and Anne Phillips (eds), *The Faith Lives of Women and Girls: Qualitative Research Perspectives* (London: Routledge, 2013), pp. 39–50. Day argues for 'reintroducing power, agency and complexity' into researching women's work (p. 41).

29 The 26 Catholic women with whom I tested this confirmed that 'ministry' has exclusive implications. Note that there will be those who disagree.

30 Dorothy Sayers, *Letters to a Diminished Church* (United States: W. Publishing Group, 2004), p. 125.

31 For a discussion on the positive and negative ways in which work is understood, see Miroslav Volf, *Work in the Spirit: Toward a Theology of Work* (Eugene, OR: Wipf and Stock, 2001), pp. 1–13.

32 Volf, *Work in the Spirit*, p. 12.

33 On 'the research process itself as a potential means of spiritual growth and social transformation', see Mary Clark Moschella, *Ethnography as a Pastoral Practice: An Introduction* (Cleveland, OH: Pilgrim Press, 2008), p. 12; Nicola Slee, 'Feminist Qualitative Research as Spiritual Practice: Reflections on the Process of Doing Qualitative Research' in Slee, Porter and Phillips (eds), *The Faith Lives of Women and Girls*, pp. 13–24.

34 I have explored with a number of interlocutors regarding how to speak of 'women of colour'. Whether one chooses 'Minority Ethnic', 'Brown, Black, and Asian', or 'women of colour', each description is developed within the construct of whiteness and is therefore problematic nomenclature. Where the women have described themselves in

particular ways, I have applied these descriptions with permission. I point readers to the work of Dr Sanjee Perera, who has researched the disenfranchisement of persons of colour in the Church of England. She has generously made available for public access important highlights of her work: 'Beyond the Lych-gate; a Strategic Diagnostic of Church Culture and Practices that Marginalise and Disenfranchise Black, Asian & Minority Ethnic People in the Church of England'. See the Anglican. org website: https://anglicanism.org/. I am thankful for her expertise and insight: she has been a generous conversation partner with whom to think through questions concerning my own voice and context.

35 A. D. A. France-Williams, *Ghost Ship: Institutional Racism and the Church of England* (London: SCM Press, 2020), p. 44.

36 I use 'we' because I am white and a member of the Church of England.

3

Gifts, Wounds and
Emerging Themes

Receptive ecumenism is a complex undertaking for 'actual' people. Some participants resisted the task of identifying weaknesses in their churches. Others focused on wounds, sins and dysfunctions to such an extent that they were unable to name even one gift or to reflect on positive aspects of working in their church. I shall explore possible reasons for these diverging responses, which were consistent throughout the research irrespective of the geographical location of the participants.

Themes of hospitality, vocation, leadership and power were prevalent through the participants' engagement in receptive ecumenism. While the themes emerged consistently, women's responses to them differed even when working in the same tradition. For example, an Anglican participant testified to flourishing in her lay vocation while another discussed how she had been bullied for attempting to explore a possible call from God. From practising receptive ecumenism, participants learnt that we cannot rightly make claims such as 'women are flourishing in X church, but not in Y church'.[1] Instead, when we engage receptively our presuppositions will be challenged. I write 'we', because my own assumptions were challenged through listening to the conversations. Towards the end of a focus group, one woman put it like this:

My biggest take-away from today is that things are hard for women in other churches too. The grass is not necessarily greener on the other side even though it can sometimes seem that way. I have learnt more about how women in a wide range of churches are handling their experiences and challenging the cultures of their churches on the treatment of women. (Catholic, 65)[2]

A further participant commented, 'When you gather together with women from diverse churches, wrong beliefs are exposed and amended' (AoG, 49). Another put it differently: 'From listening to other women, I have realized that I am happier at work than many of the women in the group, both those in my own church and those in other churches. I did not realize I had it so good!' (Methodist, 42).

After exploring hospitality, vocation, leadership and power, the chapter shines a spotlight on the most prevalent wounds, sins and dysfunctions pertinent to women's experiences of working in churches. These include sexism and sexual harassment, being a person of colour, singleness and motherhood. I will close with recommendations from the women themselves for enhancing and transforming women's experiences of working in churches in England.

Gifts and wounds

As noted in the previous chapter, I invited participants to write down on sticky notes their responses to the following:

1 Gifts according to my experiences of working in a church.
2 Wounds according to my experiences of working in a church.
3 Gifts in another's church, which would contribute to healing wounds in my tradition.

The jottings summarized each morning's conversations, providing a focus for the afternoon's exchanges. The following lists are collated from the sticky notes from the five focus groups and from verbal responses during research conversations. I will focus on the first two points below, whereas the third theme unfolds over the course of Part 2 of the book. Since these lists do not reflect the nuances of the women's responses to this task, I will offer further commentary below.

Gifts:

Catholic
Spirituality; Mary; the Pope; global; lay chaplaincy; liturgy, tradition; Mass.

Baptist
Strong tradition of preaching; down to earth.

Methodist
Methodist Quadrilateral (also called the Wesleyan Quadrilateral);[3] Connexion; Conference; women's voices; a tradition of strong women; Phoebe Palmer.

Eastern Orthodox
Liturgy; choir; the church fathers; tradition; beauty.

Anglican
Breadth of tradition; state church; creative; dynamic; women can be ordained.

Assemblies of God
Innovative; Spirit-led; Bible-based; positive; missional.

Independent Evangelical
Bible-teaching; hospitality; good leadership.

Independent Pentecostal
Freedom in the Spirit; powerful women of prayer; welcoming to people of colour.

Wounds:

Catholic
Abuse crisis; only men are priests; never hearing a woman give a homily during Mass; abuses of power; lack of lay participation in decision making; sexual abuse; 'genius of women'.[4]

Baptist
Structure prevents dealing with sexism; men in power; difficult if you are from an ethnic minority.

Methodist
Lack of innovation in mission; fewer women in positions of influence; not always welcoming to people from ethnic minorities; takes for ever to make changes.

Eastern Orthodox
Lack of women's voices; too many bearded men in power.

Anglican
Sexism; 'mutual flourishing';[5] resource churches mostly being led by men; lack of funding for women pioneers; racist; bullying covered up.

Assemblies of God
Not always good at raising up women; women often hold pastoral roles; strong leadership can be too strong.

Independent Evangelical
Men in authority; not good at being ecumenical.

Independent Pentecostal
Not always supportive of women leaders; powerful men.

Prior to gathering, I had advised the women that I would ask them to share some of the positives and negatives – or put another way, the 'gifts and wounds' – of their experiences of working in their respective churches. Only a few embraced this task comfortably. Instead, the participants tended to focus upon either positive or negative experiences. This is important to bear in mind as churches engage with receptive ecumenism, since individuals may not always be aware of which direction they lean. It is worth recognizing early on in the process that participants will approach the task of receptive ecumenism differently from one another.

A high proportion of the Baptist and Catholic participants experienced challenges with naming gifts. Some women did not name a single gift since they were, as one put it, 'a little beaten down through ministering in my denomination' (Baptist, 54). The women who could not name gifts reflected with the others on whether they should add their empty sticky notes to the large sheet on the wall labelled 'gifts'; the consensus was 'yes'. The end result was an array of blank notes placed amid those scrawled with writing, serving as a stark reminder of the difficulty of some women's experiences.[6] In certain instances, women could not name gifts because of 'extremely harrowing experiences' (Catholic, 64). A number named the abuse crisis as the greatest wound in the Catholic Church and explained that they felt this overshadowed any gifts their church might share.[7] As well as speaking on the abuse crisis, no fewer than seven Catholic women responded that they could not see how their church had enabled them to flourish in their work. They stated firmly: 'No gifts here'; 'I can't think of a single gift'; and 'What gifts? You must be joking'. While this was not the perspective of every Catholic participant, a higher proportion struggled to name gifts than those who named gifts with ease. Listening to the experiences of one Catholic, another woman burst out, 'Why on earth don't you just leave your church? I don't see what you gain by staying' (AoG, 48). The first woman responded:

> It's not that simple for me. I converted to Catholicism at a later stage in life, and my eyes were wide open about its dysfunctions, but the tradition is so important to me. I am part of something that not only reaches out globally, but has also stood the test of time. (Catholic, 69)

The participants laboured on to understand one another's traditions and perspectives. Listening to the conversation, I observed that receptive ecumenism creates a space for grappling with difference. As argued in Chapter 1, receptive ecumenism does not necessitate agreement on particular doctrines. It was possible for women to receive from one another *because of* rather than *despite* their differences.

Whereas some women focused on wounds, sins and dysfunctions in their traditions, others were uncomfortable with the task of naming these. In one group, the women explored why they felt this way and each gave different responses. One said firmly, 'There are no negative traits in my church' (AoG, 53), while another implored, 'I'd rather not focus on what's bad, can't we focus on what's positive?' (Independent Evangelical,

34). This highlights a significant challenge presented by receptive ecumenism, since it drives us to confront aspects of our churches that we might prefer to overlook. Added to this, in ecumenical settings people often present their churches in the best possible light. However, if receptive ecumenism is to work effectively, we must be willing to scrutinize our traditions. The way of receptive ecumenism forces us to diagnose unhelpful behaviours and seek help.

Overall, the Methodist and Independent Evangelical women were the most reluctant to name wounds, sins, or dysfunctions. Reflecting on this later, I asked three of the Methodist participants why they thought the Methodist women had responded in this way. Each answered differently. One said, 'We tend to be pragmatic and just get on with things. I think this means that we are prone to be positive.' Another said, 'I wonder whether it's because we are a shrinking church? Maybe no one wants to name the reasons why this might be?' Still another replied, 'We've been ordaining women for years. Because of this, we have had a chance to shape the culture. It's possible this has already healed some wounds left behind by the men!' The diversity of these responses demonstrates that Methodist women do not think alike necessarily. Only one of the Independent Evangelical participants offered a suggestion: 'I wonder whether it's because within an ecumenical group I was very aware that my church does not allow women to preach. I wanted to present the best of my church since others already see the potential difficulties without me naming them.'

Themes arising

Amid rich conversations in focus groups and research conversations, four themes emerged, often as interwoven threads: hospitality, vocation, leadership and power. These will form the focus of case studies in Part 2. The quotations below are intended to represent the broadest range of experiences shared by participants. For the purpose of anonymity, I have rarely revealed the roles of each respondent, indicating instead the age and denomination of each woman speaking. I have kept my commentary to a minimum in order to create a space for the women's voices to speak for themselves as much as possible.

I must make one further point, since the depth of compassion that the women displayed to one another may not be evident below. The practice of receptive ecumenism provides a space for facilitating not only the reception of gifts but also human kindness. Some women shared egregious experiences. Observing responses and interactions to them left me with an awareness that receptive ecumenism can create an open environment. The virtues, identified in Chapter 1 as hospitality, love, humility and hope, appeared often as the women delved deeply into their own and others' experiences, naming the shortcomings of their churches but remaining hopeful of the Spirit's healing.

Hospitality

The women's experiences of working in churches in England relate to hospitality in diverging ways. On the one hand, women are often responsible for creating a welcoming space; on the other, they experience a lack of hospitality from their own churches because they are prevented from participating in certain forms of work in churches. A recurring theme relates to racialized abuse and hospitality. One participant who is a person of colour spoke about 'the lack of welcome from predominantly white churches', highlighting the need for transformation across the traditions. Another told a story of her whole family being asked to leave a church because of the colour of their skin. I will return to this towards the end of the chapter.

Philosophers and theologians have spilt much ink over the nature of hospitality, challenging notions of the 'hospitality industry' and asking whether 'pure hospitality' is possible. I will speak to these debates in the following chapter, in which I will argue that women's practice of hospitality in churches can be interpreted as 'prophetic' and contributes significantly to informing current practice of receptive ecumenism. For our purposes in this chapter, however, hospitality is understood as 'offering refreshments' and 'creating a warm welcome', following the ways the women themselves spoke of hospitality.

No fewer than five women reported that they had been told to 'stick to making the tea' in response to their requests to explore vocations. Even in some of the most forward-thinking churches there remains an expectation that women will provide refreshments. This is not to say that only women participate in this activity, but generally women are found behind the serving hatch, catering for all kinds of gatherings.[8] When discussing the hospitality that they offered in their churches women were divided over whether or not they wanted to 'make the tea'. Some responded positively: 'I actually like making the tea. I'm quite shy and it's a way of speaking to people, while I'm safe behind the counter with a teapot in my hand' (Baptist, 68); 'I'm in favour of good coffee, and in my experience the only way that's going to happen is to make it myself' (AoG, 28); also, 'It's very useful to be organizing refreshments, as it means that the priest must communicate with me. This gives me a chance to know what's going on more widely' (Catholic, 78). The last comment points to alternative methods of accessing power.

Not all the women wanted to be responsible for refreshments, nor did they want to be on the 'hospitality committee'. One responded emphatically, 'I think we should be boycotting this kind of work and leaving it to the men. How will things ever change otherwise?' (Anglican, 30). While she believed it was important that 'churches offer hospitality', this woman thought that men might provide refreshments instead, or at the very least 'be on the hospitality rota'.

One common experience pertained to being both a leader and a woman. For example, one leader explained that at her church she was 'expected to help cater at the event as well as running it' (49).[9] It was fascinating to observe the reactions of the women listening. The nods of assent were vigorous; heads bobbed up and down, and there were many wry smiles. The non-verbal communication pointed towards the lack of surprise from most of the women in the room. One woman responded, while frowning, with two important questions:

'How can you know for certain that this happened because you are a woman? Is it possible that the people in your congregation are just really demanding?' (Independent Evangelical, 44). These questions highlight the difficulty in stipulating that a particular experience relates to being a woman. This is a question to which I will return towards the close of the chapter.

Vocation

Whether vocation was the focus of in-depth sharing or mentioned only in passing, it arose repeatedly during conversations on both gifts and wounds.[10] It is important to note that the women did not approach vocation univocally. Some talked about vocation as it relates to their discipleship: 'My vocation is to follow Jesus and to make disciples' (Independent Evangelical, 22). Others related vocation to being a mother: 'My vocation first and foremost is to be a mum to my kids' (Anglican, 39). For others, vocation related to a particular kind of call to follow Christ: 'Holy Orders'. One of the Sisters shared:

> I did not plan on living as a single woman but in the end, after many years of prayer and conversation with others, it became clear God was calling me ... I still laugh to myself about the fact that this is my vocation because I am not at all how you might imagine a Sister would be. (Catholic, 82)

Catholic and Anglican women often spoke of vocation with the prefix 'lay', observing 'the Spirit calls all Christians to serve in the body of Christ' (Anglican, 27). Irrespective of their tradition, participants observed that there is a deficit in training and support for those who want to discern any kind of lay vocation: 'What about a vocation to chaplaincy work?' (Baptist, 45); 'You'd think the only call God puts on people's lives is to be a presbyter' (Methodist, 38); 'When I thought that God might be calling me to work with people who have dementia there was no one to discern this with, other than my friends' (Catholic, 75); and, 'Sometimes, it feels as though the only thing God might call you to be is a pastor' (AoG, 41). For the Catholic and Orthodox women, exploring vocation to ordained ministries is not an option. Some thought that this is 'just something we need to live with' (Catholic, 38), whereas others could not discuss it without shedding a few discreet tears. Below, note that women respond differently to the way in which some churches do not permit the discernment of vocation to ordained ministry.

Flourishing in a vocation

When speaking of vocation, over half the women described themselves as 'fulfilled', 'flourishing', 'overwhelmingly thankful' and 'in a place of wonder at having been called by God'. The reflections below demonstrate that being a woman does not inhibit vocation necessarily:

> As a Catholic woman in local lay leadership I feel empowered and supported by the men I encounter. It's true my gender excludes me from the priesthood and diaconate, but there are plenty of other opportunities to live out my vocation to spread the Good News. (Catholic, 42)

> As a Methodist, I never considered I should leave leadership to the men, and so when I sensed God calling me to be ordained deacon, the process was straightforward. (Methodist, 38)

> Despite being divorced, a single parent, and a whole other host of potential barriers, my vicar supported my journey to becoming a youth-worker all the way. (Anglican, 46)

> My vocation to lay parish work was supported all the way. Although goodness knows what would have happened if I'd said I thought I have a vocation to priesthood. (Catholic, 82)

> It was all rather easy, really, in the sense that my pastor listened to what I thought the Spirit was saying and then began

to put me in various leadership roles so that I could gain experience. It would have been nice to have had a female role model, but somehow Jesus created a way among the men. (Independent Pentecostal, 37)

Unable to pursue a vocation

Not all women spoke positively concerning vocation. Some shared that they had a sense of vocation using words such as 'sorrow', 'loss', 'grief' and 'confusion', describing their experiences in the following ways:

Despite all I did in and around the parish, I was never able to explore a vocation ... any vocation ... there is no real lay vocation in our church. Vatican II might as well not have happened. It breaks my heart. (Catholic, 74)

I had to go to four different churches before I found a minister and church which would support my sense of vocation to ordained ministry. I got there in the end but it was hardly a pain-free journey. (Baptist, 46)

I thought I was called to be a deacon, but now I'm dying and I'll never know. (Catholic, 67)

Vocation to what? To bake the bread for the men to break it? (Orthodox, 53)

As a Pentecostal, I heard the Spirit call me to be ordained; so when my pastor would not support me because I am a woman, I went to another church because I wanted to be faithful to God. (AoG, 40)

A number of women noted their surprise that the negative testimonies spread across such diverse traditions. One Baptist (47) summed up their responses: 'I think we have learnt that just because a church ordains women, it does not mean that we will automatically flourish'. In the same group, a Catholic registered her shock at what she had heard others share:

I had no idea that whether churches are governed as autonomous bodies, or structured with a broader accountability, it can be problematic for a woman to discern a possible vocation from God, or test possible gifts. I thought it was the Catholic Church that has all the problems. I am genuinely shocked. (Catholic, 65)

One of the outcomes of this research relates to the breaking down of presuppositions. Receptive ecumenism creates space for a deeper understanding of diverse traditions, which is an important step towards unity.

'Should I leave my church to pursue a possible vocation to the priesthood?'

A Catholic woman posed this question during one of the focus groups. Her question was rhetorical, although she was curious about responses to what she described as 'my discernment dilemma'. The group itself did not attempt to resolve the woman's challenges; rather, they reflected with her on both sides of the argument. During a further research conversation, an Anglican priest who had previously left the Catholic Church to pursue vocation to the priesthood described her experience in the following way:

I felt like I was getting divorced. It was dreadful, and I received so much judgement from fellow Catholics, from men and women. My husband was supportive, but even now it pains me that he can't receive the body of Christ when I celebrate. He is Catholic, and, of course, officially Catholics can't receive in other denominations. But I know I'm in the right place, being who God has called me to be. (Anglican, 58)[11]

69

On the basis of this research, it would not be an exaggeration to say that vocation is fraught with challenges, especially when church structures and those in authority prevent women from discerning particular vocations.

While discussing 'vocation to priestly ministries', in one group the focus of conversation turned to the problems of clericalism. One Catholic made a thought-provoking comment:

> I think it's good that women are not ordained in my church. Look at all the energy there is among us women. We are out involved in mission, social justice, politics, and caring for the environment. There are some brilliant women doing Catholic theology in the academy. Do we really want all that energy to be lost to clericalism? Women are no different from men in this regard – look at the Anglicans. How many women are making any kind of radical difference to the clericalism in the Church of England? Yes, they are being role models, but do we really need to be ordained to do that? (Catholic, 69)[12]

This evoked strong reactions from others in the room. Most agreed that clericalism (across all traditions) is a problem, but not everyone agreed that 'excluding women is the most appropriate way to combat clericalism'. (Orthodox, 41)

Vocation to preach?

In a conversation with a colleague during which I was reflecting on prevalent themes, I noted my surprise at how many women during the course of the research expressed a desire to preach. In fact, no less than two-thirds of the participants mentioned preaching.[13] My colleague responded that since women cherish the Scriptures, they need to be able to hear their own voices expounding on them. She suggested that the desire to hear a woman's voice does not only stem from a wish to hear women's perspectives on the Bible, but that it is also about the need to hear an 'actual woman's voice' as a reminder that women are part of the larger Christian story. She explained that women need to be able to listen to their tradition and hear their own voices echoing back. If we only hear men's voices preaching, we miss the impact of inspirational women through the ages.[14] During a feedback session others echoed this observation, agreeing that it is important to hear and see women in churches.

Within the focus groups and research conversations, women discussed their paths to preaching:

I preach at Mass. Our priest is progressive and he often invites me to preach. No one from the parish has ever complained. I think people like hearing a woman interpret the Bible. (Catholic, 42)

I'm training to become a local preacher and I've only ever been encouraged to go for it. I'm loving it and everyone's very supportive. (Methodist, 31)

I've set up a younger preachers' group to encourage the younger members of our church who want to have a go at preaching. They love it, and so do I, especially when it's the young women who are growing in confidence. (Anglican, 48)

Since my own church does not allow me to preach, I have a licence to preach in the Anglican Church. While it's not the same as preaching in my own church, I still get to use my gifts, and my preaching is usually well received. (Catholic, 67)

The women's resilience in pursuing a vocation to preach demonstrated the lengths to which women will go to pursue God's call on their lives. Since it formed a strong theme, we will return to questions of vocation throughout the book with a particular focus in Chapter 5.

Leadership

Challenges relating to leadership arose frequently in conversations, often accompanied by reflections on power. The women's experiences range from leading children's groups, local churches, congregations, youth groups, choirs, liturgy and mission teams through to providing spiritual direction to church leaders. On some occasions, women indicated that they might be gifted leaders, or that they were skilled as leaders. All too often, they apologized when identifying their own positive attributes.[15]

During a research conversation, a woman declared to me, 'I *am* a leader, it's just that my church does not recognize this' (Catholic, 72). As she spoke, she had tears in her eyes which communicated the pain experienced through the rejection of her gifts. During a talk on receptive ecumenism at a local Catholic group, I shared this story, and one of the men became agitated while listening to me. He interrupted, 'No one should be walking around saying things like that. No one should declare themselves to be a leader.' I asked him why he was so offended, explaining that the woman had felt the need to justify her ability because her experience was one of being prevented from taking on leadership roles precisely because she is a woman. My interlocutor remained unconvinced, pronouncing that women should not make such claims. I relay this here to emphasize how contentious it is in certain contexts to claim that God bestows leadership gifts upon women. While some women reported positive experiences of leading, others made the following comments:

> I think the problem with women leading in the Orthodox Church is that we can't easily grow beards. To me the beard says, 'Men lead. Women don't.' (Orthodox, 64)

> Father knows best, does he 'eck. But there's nothing I can do about it. He won't listen to the likes of me. A woman. Despite the fact I've been a CEO. (Catholic, 78)

Saying out loud 'I am a leader' has attracted a great deal of resistance. (Baptist, 57)

I used to have a formal leadership role within my church, but I got really tired of the power games among the men, and in the end I left and became a teacher instead. (Independent Evangelical, 47)

Collaboration is sometimes tricky because not all Baptist ministers want to collaborate, especially with women. (Baptist, 62)

Do women lead differently from men?

This question arose, without being introduced by the researcher, in each of the five focus groups and in several research conversations. When women spoke for or against essential feminine qualities, they did not refer explicitly to theories of sex and gender.[16] Some participants believed that women have unique leadership gifts, 'especially with respect to collaboration' (Anglican, 46). Others disagreed, maintaining that how women lead is 'unrelated to gender' (Catholic, 38) and has more to do with 'cultural conditioning' (Baptist, 54).

I think we bring something that men don't. We are softer and more caring. (Methodist, 39)

I lead with a man. He is strategic and I am pastoral. That's where our gifts lie and I'm happy with it. (AoG, 49)

Both in my own role, and working collaboratively with colleagues, I held significant responsibilities and helped to build a more collaborative culture. (Independent Pentecostal, 41)

Women are more collaborative by nature, but collaboration in the Catholic Church is sketchy – it really depends on the priest. (Catholic, 46)

I lead no differently from some of my male colleagues and this always seems to be a problem. I don't prefer the more pastoral roles, or working with young children, and yet they always seem to want me to be in these roles because I am a woman. (Baptist, 54)

I'm not sure the Church of England has fully reconciled itself to the fact that women are gifted to lead, and that they don't necessarily lead differently from men. (Anglican, 37)

I lead happily with men in my own church, but it's not always as easy with those outside my tradition. (Methodist, 49)

Leading in ecumenical work

No fewer than eight Methodists mentioned that working ecumenically brings challenges, since 'ecumenical work brings us into contact with leaders from churches which do not support women in leadership'. One mentioned that she had moved into an area where the leaders of the various churches met together regularly. The other leaders were men and belonged to a group called 'the fraternal'. The new Methodist asked whether it would be possible to change the name to something that did not suggest a 'men-only leaders' group'. Their response was a resounding 'no'. She smiled, sighed, and said, 'You pick your battles, don't you? And this is one I just do not have the time or the energy to fight.' Even when a church creates space for its women to lead, it does not guarantee the experience of women is positive when they are working ecumenically in England.

Power[17]

Conversations often revolved around aspirations of possessing power, the seduction of power, uses and abuses of power, structures of power, men in positions of power, and whether or not women share power more willingly. Whether explicitly or implicitly, power emerged as the most prevalent theme in every conversation. Generally, the women responded negatively to the concept of power, approaching it with suspicion as a 'thing from which women need to retreat' (Baptist, 48). Opinions varied over whether women use power differently from men and the ways in which male leaders empower or disempower women:

> I suppose any group in which one gender dominates will always be at risk of dysfunction, especially if gender exclusiveness is aligned with power. (Catholic, 46)

> I recognize that the dominant feminist narrative – about the exclusion of women from any positions of real power – is forceful and largely accurate, but it is not the only story. There may have been too few, and some may see them as tokenistic, but there have been women doing serious work. (Catholic, 65)

> I think this reflection on power is fascinating, in that it seems to be something to do with the people in the positions of power. Whatever church we're in, not everyone seems to be able to hold it well. Do you think a woman would make a difference in that position? (Orthodox, 44)

> People have asked me whether, now that we have women bishops, this makes a difference with how power is used in the church. I wish I could say it does, but there are still far too many men in the positions of power, and women have not worked out how to lead as women. (Anglican, 36)

> Manipulation can be a form of power. I think that sometimes we women can be the worst offenders there, at least when it comes to flower arranging or any other of the jobs that women like to do in churches. (Methodist, 41)

> We don't have theological disagreements; we just have power struggles in our congregations. And we have power struggles

between Moscow and Constantinople. Maybe if there were more women at the top or any women at the top things would be different. We'll never know, though. (Orthodox, 69)

Men like to have power when it comes to leading the churches. They seem to like willy-waving to show how much power they have! (Baptist, 45)

The comment above resulted in a great ripple of laughter among the women in the room. I was curious because the laughter indicated that the others agreed with the statement. Some nodded their heads, recalling times in their own work they had witnessed 'this kind of behaviour from male colleagues' (Methodist, 41). The general opinion among the women was that they had each experienced this in one context or another while working for churches in England. They did not all agree, however, on whether women and men use power differently.

Further conversations ensued over whether women were empowered or disempowered by men in leadership positions. Even when women are in positions of significant authority outside of the Church, they can be treated differently when working within churches.

Some women in our church have powerful jobs within the community. They are great leaders, they are inspirational, they are entrepreneurs, they have great vision, and a compassion for the community that really stirs people to action against injustices and impoverished conditions. They fight for their community in such a powerful and dynamic way, but yet they'll go to church meetings and then the men in power say, 'Oh, you sit over there.' And this is very painful. (Independent Pentecostal, 57)

I have never felt disempowered as an Orthodox woman. In fact, one of the things that surprised me when I first began to meet Orthodox people was how seriously they all took me, especially the clergy! I have always felt respected for what you might call the creative side of being a woman. However, I have never had any vocation to ordained ministry, and maybe I would feel different if I had. (Orthodox, 63)

For years I felt that the Lord was calling me to preach, but my pastor said that women can't do that. It did not occur to me to challenge him; the women did not do that. It's not how it worked. In the end, I moved to a different church. It seemed crazy to me, given I did so much motivational speaking in my day job. (Independent Pentecostal, 53)

On the one hand I could say that the people who did not allow me to flourish are men. However, what it was is that the people who did not allow me to flourish were the people in positions of power. So it might not be as much to do with gender as power. (Anglican, 43)

Pastors have power: an enabling power and a restricting power. What's sad is that I seem to have experienced the restricting power more often than the enabling one. (Independent Evangelical, 53)

I think that we do have power, and if we would only work together, we'd have a chance of changing the culture instead of tearing each other apart and being so competitive with other women all the time. Women are not always each other's advocates. (Anglican, 38)

When I thought that God was calling me to teach the Bible, my minister explained that the Bible says women should not have authority over men or teach them. (Baptist, 56)

This comment came from a Baptist lay preacher, who reduced the room to tears with further stories of being held back in her vocation. I will return to this in Chapter 7, in which I will discuss some differences between the Baptist and Methodist traditions in England, and how these affect the disempowerment or empowerment of women.

Wounds, sins and dysfunctions

Women related tales of sexism and sexual harassment experienced while working in their churches. Furthermore, participants spoke of incidents that related to being single, being women of colour, and being mothers.

Experiences of sexism and sexual harassment

Funeral directors can be a problem. And the comments on my appearance are always as I'm about to walk the coffin in. You can't retort at that point. I've had all kinds of things, such as, 'The churches would not be dying if all the ministers had a figure like yours', through to 'Do you fancy sitting on my lap at the wake?' It's not great when you are about to take a funeral service. (Methodist, 41)

I have had inappropriate flirting from men in every single congregation I've worked in. I always wear trousers these days as I've just had too many comments on my legs. It makes me sick as I just want to get on and do the job and not be seen as a sex object. (Baptist, 53)

So, for most of the men I work alongside, I'm either the woman in the kitchen or there's a certain little flirty thing going on. They find it really hard to relate on an equal setting. My situation is I'm in a chaplaincy team and I'm in a room with all other men. (Baptist, 49)

In youth-work, often colleagues joke around. I don't think they mean to be sexist, but I still find it difficult. (Independent Evangelical, 26)

Sometimes in my job I come across a 'flirty' priest. In the main, they are fine, but there was one time when, during an interview, a priest invited me to sit on his lap. I declined. Needless to say, I did not get that job! (Catholic, 42)

Being single

As a lay leader, sometimes I'm included in dinner parties, but there's always an expectation I must be looking for someone to marry. Churches have a long way to go in understanding singleness as a gift. The family, or so it seems to me, is one of the idols of our age – at least it is in the Church of England. (Anglican, 31)

My challenges have come from being a single female in ministry. I find that women in the congregation often treat me with suspicion and they seem to think that I want to steal their husbands. It makes ministry difficult. (Methodist, 49)

No one takes into account the fact that when I get home after a funeral or something, there's no one to cook the tea. (Baptist, 56)

My challenges have not come from the institution itself, but instead they have come from congregations and also from being a single female in ministry. When I came into circuit it was just assumed that I would manage. I could run the house, I could do the garden, I could do the shopping, cleaning, washing, and do full-time ministry as well. Whereas there were a couple of my male colleagues who were single, who went into circuit, and they had women offering to help them, saying things like, 'I've made you a cake', or 'I've made you a meal'. (Methodist, 53)

Being a woman of colour

The following comments demonstrate, as one participant put it, 'the intersection of sexism and racism'. Writing in the 1980s, bell hooks argued that black women in the USA were afraid to acknowledge that 'sexism could be just as oppressive as racism'.[18] This theme arose during the conversations, despite being 30 years after bell hooks was writing and in a very different context. A black participant explained:

I have experienced both sexism and racism whilst working for my church, but I'm not always clear on which is the driving factor. Probably, those behaving badly towards me don't know either. The blind spots and prejudices run very deep both towards white women and women of colour. I do feel though that we [women of colour] get an extra dose thrown in our direction. (Anglican, age undisclosed)

Other participants commented:

I started off originally through my parents, my mother in particular, going to the Methodist Church because both my father and my mother came to this country back in the early 50s and they were already part of an established Methodist Church and they came to England expecting to join the same one, which they did. It was down the road from where we lived and I used to go there for Girls' Brigade and for Sunday service. I remember my mother being quite upset one Sunday, not understanding the full implications of it at the time, but I remember her saying to me, 'Oh, come on, we've got to find another church.' And I didn't quite understand what she meant by that, but it turns out we had a new minister that had started and he was a bit concerned about the number of black faces in his congregation. So, we found another church to go to which had more people like us. I found acceptance, a sense of belonging, and a sense of seeing people that represented and look like myself, which was key at the time, as a young woman trying to find my place in the world, where I'm going, what I'm doing, and all that stuff … I work as a chaplain now and I'm the only black woman in a white man's world. I'm rarely taken seriously. (Independent Pentecostal, 53)

I have experienced racism in every job I've had in a church. Mind you, I should say the same about sexism. (Anglican, 46)

I lead the Sunday school and I'd say that most of the time the racism is very subtle. I've had to work reasonably hard at making sure other leaders and teachers don't use pictures and illustrations of only white children. The worst is 'white Jesus'! There are so many pictures of a white Jesus in Sunday school books. I'm determined to raise a generation of youngsters who can relate to Jesus as they are and not think of the Son of God as a white man. It's easier to get hold of a picture of Mary as a black or brown woman; at least this is what I've found. (Catholic, 63)

Motherhood

When I got pregnant it was just before my curacy was due to start. I had to get legal advice, just to get maternity pay from my diocese. They were desperate to get out of it and clearly did not know what to do with me. I was a problem they did not want to deal with. (Anglican, 27)

There were lots of questions about how I would do this with a baby. And when I go to a conference, people will come up to me and say, 'Who's looking after the children?' I tell them that my husband is and they ask me, 'Will he be all right?' I hope so, he's their father! (Methodist, 42)

Those in authority assumed I would support myself during ordained ministry because I have a disabled son. So, the assumption was that I would stay at home to care for him. When I explained that my husband supported my vocation and he would take care of our son when I'm at work, they were visibly shocked. (Anglican, 38)

The women listened with compassion and expressed great sadness at what they heard of one another's experiences, whether these related to sexism, singleness, motherhood, racialized abuse, or any other source of pain. Other experiences were shared, although the women stated that they did not believe their experiences to be a 'women only' problem. These related to times when inadequate support was given to those with disabilities and/or mental health challenges, which is a further area in which churches are not yet functioning as well as they might.

Recommendations

At the close of each group and research conversation I asked participants how they might want to continue the journey of receptive ecumenism. The women made three recommendations that they believed would help make a positive change to women's experiences of working in churches in England.

Ecumenical mentoring

The participants observed the need for younger women to be mentored across the traditions. One young Catholic put it like this: 'I never get the chance to spend time with ordained women like I have today. It's been inspirational, and I'd love to learn from women outside my church, as well as inside my church. Mentoring would be a great way forward.' Mentoring across diverse traditions presents some challenges, but participants were unanimous that the benefits are great both for the mentors and the mentees.

Receptive ecumenism network

Some participants suggested a network, since they 'recognized that life in the twenty-first century is busy with women juggling a number of roles'. The women identified the need to journey together, suggesting that a space in which relationships can grow over time would work best. This has begun through informal Facebook groups which allow for communication amid the demands of working in churches.

Publication

A number of participants mentioned that they would like to see this research published as a book. I hope that what is written here both honours their contributions and inspires others to practise receptive ecumenism.

Conclusion

Women possess a broad range of gifts

- Some gifts are received in churches unequivocally.
- Particular gifts – such as Bible-teaching, preaching, leadership, and process implementation – are rejected by numerous churches.

Women are called by God to use their gifts

- Some are able to respond to this call, enabling their churches to flourish in a variety of ways, and are fulfilled in their vocations.
- Others experience great resistance when they respond to Christ's call amid the abuse of power in flawed institutions.
- Women have pushed through the limits to find places where they can use their gifts, even though the gifts are not officially recognized.

Women's views and experiences are diverse

- Women do not all think alike!
- Some believe that women work differently than men and others disagree with this. We cannot simply say 'women believe X'.

Practising receptive ecumenism

- Some participants prefer to focus only on positive experiences, preferring not to name the difficulties of working in a particular tradition. For others, directing attention to gifts is not always easy, especially if they have experienced rejection or abuse. Self-awareness and self-management help when journeying according to the way of receptive ecumenism. Added to this, whether we speak of 'power dynamics', 'power games', or 'powers that be', those involved in the receptive journey enter into relationships of power. When churches come together to practise receptive ecumenism, an explicit recognition of these factors will demonstrate care for the participants and enable productive conversation and learning.

Walking towards healing

Since receptive ecumenism encourages honest engagement with churches' wounds, I have aimed to interrogate the ways in which women have spoken about dysfunctions in the churches in which they work. I hope that the findings will provide inspiration for individuals and churches to engage in their own reflection, following the way of receptive ecumenism. Part 2 reflects theologically on themes emerging from the women's conversations and engages receptive ecumenism across diverse churches, aiming to move towards healing some of the wounds identified from the focus groups.

Notes

1 See, for example, the book by Kate Coleman, *7 Deadly Sins of Women in Leadership: Overcome Self-Defeating Behaviour in Work and Ministry* (UK: Next Leadership, 2010). Coleman outlines common traits among women in leadership, which shows that the problems are not specific to particular denominations.

2 The women's ages are listed next to the tradition in which they work.

3 For further information, see the Methodist Church's website: www.methodist.org.uk/about-us/the-methodist-church/what-is-distinc tive-about-methodism/the-methodist-quadrilateral/.

4 The 'genius of women' refers to a phrase used by John Paul II. Chapter 4 draws on these words to explore the lack of recognition of the full breadth of women's gifts.

5 'Mutual flourishing' refers to a catchphrase in the Church of England, which I will explore in Chapter 6.

6 I have not included photographs of the sheets filled with sticky notes in order to preserve the anonymity of the participants.

7 Members of the Centre for Catholic Studies at Durham University are leading a multi-disciplinary research project entitled 'Boundary Breaking: Ecclesial-cultural Implications of the Sex Abuse Crisis within the Catholic Church', www.dur.ac.uk/boundarybreaking/.

8 For an ethnographic study of the roles taken by women in churches, see Abby Day, *The Religious Lives of Older Laywomen: The Final Active Anglican Generation* (Oxford: Oxford University Press, 2017). In the book, Day explores in depth the role of hospitality as a means of community-building.

9 I have not included the denomination here in order to protect the anonymity of the participant.

10 The following volumes draw together work on vocation from a variety of faith perspectives: Kathleen A. Cahalan and Douglas J. Schuurman (eds), *Calling in Today's World: Voices from Eight Faith Perspectives* (Grand Rapids, MI: Eerdmans, 2016); John C. Haughey, *Revisiting the Idea of Vocation: Theological Explorations* (Washington, DC: Catholic University of America Press, 2004).

11 When the woman explains that her Catholic husband cannot receive the Eucharist from her, she is referring to Canon 844 which states, 'Catholic ministers administer the sacraments licitly to Catholic members of the Christian faithful alone, who likewise receive them licitly from Catholic ministers alone'; see www.vatican.va/archive/ENG1104/_P2T.HTM.

12 Her comment echoes an article by Linda Woodhead, 'A Woman's Place', *The Tablet* (1 December 2012), p. 20. She argues, 'It's easier to name prominent Catholic women in British society than prominent Anglicans.'

13 Catholic women are not officially allowed to preach the homily after the Gospel reading, since this privilege is reserved for the priest.

14 I am grateful to Anna Rowlands, an insightful colleague whose work provokes much to think about.

15 This behaviour is common; see Karina Schumann and Michael Ross, 'Why Women Apologize More Than Men: Gender Differences

in Thresholds for Perceiving Offensive Behavior', *Psychological Science* 21.11 (2010), pp. 1649–55, https://journals.sagepub.com/doi/abs/10.1177/0956797610384150.

16 See Chapter 4 for further discussion on essentialism.

17 I will explore characterizations of power in Chapter 7.

18 bell hooks, *ain't I a woman: black women and feminism*, 2nd edition (New York and London: Routledge, 2015), p. 1.

PART 2

4

The Gift of Hospitality

Part 1 explored how receptive ecumenism precipitates the good of the church not as a quick fix to the ecumenical winter, but as a long-term process of conversion in which a church, recognizing its own weaknesses, becomes more fully itself through learning and receiving from another. Having surveyed receptive ecumenism, Part 1 moved on to analyse how women engaging in receptive ecumenism explored together the wounds and gifts of working in their respective traditions. Even women working in the same tradition testify to very different experiences, since no single tradition is free from difficulties relating to doctrines, structures and practices. Part 2 constructs case studies that reflect theologically on the principal themes emerging from the research: hospitality, vocation, leadership and power. As identified in the Introduction, the following chapters adopt different approaches in order to demonstrate a breadth of ways to draw on and engage with receptive ecumenism.

This chapter reflects on the gift of hospitality to which the women's experiences of working in churches in England relate in diverging ways.[1] On the one hand, women are often responsible for creating a welcoming space and for being hospitable; on the other, many experience a lack of hospitality from their own churches. Since what constitutes hospitality is debated widely, while probing these debates I will argue that even through tea and biscuits, work is undertaken, and power and difference are negotiated; and, as such, this negotiation can be an important part of pursuing common flourishing. Following the way of receptive ecumenism, I will begin by considering the 'wound' identified by Catholic participants who spoke frequently of papal teaching on the 'genius of women'.[2] A number observed that this teaching signifies a 'harmful theological anthropology', one outcome of which is the limitation of women's roles in the Catholic Church or, put another way, 'a rejection of the full range of gifts that the women bring to their church'. This results in the absence of women's minds and voices during Mass, or in decision-making in the Church, or both.[3]

To critique the 'genius of women', I will draw on a case study concerning a group of Catholic women in the Midlands, UK, who organize small-scale, women-only receptive ecumenism gatherings at grass roots. As we shall see, hospitality is at the heart of their work.[4] Through reflecting theologically with them upon the rationale for their practices, important learning arises which (a) highlights some of the difficulties with the Pope's depiction of the 'genius of women', and (b) shapes the way we conceive hospitality and its significance to receptive ecumenism. I will bring the women's work into conversation with Letty Russell and Luke Bretherton, who have engaged theologically with the theme of Christ's radical hospitality. Against this backdrop, a prophetic call unfolds concerning the women's practices which challenges the Catholic Church on its lack of hospitality to women and lack of reception of women's gifts. While receptive ecumenism suggests that one tradition receives the gifts from another, we shall see that the practice of receptive ecumenism also brings to the surface gifts within one's own tradition that can help to heal particular wounds.

The 'genius of women'

The previous chapters described how I drew on the core commitments of receptive ecumenism in order to create a space for women to explore their experiences of working in churches in England. Recall that participants wrote on sticky notes according to the following three points:

1 Wounds according to my experiences of working in a church.
2 Gifts according to my experiences of working in a church.

3 Gifts in another's church, which would contribute to healing wounds in my tradition.

Having explored the first two points in the previous chapters, I turn now to focus on a response to the third point. Unequivocally, Catholic women stated that the gifts they would most like to receive into their church – if they were in the position to make this kind of decision – would be 'to see women priests', 'women involved in decision-making', and 'to hear the sound of a woman's voice preaching the homily at Mass'. As I listened to the Catholics speaking, it struck me that 'preaching' in particular was mentioned repeatedly. In fact, nearly two-thirds of the Catholic participants spoke of a desire not only to hear a woman preach but 'to preach at Mass'. One of the oldest participants, a woman well into her eighties, said, 'How awful it is and what rubbish that women can't interpret the word of God – officially, anyway. I think the Church is the worst for it you know, we're missing out.' A similar point was made by a much younger woman in her early twenties:

> My church does not want my gifts just because I am a woman. Sometimes, when I read the Gospel before Mass, I really want to preach on it. I feel like I have a gift that I could give here and a way of interpreting the Gospel. And even though I studied theology and I have the background that maybe they'd expect for someone to preach, I'm not allowed to do this because I'm not the priest.

Despite not being permitted to preach, at least officially, numerous Catholic women testified to exercising the ministry of preaching, believing themselves to be called by God to preach. Personally, I have benefited greatly from their ministries on the occasions I have been able to listen to them. One or two are encouraged by their priests to preach at Mass despite the Catholic teaching that disqualifies them from doing this. Some preach in ecumenical services; some in university chaplaincies; and others hold licences to preach in Anglican churches. One Catholic commented that, on the one hand, she was delighted to be able to use her gifts in the Church of England, but she was grieved at her own church not recognizing her skills. She closed her comments with 'it would be nice to be welcome in my own home'. As I observed in the previous chapter, drawing on the insights of a colleague, this is not principally about women's 'rights', but about being able to hear women's voices echoing through the tradition, and women hearing themselves in the stories. It is also about recognizing that God has given women a way of speaking and interpreting that means those listening are able to encounter Christ through their exposition of the Bible.

When they spoke about the restrictions regarding preaching and vocation in the Catholic Church, the participants referred repeatedly to Pope John Paul II's letter *To Women*. The letter was written for the Fourth World Conference on Women, entitled 'Action for Equality, Development and Peace', and convened by the United Nations in September 1995 in Beijing.[5] The Pope writes to counteract the long tradition of Christian theologians who draw conclusions about women concerning their irrationality and inferiority to men. He argues against these views by insisting upon the equal value of women. However, aspects of the letter are decidedly 'hard to swallow' (Catholic, 78), added to which the timing of the letter meant that it was not well received by many women – *To Women* was circulated just one year after the Pope's reaffirmation of Catholic teaching on the ordination of priests:

[The Church] holds that it is not admissible to ordain women to the priesthood, for very fundamental reasons. These reasons include: the example recorded in the Sacred Scriptures of Christ choosing his Apostles only from among men; the constant practice of the Church, which has imitated Christ in choosing only men; and her living teaching authority which has consistently held that the exclusion of women from the priesthood is in accordance with God's plan for his Church.[6] (§1)

This account of God's plan suggests that whatever the contents of John Paul II's letter *To Women*, it will not explore the possibility of broadening women's vocations. *To Women* begins:

> I would now like to *speak directly to every woman*, to reflect with her on the problems and the prospects of what it means to be a woman in our time. In particular I wish to consider the essential issue of the *dignity* and *rights* of women, as seen in the light of the word of God. (§1)

One woman referred to the opening lines of the letter as 'particularly egregious', on the basis that 'the Pope clearly has no idea what the problems are in being a woman in the present day. He seems to be oblivious to the fact that this letter perpetuates my problems, rather than alleviating them.' The Pope proceeds to give thanks for five ways in which God calls women to be in the world. Mothers form the first group; by 'mothers', he speaks of those women who have actually given birth, although towards the end of the letter he broadens his notion of motherhood to include spiritual mothering. He then thanks women who are wives, daughters and sisters, women who work, and women who are consecrated (§2). While it appears to be an attempt at inclusivity, it is an odd list at best.[7]

The letter moves on to recognize that throughout history women's voices have not been heard as they should and that their participation in politics and society has been limited. In response to this, the Pope calls for the greater participation of women in social, economic and political life on the grounds that

> this is a matter of justice but also of necessity. Women will increasingly play a part in the solution of the serious problems of the future: leisure time, the quality of life, migration, social services, euthanasia, drugs, health care, the ecology, etc. In all these areas a greater presence of women in society will prove most valuable, for it will help to manifest the contradictions present when society is organized solely according to the criteria of efficiency and productivity, and it will force

systems to be redesigned in a way which favours the processes of humanization which mark the 'civilization of love'.
(§4)

This extract exhibits a particular view that continues to develop
throughout the letter, namely, John Paul II's complementarian
theological anthropology in which women work according to
'love', while men work according to 'the criteria of efficiency
and productivity'. Sections seven and eight bring this view to
the fore as the Pope draws on an interpretation of the first two
chapters of Genesis in which God creates human beings:

> Woman complements man, just as man complements woman:
> men and women are *complementary*. Womanhood expresses
> the 'human' as much as manhood does, but in a different and
> complementary way. (§7)

Complementarianism encapsulates the belief that God created
men and women with essential qualities, resulting in different
roles.[8] Towards the close of the letter, the Pope coins these
essentialist and complementarian views by employing two
phrases: 'genius of women' and 'feminine genius'. These phrases
have since become intrinsic to popular Catholic thought about
women, although I have yet to meet more than a few Catholic
women working in England who speak positively about this
designated 'genius'. The letter depicts the feminine genius as
'service', 'helping', and the capacity to 'see persons with their
hearts' (§§9–12). The Pope does not extend the reflection to
include women's minds and voices. On this, one participant
said, 'I am a mother and I take my role and my children seriously, but I have other gifts too which I believe are important,
although my church does not receive them.' Whenever the
Catholic women referred to the theme of this letter it was
always with the suggestion that 'women have more to offer than
this'.

I am uncomfortable with the notion of a 'feminine genius'
for a number of reasons. Drawing on the contributions of
women in the focus groups, I suggest that if one must speak of

the 'genius of women', one might better describe it in terms of 'tenacity' and 'resilience'. That said, this would not adequately describe 'all women'.

Overall, the letter exhibits a limited view of women based on a complementarian theological anthropology, one result of which is a continued lack of hospitality to women and rejection of the full breadth of women's gifts and skills. In light of this letter and the women's responses to it, I will turn very shortly to a study involving Catholic women based in the Midlands, UK. In order to create a space in which women flourish and contribute to ecclesial learning, they initiated small-scale, women-only receptive ecumenism conferences; and, as we shall see, hospitality is at the heart of their work. Through reflecting theologically with them upon the rationale for their practices, important learning arises which both highlights some of the difficulties with the Pope's depiction of the 'genius of women', and shapes the way we conceive hospitality and its significance to receptive ecumenism. Before analysing these gatherings, let us interrogate the women's understanding of hospitality and how this relates to debates on the practice of hospitality within the Christian tradition.

What is hospitality?

At the turn of the millennium Jacques Derrida asked, 'Will we ever know what hospitality is?', acknowledging that despite writing in depth on the nature of hospitality, he had not yet arrived at an answer.[9] Hospitality conjures up myriad images: one might imagine the food eaten at the house of a friend or family member, a warm welcome in an otherwise hostile environment, or a costly meal in a hotel, which draws us towards images of the hospitality industry. Scripture and the Christian tradition witness to God's hospitality.[10] The belief that hospitality begins in God has long been acknowledged by those writing in the Christian tradition; for example, the fourth-century bishop Gregory of Nazianzus writes:

You will never surpass God's generosity even if you hand over your entire substance and yourself into the bargain ... No matter how much you offer, what always remains is more; and you will be giving nothing of your own because all things come from God ... we cannot outdo God in our gifts, for we do not give anything that is not God's or that surpasses God's own bounty.[11]

For centuries, Christians have recognized a particular kind of hospitality that is rooted in God. This is evident in the uniqueness of the incarnation of Christ, in which God demonstrates radically God's hospitality to the whole world, through to the simple breaking of bread shared on the road to Emmaus, in which Jesus is revealed as both host and guest (Luke 24.13–35).[12]

Over the past few decades, theologians have urged that we do not confuse hospitality with 'entertaining'.[13] The kind of entertaining to which they refer encompasses hosting family and friends in one's home through to commercial catering. For example, Letty Russell argues that in any Christian understanding of hospitality, 'tea and crumpets' must be excluded. These, she proposes, conjure up notions of 'terminal niceness' to which she would refuse a place at the hospitality table.[14] She also cautions against a false or shallow interpretation of hospitality that could 'deform' this virtue, such as the way in which those with greater advantages might condescend to share their wealth with 'inferior people'. Appropriately scathingly, she refers to this attitude as 'lady bountiful'.[15] Instead, Russell advocates for hospitality as 'the practice of God's welcome, embodied in our actions as we reach across difference to participate with God in bringing justice and healing to our world in crisis'.[16] While Russell is speaking about the injustices caused by the colonizer/colonized divide, her words might also be used to describe the women's ecumenical gatherings, as we shall see shortly.[17]

Continuing to identify the distinctiveness of Christian hospitality, in *Making Room: Recovering Hospitality as a Christian Tradition* Christine Pohl argues, quite rightly, that hospitality should only be called 'Christian' if it involves a welcome of the stranger. She draws on the New Testament writing of hospitality as *philoxenia*, which means literally 'love of strangers'. The case study in her book locates 'the strangers' as the persons who are most vulnerable in our communities. Her predominant argument aligns with Russell's, suggesting that there is more to be said of Christian hospitality than simple provision of refreshments.[18]

I wholly support the arguments for a radical hospitality that entails that churches open their arms to those who are refugees, those who are homeless, and those who are vulnerable in such a way as not to demean those who do not share the privilege of wealth.[19] These reminders are timely and enable Christians to think through how we image God's hospitality and welcome. I pause to offer a caution over the risk of devaluing everyday cultural practices through which the Spirit reveals God's presence at the expense of recovering a wholly radical interpretation of hospitality. Since 'our hospitality both reflects and participates in God's hospitality',[20] the Christian tradition needs an account of hospitality that reflects the multitude of ways in which the Spirit reveals God's hospitality on earth.

An understanding of hospitality should be able to encompass different kinds of welcome, both the radical and the everyday. As Elizabeth Johnson argues, 'God's presence in the world through the power of the Spirit is evidenced by ordinary people in ordinary time'.[21] The context of Johnson's argument is one in which she calls for a fresh vision of the communion of saints which, rather than depicting paradigmatic characters, should encompass the whole body of Christ. In the same way, if we define hospitality in such a way as to refer to radical acts of welcome only, we risk undermining the broader practices of welcome through which God is present. Overlooked in discussions on Christian hospitality is that, in England at least, the consumption of tea and biscuits (or some such equivalent) often forms the opening ritual which is an important aspect of the broader hospitality offered. As observed earlier, the personal is the political: even through tea and biscuits, work is undertaken and power and difference are negotiated; and, as such, this negotiation can be an important part of pursuing common flourishing.

Thus far, I have argued that hospitality begins in God and concerns the reception and welfare of the stranger, and that this reaches from offering refreshment through to ensuring those received are in a place of safety. Let us turn now to the case study that explores the practices of hospitality at the women's receptive ecumenism gatherings. We will observe a hospitality that incorporates a range of practices: not only welcoming and learning from the stranger, but also aiming to create a safe space for gifts to be received.

Receptive ecumenism gatherings for women

Paul Murray, David Pascoe and Antonia Pizzey have discussed hospitality conceptually, arguing that it is one of the core values or virtues required for receptive ecumenism. I extend their work by analysing for the first time both the theological and practical implications of the outworking of hospitality within receptive ecumenism.[22] The following case study involves members of the Ecumenical and Interfaith Group (EIG) of the National Board of Catholic Women (NBCW) who, in 2013, initiated women-only receptive ecumenism gatherings, as discussed in Chapter 2.[23] I conducted research conversations with eight of the women, and spent over 50 hours as a participant observer, attending their planning meetings and events in order to explore their approach to receptive ecumenism as fully as possible.

In various forms, the women have worked ecumenically across a number of traditions for over 30 years. They lead ecumenical collaborations such as winter night shelters, as well as chairing the local Churches Together in England committee, leading ecumenical services and participating in local groups for Women's World Day of Prayer.[24] Since I regularly meet Christians who have not heard of receptive ecumenism, I was curious to learn what it was about this way of ecumenical engagement that had inspired the women to the extent that they should want to put it into action. They explained that they had initially heard about it through their connections with the Centre for Catholic Studies at Durham University. The women's relationship with the Centre stems from a shared Catholic faith and the desire to 'support the public witness and engagement which is promoted through the Centre'.[25] On learning about receptive ecumenism, the women had been drawn initially to the emphasis on 'listening, learning and receiving gifts' from other Christian traditions. The women spoke about how 'the Holy Spirit has inspired and guided' their work, showing them 'new possibilities for ecumenism through the fresh approach offered by receptive ecumenism'.

When I asked the women about their motivations for pioneering these conferences, they explained that 'women have a great deal to contribute to ecumenical learning' and that they wanted 'to create a safe space for women to speak freely about their experiences', since the women believe that sometimes the presence of priests inhibits the laity from speaking candidly. Their practice of hospitality emerges through the formation of the receptive ecumenism conferences in which women participated from diverse traditions. They explored together a wide range of themes, such as 'prayer', 'ministry', and 'affirming women's gifts'. Observe below an outline of a typical gathering:

- Welcome with refreshments
- Prayer and Scripture reflection
- Introduction to receptive ecumenism
- Four short presentations by women from different traditions
- Gathering together in small groups to discuss the talks
- Lunch
- Group discussions based around the theme and talks; the practising of receptive ecumenism
- Gathering together the themes and feedback
- Closing prayer and farewell

From enveloping the day in prayer and Scripture reflection through to providing refreshments and lunch, the women's beliefs about and practices of hospitality undergird both the organization and duration of the gatherings. I shall begin by analysing the significance of location to their overall project, since the group devoted no small amount of time to thinking about where they should hold the first conference.

Derrida's discussions of narcissism draw attention to the way in which the host maintains a degree of power over the guest, since the host may invite the guest into their space in order to be in control of the encounter.[26] When hospitality occurs without room for reciprocity, the encounter becomes a breeding ground for reliance and debts. Ideally, the host creates space not only for giving, but also for receiving. In light of this, the Catholic women initiating the receptive ecumenism conferences decided it was crucial not to hold the primary gathering on Catholic ground. One commented, 'We wanted to create a space into which we were received because receptive ecumenism is a journey and we wanted our journey to set off in the right spirit. We believed it was important to begin well.' Another said, 'The Catholic Church often thinks of itself as the true church, and by not hosting the event we wanted to show that we respect the holy ground of others' churches.' In short, as one woman put it, 'place matters'. The Catholic women and those from other churches with whom they were collaborating opted to host the first conference in a nearby Methodist hall. Catholics and Methodists shared the hosting through which the Catholics aimed to 'hand over our complete ownership of the gathering'.[27] In several instances, when non-Catholics have organized a gathering, the Catholics have welcomed them into parish rooms.[28] Through this, they entered into a relationship of reciprocity intentionally. A further factor of great importance was easy access to the building. The result of this was that gatherings only took place in buildings with access for wheelchair users and sound systems for those requiring hearing technologies.

After settling on an apposite location, the women began to discuss how best to create a receptive space in which to welcome others. Aware that hospitality consists of human 'exchanges which restore the spirit', they began by making room for initial conversations among participants.[29] Food and drink formed a thread in their thought about how best to facilitate relaxed conversations. The result of this was that the attendees travelling from various parts of the Midlands arrived to find tea, coffee, biscuits, cake and fruit. The provision of refreshments performs an important function here: as one woman said, it 'offers refreshment for those who have travelled to the gathering, at the same time, providing a space for women to gather themselves for the day ahead. Many people are not comfortable to meet strangers and begin talking without some kind of initial ice-breaker.' To some it might appear that a cup of tea is a relatively inconsequential aspect of the overall ecumenical vision of receptive ecumenism; nevertheless, I cannot overstate the significance of offering a cup of tea. To drink a cup of tea signifies something particular in the English psyche, for better or for worse.[30] In this instance it sets the scene for a comfortable space in which guests feel safe. Safety of the participants is crucial to the receptive journey, as I shall discuss shortly.

After refreshments, the gathering begins in prayer and with a reflection on Scripture shared by a number of women. Not unlike the view expressed by Gregory of Nazianzus, the group's rationale for beginning in prayer is 'hospitality begins in God, expressing an aspect of God's character'. Through beginning in prayer, we locate ourselves and our stories in God. Ecumenist Michael Putney has highlighted, quite rightly, that it 'would be a mistake when talking about unity between the churches or the unity within any one Christian community to start with or focus upon the relationship of Christians with each other'.[31] Moreover, as one woman commented, 'prayer together affirms that it is the Spirit who we trust to lead us forward into unity'. Through prayer, both the hosts and guests locate God as the host who provides for their needs.

After a brief introduction to receptive ecumenism, three to four women speak about their experience of being in their respective traditions, focusing on a particular theme. The short talks comprise around 15 minutes in which a speaker shares her experience on a particular topic; for example, on 'prayer' and 'women in the church'. During one conference, women gave presentations on various forms of ministry. The women in the NBCW were keen to emphasize that they 'discussed ministry with a small "m", since Catholic women are not permitted to enter into ordained Ministry'. When I asked about why they chose these particular subjects, one woman responded:

> We thought long and hard about the topics because we wanted to address issues which are relevant to women, but we felt that we were walking a rather tight line. We did not want to be too controversial so as to include as many women as possible ... we wanted to create space for women to receive from one another in a way which is meaningful to them.[32]

Following these talks, the women gather into small groups to begin to reflect on what they have heard in relation to their own context and church tradition. After lunch the groups continue to reflect together, and through careful facilitation they discuss challenges and think about gifts that might be received.[33] One purpose of these talks is to allow women to enter into one another's worlds, at least with respect to their diverse churches in the Midlands, UK.[34] Hospitality necessitates a way of thinking that is not presumptuous, since it is all too easy to assume that we know and understand one another's contexts, and even what might be in another's mind. To move beyond this we must enter into dialogue with a willingness to listen, since 'to welcome the other means the willingness to enter the world of the other'.[35] Through entering the world of another, a further move occurs that recalls the heart of receptive ecumenism, namely, the women are able to discern more clearly the wounds and gifts of their own traditions.

Participants must feel as safe as possible for the facilitation of candid conversations. For this reason, among others, the NBCW created a space for women only. This decision brings to the fore questions concerning asymmetrical relations and power dynamics that arose in research conversations with the NBCW and also during focus groups.[36] Some women explained that it might present certain challenges to do the work of receptive ecumenism with those who are unsupportive of women in leadership, especially if those who are unsupportive occupy positions of authority in the churches. One woman put it this way: 'Why would I feel safe receiving a gift from someone who will not recognize my vocation? You need to trust someone to receive a gift, and not all those in authority are trustworthy when it comes to women.' She added, 'I am not sure I would want to come vulnerably with wounded hands into a space where my ministry is not recognized.'[37] While she was not speaking on behalf of all the women present, this participant raises a serious question with which we must grapple in relation to hospitality within receptive ecumenism. Hospitality should include the wellbeing of participants.[38] The best practice creates the space for women to contribute safely. Believing that 'God affirms all women', the NBCW and their ecumenical colleagues create a space in which women may freely and safely share their gifts.

Next I will bring the NBCW's practices of hospitality into conversation with Luke Bretherton's work on Christian hospitality in which he argues that hospitality 'is not an essentially domestic and apolitical kind of action'.[39] My primary reason for incorporating Bretherton's work emerges from conversations with the NBCW about what they believed they were accomplishing through the receptive ecumenism conferences. As one put it:

> We want to make clear that a receptive ecumenism conference is about more than just a nice tea party. We are creating a safe space for women to receive gifts from others, to have the opportunity to have their voices heard, and by being heard to begin to heal. During a gathering, women are able to dare to imagine a church in which they experience full participation and one in which their gifts are taken seriously.

This comment was made in a meeting of the Ecumenical and Interfaith Group of the NBCW. We were discussing the draft of a paper that I had written following research conversations with the principal women involved in organizing the receptive ecumenism conferences. I sent a draft of the paper through two weeks prior to the meeting so that they would have the opportunity to read, digest, and prepare their comments. I wanted to be sure that they were able to resonate with what

I had written. This meant that I was ready to make changes where necessary so that the final version reflected their own voices, intentions, and insights. Two of the women were keen that I brought to the fore the radical nature of the hospitality they were offering. This entailed further reading, reflecting and writing, as well as further conversations with the women themselves. I note this to identify that the theology and insights in this chapter came about through an iterative process that involved the women and me talking together, listening to one another, praying together, and discerning together the work of the Spirit. The process itself was non-prescriptive and as such provides one way of interpreting the women's practices.[40]

In the following section I will argue that the women's practice of receptive ecumenism, during which they receive one another's gifts and skills, embodies the kind of radical hospitality practised by Christ in the New Testament. To make sense of this claim, we turn to the themes of purity and holiness that run through Scripture.

Hospitality, purity and holiness

In *Hospitality as Holiness*, Bretherton writes, 'Through his hospitality, which has as its focal point actual feasting and table fellowship, Jesus turns the world upside down.'[41] Bretherton argues this during a discussion of the continuity and discontinuity between hospitality in the Old Testament and the New Testament. In the Old Testament hospitality is apparently somewhat paradoxical. For example, Leviticus 19.34 exemplifies the way in which God calls Israel to be a people of hospitality: 'the alien who resides with you shall be to you as the citizen among you; you shall love the alien as yourself, for you were aliens in the land of Egypt: I am the LORD your God'. At the same time, an issue prevails regarding purity and how Israel must keep itself clean.[42] Leviticus 11—15 and Numbers 19 describe the ritual impurity that results from contact with a variety of natural processes and substances. Hence the Torah contains numerous purity rituals in order to protect Israel from becoming polluted by those with whom she comes into contact. In short, it is concerned with the holiness of Israel.[43]

Moving forward to the New Testament, Jesus does not simply resolve the 'tension between hospitality and holiness present in the Old Testament'.[44] Rather, he brings together 'these two imperatives in a particular way. Jesus relates hospitality and holiness by inverting their relations: hospitality becomes the means of holiness.'[45] Neyrey's earlier work affirms Bretherton's thesis. He explores the relationship between meals and the purity system in Luke-Acts, arguing that the Pharisees eat with those with whom they share the same values. He writes, 'Hence, the Pharisees criticise Jesus ... for eating with tax collectors and sinners, because shared table fellowship implies that Jesus shares *their* world not God's world of holiness.'[46] Said another way, Christ's hospitality of pagans, sinners and those who are 'tainted' demonstrates his holiness because he restores them rather than being contaminated by them, thus requiring cleansing himself.

Let us consider how this works in action by examining Luke 8.43–48, which describes the encounter between Jesus and a woman who has been bleeding for many years: 'She came up behind him and touched the fringe of his clothes, and immediately her haemorrhage stopped' (verse 44). Following usual purity laws, Jesus would have gone to the temple to be cleansed after experiencing physical contact from a bleeding woman, since she would be considered unclean. However, rather than requiring cleansing, Jesus's holiness contagiously cleanses the woman.[47] He heals her, restoring her to a right place among her people rather than her tainting him. Later in Luke 10, Jesus tells the well-known parable of the Samaritan man, which recalls the demonstration of hospitality by a man who would be considered unclean by the Pharisees. Rather than using the parable to endorse purity teachings, Jesus tells those listening to 'go and do likewise' (10.37) – that is, to go and show mercy to those outside the confines of their social and religious world. Thus through actions and parables, Jesus establishes a way of being in which mercy and hospitality to those who are 'unclean' is prized. It is noteworthy that not only is this approach to holiness and hospitality inhabited by Jesus, but that Christ establishes this as the preferred behaviour of his followers. This is mapped on to Acts 10, when Peter visits Cornelius, a Roman centurion, and declares, 'You yourselves know that it is unlawful for a Jew to associate with or to visit a Gentile; but God has shown me that I should not call anyone profane or unclean' (10.28). Later in the chapter (10.44), the Holy Spirit falls upon the Gentiles present, thus affirming Peter's inclusion of them.

In light of this, let us recall the women gathering to engage in receptive ecumenism and the hospitality offered to each woman present. While many women flourish in churches and are fulfilled in various vocations, this is not the experience of every woman.[48] There is not enough space to cite the vast body of literature that calls for a reception of each woman's gifts in the body of Christ.[49] Even today, women's gifts are frequently rejected, especially if the gifts relate to teaching and preaching or leadership. Added to this, Catholic women have observed that little hospitality is offered regarding their involvement in the processes of decision-making.[50] Through practising receptive ecumenism, a space is created for the women gathered to receive one another's gifts, even when these gifts are being rejected within the structural level of their own churches. For example, women who testify to a vocation to preach but are not allowed to pursue this in their own church are provided with a space not only to be affirmed but also received as preachers.

Thus, in the same way that Jesus radically redefines hospitality by receiving and affirming those who are previously impure in relation to Torah, these gatherings of women function as a safe space where their gifts, which are otherwise rejected by their churches, are received. In light of this, the hospitality offered through these gatherings embodies the radical hospitality of Christ.

Conclusion

As Chapter 1 described, the commitment of receptive ecumenism is for one tradition to receive gifts from another to address the difficulties in its own. This chapter suggests that the practice of receptive ecumenism also brings to the surface gifts within one's own tradition. In this instance the gifts are women, who are often not expected to bring particular gifts. Just one month prior to the publication of *To Women*, John Paul II distributed the encyclical on commitment to ecumenism *Ut Unum Sint* ('That They May Be One').[51] In this, he explains that Christian unity is integral to the life of the faithful, stating quite rightly that ecumenical dialogue is not simply an 'exchange of ideas' but 'an exchange of gifts' (§1). In light of the fact that Catholic women pioneer receptive ecumenism gatherings, preach and teach in Anglican churches, and mentor and work as spiritual directors for those in different traditions, we might say that they are themselves gifts being received, albeit not in their own tradition.

Following the way of receptive ecumenism, Catholic participants identified the papal teaching on the 'genius of women' as a 'wound' in their tradition because it upholds a commitment to the lack of women's voices in formal decision-making and denies the possibility of women's vocation to the priesthood. As noted at the beginning of the chapter, the bright array of sticky notes containing scribbles by Catholic participants stated that they most eagerly desired the following gifts in other traditions: 'to see women priests', 'women involved in decision-making', and 'to hear the sound of a woman's voice preaching the homily at Mass'. These gifts exist in other traditions, albeit imperfectly; however, the ordination of women is the reason most often cited for disunity between the Catholic Church and the Anglican Communion, therefore it is unlikely that these gifts will be received into the Catholic Church any time soon. For now, Catholic women find innovative ways of making their voices heard, through using their gifts and skills in other churches, and through working ecumenically.

Turning to the NBCW receptive ecumenism conferences, we

see that reflecting upon their practice of hospitality highlights vital learning for churches intending to engage in receptive ecumenism. First, these gatherings emphasize the importance of prayer for receptive ecumenism. Through prayer, each tradition locates the desire for Christian unity in God. Prayer creates the space to acknowledge that all gifts come from God, while serving as a reminder that we look to the Spirit to lead the churches into transformation.

Second, the conferences establish that location matters and call to mind the power dynamics involved in hosting events. The role of reciprocity in receptive ecumenism comes to the fore through the location of events through which the hosts look to both give and receive.

Third, refreshments signify more than the need to quench thirst. Even through tea and biscuits, work is undertaken, and power and difference are negotiated; and, as such, this negotiation can be an important part of pursuing common flourishing.

Fourth, the women's considerations underline the importance of considering asymmetrical relations. While it might not be possible or even preferable to bring about symmetry in the relationships of those involved in receptive ecumenism, an ethical practice of receptive ecumenism must begin with an account of the power relations between those taking part.

Finally, reflecting theologically on the practice of receptive ecumenism by Catholic women in conversation with Christ's own radical hospitality which receives and restores the stranger, I argue that the women's gathering for receptive ecumenism serves as a prophetic voice which not only calls to account the hospitality of our churches to women, but also calls for the reception of the whole breadth of women's gifts across the churches.

Notes

1 Many interlocutors have contributed to this chapter which draws on Gabrielle Thomas, 'A Call for Hospitality: Learning from a Particular Example of Women's Grass Roots Practice of Receptive Ecumenism in the UK', *Exchange* 47.4 (2018), pp. 335–50 (used with permission).

Nigel Rooms critiqued an early draft of a related paper, pointing me to Luke Bretherton's work. I first presented a section of the chapter at the annual conference of the Society of the Study of Theology in Nottingham, UK, in April 2018, to which Julie Gittoes, Mike Higton and Tarah Van de Wiele gave helpful, critical responses. During my presentation at the Ecclesiology and Ethnography Conference, St John's College, Durham, UK, in September 2018, I received encouragement and important feedback from both academics and practitioners. Antonia Pizzey and Sara Gehlin shared unpublished work with me, and through a patient reading of the text, Jenny Leith helped me to articulate my argument.

2 Tina Beattie argues that the sins of the Church must be 'recognized as male sins' in *New Catholic Feminism: Theology and Theory* (New York: Routledge, 2006), p. 280.

3 There were two notable exceptions among the Catholics who commented that they did not share the others' feelings.

4 See Chapter 1 for a discussion of my usage of 'Catholic' and 'Roman Catholic'. Throughout this chapter, I apply 'Catholic', since this is how the women speak about themselves.

5 For the letter, see www.vatican.va/content/john-paul-ii/en/letters/1995/documents/hf_jp-ii_let_29061995_women.html.

6 *Ordinatio Sacerdotalis*, available at www.vatican.va/content/john-paul-ii/en/apost_letters/1994/documents/hf_jp-ii_apl_19940522_ordinatio-sacerdotalis.html.

7 Catholic theologian Karen Kilby offers a reflection on the letter entitled 'Second Sex?' in *The Tablet* (9 November 2013), pp. 14–17.

8 John Paul II's book echoes the work of Hans Urs von Balthasar and remains a much-read and much-cited text on theological anthropology; see *Man and Woman He Created Them: A Theology of the Body*, reprint edition (Boston, MA: Pauline Books & Media, 1997). An early challenge to this reading of Genesis can be found in Phyllis Trible, 'Adam and Eve: Genesis 2—3 Reread' in Carol Christ and Judith Plaskow (eds), *Womanspirit Rising: A Feminist Reader in Religion* (San Francisco, CA: Harper and Row, 1979), pp. 74–83. Danielle Nussberger's essay summarizes responses to these themes: 'Catholic Feminist Theology' in Lewis Ayres and Medi Volpe (eds), *The Oxford Handbook of Catholic Theology* (Oxford: Oxford University Press, 2019). For a foundational critique of essentialist approaches to gender, see Judith Butler, *Gender Trouble: Feminism and the Subversion of Identity*, second edition (Abingdon: Routledge Classics, 1999).

9 Jacques Derrida, 'Hostipitality', *Angelaki: Journal of the Theoretical Humanities* 5.3 (2000), pp. 3–18. Both Emmanuel Lévinas and Derrida relate hospitality to identity; see Emmanuel Lévinas, 'Responsibility for the Other' in *Ethics and Infinity*, translated by Richard Cohen (Pittsburgh, PA: Duquesne University Press, 1985).

10 For example: David B. Gowler, *Host, Guest, Enemy, and Friend: Portraits of the Pharisees in Luke and Acts* (New York: Peter Lang, 1991); Brendan Byrne, *The Hospitality of God: A Reading of Luke's Gospel* (Collegeville, MN: Liturgical Press, 2000); Luke Bretherton, *Hospitality as Holiness: Christian Witness Amid Moral Diversity* (New York: Routledge, 2006); Andrew Arterbury, *Entertaining Angels* (Sheffield: Sheffield Phoenix Press, 2005).

11 Gregory of Nazianzus, Oration 14.22, in Martha Pollard Vinson (ed.), *St. Gregory of Nazianzus: Select Orations* (Washington, DC: Catholic University of America Press, 2003), p. 55 (with amendments).

12 For an excellent theological summary of hospitality, see Craig Dykstra and Dorothy C. Bass, 'A Theological Understanding of Christian Practices' in Miroslav Volf and Dorothy C. Bass (eds), *Practicing Theology: Beliefs and Practices in Christian Life* (Grand Rapids, MI: Eerdmans, 2002), pp. 13–32 (p. 19).

13 See Arthur Sutherland, *I Was a Stranger: A Christian Theology of Hospitality* (Nashville, TN: Abingdon Press, 2006), p. xiii; Elizabeth Newman, *Untamed Hospitality: Welcoming God and Other Strangers* (Grand Rapids, MI: Brazos Press, 2007), p. 24.

14 Letty M. Russell, *Just Hospitality: God's Welcome in a World of Difference* (Louisville, KY: Westminster John Knox Press, 2009), p. 19.

15 Russell, *Just Hospitality*, pp. 80–1.

16 Russell, *Just Hospitality*, p. 2.

17 Henri Nouwen has also critiqued 'soft sweet kindness, tea parties, bland conversations and a general atmosphere of cosiness', arguing that hospitality is about learning from the 'other' in a space where we exchange roles with those who we consider different; see *Reaching Out: The Three Movements of the Spiritual Life* (London: Collins, 1976), p. 64. Also see Kate Ward, 'Jesuit and Feminist Hospitality: Pope Francis' Virtue Response to Inequality', *Religions* 8.71 (2017).

18 Christine Pohl, *Making Room: Recovering Hospitality as a Christian Tradition* (Grand Rapids, MI: Eerdmans, 1999).

19 In an essay on hospitality in a Nordic context, Paula Merikoski explores ways of overcoming dichotomies of guest/host: 'Hospitality, Reciprocity, and Power Relations in the Home Accommodation of Asylum Seekers in Finland' in Synnøve Bendixsen and Trygve Wyller (eds), *Contested Hospitalities in a Time of Migration* (New York: Routledge, 2019), pp. 113–28.

20 Pohl, *Making Room*, p. 172. See also Hans Boersma, *Violence, Hospitality, and the Cross: Reappropriating the Atonement Tradition* (Grand Rapids, MI: Baker Academic, 2004), p. 27.

21 Elizabeth A. Johnson, *Friends of God and Prophets: A Feminist Theological Reading of the Communion of Saints* (New York: Continuum, 1998), p. 228.

22 Paul D. Murray, 'Receptive Ecumenism and Catholic Learning

– Establishing the Agenda' in Paul D. Murray (ed.), *Receptive Ecumenism and the Call to Catholic Learning: Exploring a Way for Contemporary Ecumenism* (Oxford: Oxford University Press, 2008), pp. 5–25 (p. 16); David Pascoe, 'Hospitality Grounded in Humility: A Foundation for Inter Ecclesial Learning', paper presented at Receptive Ecumenism and Ecclesial Learning: Learning to be Church Together (Durham University, UK, January 2009); Antonia Pizzey, 'The Receptive Ecumenical Spirit: The Role of the Virtues in Guiding Receptive Ecumenical Discernment and Decision-Making', paper presented at the Fourth International Conference on Receptive Ecumenism: Discernment, Decision Making and Reception (Canberra, Australia, November 2017), http://arts-ed.csu.edu.au/__data/assets/pdf_file/0005/2875415/Leaning-into-the-Spirit-Conference-booklet.pdf.

23 Women have attended their conferences from traditions as diverse as the Assemblies of God, the Salvation Army, Anglican, Catholic, Methodist, Baptist, and the United Reformed Church.

24 https://worlddayofprayer.net/index.html. The World Day of Prayer is a global ecumenical movement led by Christian women who welcome all people to join in prayer and action for peace and justice.

25 I apply quotation marks when I cite the women directly.

26 Boersma, *Violence, Hospitality, and the Cross*, p. 34.

27 Theological reflection on power forms the basis of Chapter 7.

28 I am not aware of scholarship that explores the significance of place to receptive ecumenism. The importance of place, however, is not a new discovery to Christian theology more broadly. Theologians such as Willie Jennings have established the impact of location and, more specifically, of geography on the formation of Christian theology; see Willie James Jennings, *The Christian Imagination: Theology and the Origins of Race* (New Haven, CT: Yale University Press, 2010). Likewise, the women's attention to location establishes that it is critical to the practice of receptive ecumenism.

29 John Koenig, *New Testament Hospitality: Partnership with Strangers as Promise and Mission* (Philadelphia, PA: Fortress Press, 1985), p. 19.

30 For a practical consideration of how we consider both being English and Christian, see Nigel Rooms, *The Faith of the English: Integrating Christ and Culture* (London: SPCK, 2011).

31 Michael Putney, 'A Catholic Understanding of Ecumenical Dialogue' in Elizabeth Delaney, Gerard Kelly and Ormond Rush (eds), *My Ecumenical Journey* (Adelaide: ATF Theology, 2014), pp. 173–90 (p. 184).

32 As noted in Chapter 1, 4 of the 22 participants involved in the most recent phase of ARCIC are women; see www.anglicancommunion.org/media/305352/communiqu%C3%A9-from-the-meeting-of-arcic-iii-in-erfurt-2017.pdf.

33 For information on group facilitation, see Appendix 1.

34 Miroslav Volf writes, 'The will to embrace precedes any "truth" about others'; see *Exclusion and Embrace: A Theological Exploration of Identity, Otherness, and Reconciliation* (Nashville, TN: Abingdon Press, 2006), p. 29.

35 Lucien Richard, *Living the Hospitality of God* (New York: Paulist Press, 2000), p. 12.

36 Sara Gehlin, 'Asymmetry and Mutuality: Feminist Approaches to Receptive Ecumenism', *Studia Theologica: Nordic Journal of Theology* (2020), pp. 197–216. Gehlin argues that feminists should engage in receptive ecumenism, and does so by drawing on Sylvia Stoller, who in turn argues for a positive understanding of asymmetry; see Sylvia Stoller, 'Asymmetrical Genders: Phenomenological Reflections on Sexual Difference', *Hypatia* 20.2 (2005), pp. 175–82.

37 It is worth noting that while the Catholic Church formally and as an institution does not currently accept the validity of women's ordination, many individual members of the Catholic Church recognize the validity of women's ordination.

38 Pizzey, Murray and Pascoe do not point to this in their work on hospitality and receptive ecumenism.

39 Bretherton, *Hospitality as Holiness*, p. 126.

40 I am borrowing 'non-prescriptive' from Clare Watkins's most recent book in which she uses this phrase to describe her own work. For a thorough review of the contemporary questions concerning ecclesiology, see the introduction in Clare Watkins, *Disclosing Church: An Ecclesiology Learned from Conversations in Practice* (Abingdon: Routledge, 2020). The ongoing conversation about what constitutes ecclesiology and whose voices respond to this question can be found in Pete Ward, 'Is Theology What Really Matters?' in Tone Stangeland Kaufman and Jonas Idestrom (eds), *What Really Matters: Scandinavian Perspectives on Ecclesiology and Ethnography*, Church of Sweden Research (Eugene, OR: Pickwick Publications, 2018), pp. 157–72, and Paul Avis, 'Ecclesiology and Ethnography: An Unresolved Relationship', *Ecclesiology* 14.3 (2018), pp. 322–37.

41 Bretherton, *Hospitality as Holiness*, p. 129.

42 Bretherton, *Hospitality as Holiness*, p. 130.

43 Also see Baruch J. Schwartz, David P. Wright, Jeffrey Stackert and Naphtali S. Meshel (eds), *Perspectives on Purity and Purification in the Bible* (London: T&T Clark International, 2008).

44 Bretherton, *Hospitality as Holiness*, p. 130.

45 Bretherton, *Hospitality as Holiness*, p. 130.

46 Jerome H. Neyrey, 'The Social World of Luke-Acts' in Jerome H. Neyrey (ed.), *The Social World of Luke-Acts* (Peabody, MA: Hendrickson Publishers, 1992), pp. 361–88 (p. 364).

47 Marcus J. Borg, *Conflict, Holiness and Politics in the Teachings of Jesus* (Lewiston, NY: Edwin Mellen, 1984), p. 135.

48 For more on the idea of taint and disgust, see Richard Beck, *Unclean: Meditations on Purity, Hospitality and Mortality* (Eugene, OR: Cascade, 2011).

49 See, for example, Elisabeth Behr-Sigel, *The Ministry of Women in the Church*, translated by Fr Stephen Bigham (Pasadena, CA: Oakwood, 1991); Rosemary Radford Ruether, 'Imago Dei, Christian Tradition and Feminist Hermeneutics' in Kari Elisabeth Børresen (ed.), *The Image of God and Gender Models in Judaeo-Christian Tradition* (Oslo: Solum Forag, 1991), pp. 258–81; Celia Viggo Wexler, *Catholic Women Confront their Church* (Lanham, MD: Rowman & Littlefield, 2016); Eileen R. Campbell-Reed, 'Living Testaments: How Catholic and Baptist Women in Ministry Both Judge and Renew the Church', *Ecclesial Practices* 4.2 (2017), pp. 167–98.

50 FutureChurch, 'Tips for Advancing Women in Church Leadership', *FutureChurch*, www.futurechurch.org/women-in-church-leadership/women-in-church-leadership/action/tips-for-advancing-women-in-church.

51 John Paul II, *Ut Unum Sint*, www.vatican.va/content/john-paul-ii/en/encyclicals/documents/hf_jp-ii_enc_25051995_ut-unum-sint. The title of this encyclical draws from Jesus's prayer for his followers in John 17.

5

The Gift of Vocation

Chapter 5 begins with the story of a group of Eastern Orthodox theologians in England who are walking the way of receptive ecumenism.[1] Along with a number of Orthodox participants, they have identified an area of their life together which they believe would benefit from being re-examined. This relates to the themes in the previous chapters and concerns the lack of women's voices in decision-making, ecumenical dialogues, preaching and the absence of women from ordained ministries in the Orthodox Church. As a response to this absence, they are reflecting on women's vocation to ordained ministry in the Orthodox Church because as members of a church which does not ordain women, they believe it is time to explore the possibility of expanding the vision of ordained ministries to embrace women and consequently have invited Anglicans to join their conversations.

I do not suggest that other forms of vocation are unproblematic for Orthodox women, or indeed for women working in any church. It is important to note that women's lay vocations are also often unrecognized, and that formal structures of discernment are lacking for these. For example, in the weeks surrounding Petertide, which along with Michaelmas is one of the principal seasons for ordination in the Anglican Communion, each year my Twitter feed shows a deluge of photographs of deacons and priests with a newly ordained 'glow', all celebrating the day of their ordination.[2] While looking at the pictures this year with the words of the participants reverberating in my mind, it struck me that churches need to find a way of celebrating lay vocations with as much energy as it celebrates ordained vocations. As recommended in Chapter

2, lay vocation is an area that would benefit from further research and reflection. However, a core principle of receptive ecumenism is that a church identifies its own wounds; in this instance, some members of the Orthodox Church have identified a weakness in the Church's teaching on the vocation to ordained ministries. Having identified this weakness, according to the way of receptive ecumenism, they invited me to share with them experiences of working out my own vocation as a priest in the Church of England. This chapter offers one way of responding to their invitation. It is not the definitive model of gift-giving, but a lived example of receptive ecumenism from the perspective of one being asked to share a particular gift.

To share this gift is to take a considerable risk. This journey is risky both for those giving and those receiving, since this conversation is fraught in various parts of the Orthodox Church across the world.[3] Added to this, the gift of vocation to ordained ministries is accompanied by its own set of challenges, one of which is clericalism. As observed by participants in Chapter 3, women are not exempt from the temptations of clericalism, and it is possible that a conversation about women and ordination might contribute to raising vocation to the priesthood above vocations to lay and diaconal ministries. This is not my intention. I am also conscious of the many ordained women who have been subject to bullying, and for whom being ordained comes at a great cost which moves beyond the expected costs of being in full-time ministry. Consequently, I aim to share this gift while recognizing some of its weaknesses. This point applies, of course, not only to the gift of the ordination of women, but to any gift being offered; those involved in receptive ecumenism must give and receive mindfully.

This chapter does not aim to serve as an apology for the ordination of women priests in the Orthodox Church, or indeed in any church. The following contribution differs from the typical approach to the debate by shifting the argument away from binary forms, as discussed in Chapter 1, and instead to walking the way of receptive ecumenism by reflecting on my own vocation as an ordained woman. I am not proposing a definitive view of the priesthood in the Church of England; as Rowan Williams once wrote, 'there is no one way of being a priest'.[4] Therefore, I shall reflect theologically upon aspects of my experience of being ordained, acknowledging that others would compose their reflections differently. What follows then is not all that I might say on the matter, but will provide a glimpse into the particular role I inhabit. My principal interlocutor is a priest who lived in the fourth century, Gregory of Nazianzus. I make this move because Gregory is a much-loved saint in the Eastern Orthodox Church, and therefore well suited for a conversation between Orthodox and Anglican theologians. In conversation with Gregory's teaching, I will consider the vocation to ordained ministry as one of many vocations which are God-given gifts. Drawing upon Gregory's insights to form the shape of the reflection, I focus upon three features of my ministry as a priest, namely, priest as theologian, priest as healer, and priest as leader among the people of God. Before I turn to these, I will discuss more fully the journey out of which this reflection arose.

Women and ordination in the Orthodox Church

On a warm, early autumn day in September 2018, an eclectic mix of people gathered, some through curiosity and others with a keen expectation, for a conference on women and ordination in the Orthodox Church at Pusey House, Oxford. For several years, Orthodox Christians have been gathering together twice a year for study days which belong to a series entitled 'Women's Ministries Initiative', although they are in fact open to all interested parties and well attended by people from all walks of life and from numerous faith perspectives. Dr Elena Narinskaya, an Orthodox theologian based in Oxford, is the pioneer of these gatherings and is joined by Professor Mary Cunningham, Fr Andrew Louth, Metropolitan Kallistos Ware, and others. After five years of meeting together, Elena and some of the regular members decided that it was time to think through the implications of ordained roles for women in the Orthodox Church and hosted a study day entitled 'Ordination of Women: Pros and Cons'. Orthodox, Catholic and Anglican theologians spoke on different aspects of priesthood and explored questions pertaining to the ordination of women as deacons and priests.

Years earlier, Metropolitan Kallistos Ware had argued firmly in print against the ordination of women on the basis that he believed Scripture to present a clear and decisive view on this question.[5] He set the tone at the conference by explaining why after many years of arguing against the ordination of women in the Orthodox Church, he had changed his mind. He explained that he believed it is time for the Orthodox Church to explore this question with serious consideration, which contributed to the open conversations taking place during the conference. As the principal organizer, Elena thought that it would be helpful to include a talk by a woman who is ordained; therefore, she reached out to me, a woman ordained in the Church of England. Her invitation was preceded by a pre-existing relationship between members of the group and myself, including some who participated in the wider research of this book.

Women's vocation to ordination in the Orthodox Church is not a new debate.[6] The most significant contribution to date comes from Orthodox theologian Elisabeth Behr-Sigel (1907–2005). The breadth of her work is beyond the scope of this chapter, but it is worth observing that Behr-Sigel departs from an essentialist position on women found in much Orthodox theological anthropology, a position similar to the work of John Paul II discussed in the previous chapter. During the course of her life's work, Behr-Sigel shifted the debate away from questions of gender and sex – the usual preoccupation in these debates – and on to considerations of personhood.[7] As Sarah Hinlicky Wilson puts it:

What makes the evolution of her thought so striking is that it started with revised ideas about *women*, but these were displaced by revised ideas about *persons*. To put it another way, her thought evolved from having an anthropological center to having a trinitarian center.[8]

Behr-Sigel's work developed over several decades; in fact, she made her most critical contributions towards the end of her life.

Vocation as gift

Let us turn now to Saint Gregory of Nazianzus, my theological interlocutor for this chapter, also known as 'the Theologian'. It is perhaps unusual in the twenty-first century, although not unique, for an Anglican priest to find one of her primary sources of inspiration for ordained ministry in the form of a fourth-century church father from the Christian East. Yet Gregory's theological work has been and continues to be key to my vocation. I first encountered his work while training for ordination, during which time I spent many happy hours translating his sermons and poems.[9] As a bishop in the fourth century, Gregory was heavily involved with the theological controversies of his day. In particular, he took a leading role in the Council of Constantinople in AD 381, which was the second ecumenical council of the Christian church. It is known for, among other issues, discussing at length the divinity of the Holy Spirit, an important doctrine to which Gregory was greatly committed as evidenced throughout his work.[10] Along with myriad orations, letters and poems, Gregory wrote an oration on pastoral ministry which comprises one of the first extended reflections on ordained ministry in the early church, and offers a defence of his flight to Pontus after his ordination to the priesthood. The oration highlights the challenges of pastoral ministry and the kinds of characteristics required in order to be a pastor of integrity, which include a correct reading and use of Scripture, doctrine, and a life of prayer.[11]

One word on reading the texts. Early in his oration on pastoral ministry, Gregory explains why he ran away so soon after his ordination: 'I did not consider myself qualified, nor do I now ... to have the care of the souls of human persons.'[12] Anyone who is aware of the gravity of vocation, either to lay or ordained ministries, might well nod their head while reading this and assume that it was an act of humility on Gregory's part to admit how ill-equipped he felt. Indeed, in the past scholars have made this assumption about Gregory's motivations, arguing that he was 'a sensitive man who entered the arena of world affairs'.[13] However, by attending to the scope of Gregory's work and his expert use of rhetoric against the backdrop of 'political, intellectual and ecclesiastical developments',[14] it becomes clear that he establishes himself as one who 'fashioned himself a life that embodied and presented authority, even power'.[15] Through his letters, poems and orations, Gregory positions himself alongside figures as wide ranging as classical autobiographer Libanius of Antioch and Saint Paul who, like Gregory, speaks of stonings by opponents, sea storms and bouts of illness. When reading Gregory's reluctance to begin pastoral ministry, it is important not to paint an idealized portrait of this theologian. Instead, reading Gregory in light of his context we observe the life of a person who was deliberate and strategic about the choices he made throughout his ministry. For him, the vocation to ordained ministry was a gift which he received and to which he devoted a significant amount of time and energy.

Vocation to ordained ministry is a gift that relates to the vocation of all the baptized. Baptism is prior to and grounds vocation to ministry as a priest in the church of God. The logic of vocation understood as gift is that it does not serve the church to speak of women's vocation to the priesthood in terms of 'rights'. To campaign for the ordination of women using arguments of justice and equality suggests that ordained ministry itself is somehow deserved or earned, or that it is a person's 'right'. No person has the 'right' to become a priest. A vocation to priesthood, like a lay vocation, is a gift of God, and one that includes a mixture of joy and at times sorrow. When speaking of women's ordination to the priesthood I do so because it makes good theological sense, and because through the centuries countless women have testified to being called by God to such a vocation and are also, dare I say, gifted by God for this purpose. Added to this, for some time now the faithful have been asking questions about the ordination of women and calling for women's gifts to be used in the service of Christ in this way. Those 'above' would do well to listen to those 'below', as suggested in the previous chapter.

My own sense of vocation grew over the course of many years. When I was a young child of about four or five, my mother used to take me along to the local parish Eucharist every Sunday morning. I remember experiencing a sense of belonging and safety within the building. Just within the porch there was a very small vestry in which the priest used to put on his vestments, and I was always curious to know what the inside looked like; in fact, most aspects of the building and the Eucharist itself intrigued me. I followed some of the celebration, becoming familiar over time with the pattern of the liturgy, if not the actual words. I was transfixed by the actions of the priest at the altar and was absorbed by the movements relating to the bread and the chalice; I was thoroughly caught up in the drama. At a young age I remember informing our priest that I was going to do what he did when I grew up. No doubt he was somewhat surprised to find a young girl confidently pronouncing this, since it was many years before women were granted permission to be ordained in the Church of England. Looking back, the Spirit first began to stir my heart for this ministry on those Sunday mornings with my mother.

Much later in my early twenties, I set aside some time to fast and pray about how God might be calling me to serve as a member of the body of Christ. By then, I had developed a sense that God was calling me to ordained ministry. This was tested by leading and preaching in safe contexts and being told by teams I had led that this was something I should consider. At the same time, I was aware of feeling thoroughly inadequate. I shared this with my priest, with whom I had a good relationship and whom I respected greatly. His response was, 'Oh dear me, no, Gabrielle, God would not ever call a woman.' While he commented that I was a gifted leader, suggesting that I might want to think about politics, he was adamant that God was not – and never would be – calling me to ordained ministry. I was a little confused by this, as the Church of England had been ordaining women for three years by then. I decided to go to theological college anyway and pursue this vocation, having other voices who had encouraged me. During this time, I studied alongside those training for the priesthood, becoming more and more convinced that God was calling me also to this ministry.

For various reasons, I found myself with this same sense of vocation over a decade later at a time when it became possible to take concrete steps forward. A series of interviews followed, and a few years later I trained full-time for ordained ministry. The process of discernment and numerous interviews were reassuring to me, since there were a number of people who believed that this was not simply a good idea, but a vocation to which God and the Church of England were calling me. Vocation to the priesthood is not about a warm or fuzzy feeling, but a calling that is tested rigorously and discerned by the Church, through which God calls persons to all kinds of ministries.

I share this story, conscious of my Orthodox and Catholic sisters who also testify to God's call to ordained ministry, and whose voices reverberate throughout this book. For them, there is no opportunity to explore this with others through a process of discernment, and it is clear from the testimonies of women in this book (and elsewhere) that this can be a great source of pain. While it is not within my gift to change this, I acknowledge their pain and their testimony of hearing God's voice. Added to this, countless women are prevented from exploring ordained ministries even in churches that ordain women, as discussed in Chapter 3. Bearing this in mind, I turn to the first aspect of my priestly experience: priest as theologian.

Priest as theologian

Many qualifications accompany 'priest as theologian', two of which I will mention here. All too often, theology is associated with an academic discipline that people study in universities and as that which is distinct from spirituality. I shall not rehearse the decades of debates on the integrity of theology and spirituality, as these would fill a book in themselves. Important to note is that early Christian theologians did not split theology and spirituality; instead, these were tightly interwoven aspects of early Christian thought.[16] Since my conversation partner is a fourth-century theologian, I will assume here an integrity between theology and spirituality.[17] My second qualification is that when Gregory speaks of the theologian as one who 'knows God', assumed is that complete knowledge of God is impossible or, put another way, Gregory's knowledge of God is apophatic. In his oration on the doctrine of God, Gregory describes the experience of sheltering in the rock, which he understands metaphorically as Christ. He writes that we can only see God in the way that we see 'shadowy reflections of the Sun in water'.[18] As close as Gregory comes to God, ultimately he finds that God is unknowable, from which he concludes: 'to tell of God is not possible ... but to know him is even less possible'.[19]

For Gregory, the desire for God compels us to continue to seek God and to know God. This requires purification, as described in the first of the so-called *Theological Orations*:

> Discussion of theology is not for everyone, I tell you, not for everyone – it is no such inexpensive or effortless pursuit. Nor, I would add, is it for every occasion, or every audience; neither are all its aspects open to inquiry. It must be reserved for certain occasions, for certain audiences, and certain limits must be observed. It is not for all people, but only for those who have been tested and found a sound footing in contemplation [*theoria*], and more importantly, have undergone, or at least are undergoing, purification of body and soul.[20]

Knowledge of God involves the purification of theologians themselves because right doctrine, a life of prayer and Scripture reflection within the Christian tradition work together in every instance. Thus the priest as theologian is one whose knowledge of God encompasses the whole of their life. I shall discuss the implications of this shortly, but first let us consider with Gregory the way in which we speak of God.

Gregory spends much of his ministry explicating the doctrine of the Trinity, 'Father, Son and Holy Spirit',[21] who is 'one divinity and power'.[22] Thus he demonstrates that the ministry of the priest-theologian is to delineate – to the extent that this is possible – the mystery of the Trinity and make Christ known. Priests do their theological work in light of the Scriptures and the Christian tradition, as Gregory emphasizes throughout his writing on Christian pastoral ministry. In his oration on the priesthood, Gregory describes the continuity that exists between the 'economy of salvation recorded in the Scriptures and the work of the Christian priest in the contemporary church'.[23] After discussing the law and the prophets, he points to the healing brought through Christ's incarnation, life, passion and resurrection. Gregory connects this to the Christian priest who, as another shepherd, is called to continue this ministry of healing until Christ's return.[24] This is Christ's ministry in which priests participate, which is one of the reasons why it is important to reflect continually upon the Scriptures in light of the Christian tradition, for it is through the Scriptures that the Church comes to know its healing and vocation within the economy of salvation.

Making Christ known is possible only through the Holy Spirit. As Gregory teaches, it is through the Spirit that the 'Father is known and ... the Son is glorified and known'.[25] Furthermore, Gregory states that the Spirit reveals correct doctrine, calls those who are pastors and bishops, guides the leaders of the church,[26] purifies through fire, and inspires preaching. It is worth recalling that Gregory went to great lengths to argue for the consubstantiality of the Holy Spirit within the Trinity. Thus, when Gregory writes that the Spirit calls, he is emphasizing that it is God who calls and forms the baptized. One of the important beliefs shared by Orthodox and Anglican Christians, agreed in the Moscow Statement, is 'the Church is that Community which lives by continually invoking the Holy Spirit'.[27] Therefore, these two churches (along with many others) continue to sing praises to the Spirit who performs these marvellous deeds:

Soul, why do you delay? Sing praise of the Spirit ... Let us stand in awe of the mighty Spirit, who is the same as God, through whom I know God, through whom God is present, and who forms me into a god in this world.[28]

As I observed earlier, the formation of the theologian is a process that Gregory advises should not be entered into lightly, since it requires attention to character and extensive purification. In his oration on the conduct of bishops, he writes:

Wary theologian ... ascend by an upright life; through purification obtain the pure. Do you wish to be a theologian one day, worthy of divinity? Seek to keep the commandments; walk in [God's] statutes. Conduct is the stepping-stone to contemplation.[29]

Gregory makes clear the importance of integrity in all aspects of the life of the theologian. What might this mean in day-to-day life? The performance of a stage play is an effective metaphor to employ when thinking about the integrity of the theologian since priest-theologians might be able to teach well on doctrine, preach on the Scriptures, conduct a 'good' funeral or wedding, lead a lively church, 'do' social justice, publicly support black and brown colleagues, and, if they are really savvy, cultivate a social media following – you get the picture – but if their conduct behind closed doors does not reflect some of what they perform publicly, then this work has little value ultimately. The 'onstage' and 'offstage' lives must reflect one another. In light of the abuse crises across the churches, I cannot underscore strongly enough the importance of this point which applies, of course, not only to theologians who are ordained, but to lay theologians and scholars working in the academy. During the time of writing and revising this book, news reports have stated that the much-loved and trusted lay-Catholic theologian Jean Vanier, founder of the L'Arche community, sexually abused six women during a period of 35 years.[30] This kind of behaviour exemplifies my point: integrity matters. While Gregory's comments do not suggest that he has abuse in mind, an important thread runs through his work that speaks to the significance of the integrity that must be at the heart of what it means to be a priest-theologian.

Prayer creates a space for becoming a person of integrity. Anglican priests commit (among other things) to a pattern of praying daily offices, during which time those gathered pray for the world, the Church, and any issues of the day. The offices, comprised mostly of Scripture, provide a gentle rhythm through a cycle of readings and prayers. This is a tradition for which I am thankful and upon which I rely heavily. It keeps me praying when I'm feeling apathetic, and through it I'm reminded daily that I belong to a global community of prayer. That said, as Nicola Slee has commented in her own reflections on the offices, it is important to recognize that the space to participate in the offices is a huge privilege that is not open so readily to everyone, such as those who work night shifts or struggle to feed families.[31]

When I am asked to speak about prayer, I often turn to Gregory of Nyssa – readers will notice I'm rather fond of these early theologians! He composed five sermons on the Lord's Prayer, all of which are superb reflections on the power and purpose of prayer. His account of prayer in the first of his sermons offers a beautiful response to the question, 'What is prayer?'

> Prayer is intimacy with God and contemplation [*theoria*] of the invisible. It satisfies our yearnings and makes us equal with angels. Through it good prospers, evil is destroyed, and sinners will be converted. Prayer is the enjoyment of things present and the substance of things to come ... Now I think that, even if we spent our whole life in constant communion with God in prayer and thanksgiving, we should be as far from having made God an adequate return as if we had not even begun to desire making the Giver of all good things such a return.[32]

When reading Nyssa's work on prayer I find myself inspired to pray, since he presents a beautiful vision of the life lived in communion with God. Through prayer, priests are sustained to meet the challenges of ministry and of life. This also occurs through studying, reflecting on, and preaching the Scriptures, and for me by spending a significant amount of my time dwelling in the writings of the early church. In these, I search for treasures from a living tradition which continues to breathe life into my theological work. As a priest who is currently working out their vocation in an academic institution, I bring these treasures into the classroom, aiming to create a safe space of learning, creativity and imagination to encourage the flourishing of budding theologians as they work out their own vocations.

I draw this section to a close by returning to Gregory Nazianzen, who closes his oration *On the Holy Spirit* with the declaration that the purpose of the priest-theologian is to

persuade all humankind as best as I am able, to worship the Father, and the Son and the Holy Spirit, one divinity and power, for to God belongs all glory, honour, authority, for age upon age. Amen.[33]

Put less elegantly: worship and mission are at the heart of this work.

Priest as healer

Let us move next to the priest as healer. Among other descriptions, Gregory summarizes pastoral ministry as a ministry of healing. This is a theme that continues throughout the history of the church, culminating in the reflection by Henri Nouwen, *The Wounded Healer: Ministry in Contemporary Society*.[34] While I have chosen not to include 'wounded' in the title of this section, the reflection assumes that the priest, like anyone else, is on a journey to becoming a healed human person. By 'healing', Gregory includes the ministry of reconciliation in which the priest participates in the reconciliation of people with God and with one another through the sacraments and through blessing those in his care. His description of healing is well known, being cited in books on pastoral ministry through the ages:

> The scope of our art is to provide the soul with wings, to rescue it from the world and give it to God, and to keep safe that which is according to God's image if it abides, to take it by the hand if it is in danger, or to put it back together if it is broken, to make Christ dwell in hearts through the Spirit, and in sum, to deify.[35]

Gregory's summary raises some questions: What does it mean to rescue a person from 'the world' and give them back to God? Does this mean that the world is a wholly bad and dangerous place? This is not what Gregory is suggesting, since his view of the world is that it is inherently good because it is created by God. However, following Saint Paul, Gregory also speaks of the world as the place in which sin and death reside, and it is from these that each human person needs rescuing. This is a ministry in which the priest participates but does not initiate, since it is God who rescues and heals. Gregory grounds his work on healing in the incarnation, beginning with an overview of the Old Testament. He explains that despite God giving the law and sending the prophets, humankind remained stuck in patterns of evil and that Christ, through the incarnation, made possible the depth of healing required:

> [Christ is] the very Word of God, the eternal, the invisible, the incomprehensible, the incorporeal, the beginning from the beginning, the light from the light, the source of life and immortality [and] the identical Image, the definition and explanation of the Father. He proceeds to his own image and bears flesh on behalf of flesh and mingles with a spiritual soul for the sake of my soul, purifying like with like.[36]

Baptism is the way in which human persons, as images of God in need of restoration, begin to receive this healing and renewal. Baptism serves the initial purpose of 'rescuing a person from the world and giving them back to God'; therefore, it is one of the most important moments in the life of the church. Gregory extols the virtues of this sacrament at great length in his oration *On Baptism*, in which he describes baptism as a gift, grace, unction, garment of incorruption, seal and bath.[37]

While all baptisms are cause for celebration, one particular baptism in which I was involved will remain with me as a perpetual source of encouragement. As a recently ordained curate, I was asked to lead a youth group consisting of young people in their early teens. The youth group proved to be popular with young people from the church bringing their friends to the church hall on a Sunday evening for fellowship. After about six months, I took 12 young people on a weekend away, during which we took part in outdoor pursuits, worshipped, prayed, and read the Bible together. On returning from this weekend, one of the young people, who had not been baptized as an infant, asked me what she needed to do to be baptized.

After some serious conversations with her parents, we agreed that she should be baptized, and I proceeded to meet with her, both as a way of exploring the Christian faith together, and to listen to her as she shared about her journey of discovery. During one of the sessions, we worked our way through the baptism service and came to discuss the moment in the service in which I would anoint her with oil. Before I began to explain some of the received meaning of this, I asked her what she thought about it. The answer from a child of 12 was one that I shall never forget: 'I think you use oil, because oil seeps into the skin. The skin is porous and so it's a sign that the Spirit is always with me, because the oil has seeped into my skin and can never be washed off.' This child's explanation of anointing was not so very different from Gregory's when he describes the gift of the Trinity at baptism as that which endures throughout the whole of life:

> I entrust [the confession of the Father, and the Son and the Holy Spirit] to you today; in this I will baptize you together, and I will raise you up together. I give you this companion and patronage throughout all of life.[38]

Baptism marks the moment of belonging to the body of Christ, the church, as well as being a significant step of a lifelong journey towards God. All those who are baptized are commissioned to glorify God and make Christ known. Let us recall Gregory's advice in the passage cited earlier: 'keep safe that which is according to God's image if it abides'. In order to keep safe those created according to the image of God, a priest walks alongside people, enabling the continuation of the spiritual growth that begins at baptism. One way of walking alongside people is through the weekly (or daily) Eucharist, as this is a regular point of connection between the members of church communities.

Unlike baptism, Gregory does not offer an oration dedicated to the subject of the Eucharist, nor does he offer details about the rite itself.[39] On the few occasions he mentions the Eucharist, it is as a 'mystery', a 'sacrifice', 'spiritual bread' and as a path to theosis.[40] He does, however, connect the Eucharist directly to the ministry of healing on more than one occasion. In the case of his father, Gregory describes in great depth how his father had a fever along with severe aches and pains and that he could not eat or sleep. The doctors were unable to help him despite all their efforts, and yet this man was restored to health through the Eucharist, as his son tells it.[41] Likewise, in his sister's funeral oration, Gregory includes a short story about a time when Gorgonia was cured miraculously from an illness (we are not told which illness) after she steals into a church one night and consumes a portion of the consecrated body and blood of Christ.[42] As far as Gregory is concerned, it is important to provide evidence of the ways in which the Eucharist heals those who participate in it. I do not compare the following story of healing to those told by Gregory since my own context is radically different from his, but I do know one person who after receiving the sacrament testified to being physically healed from a painful, twisted wrist. He explained that on walking back from the altar rail he became very suddenly free from pain, an experience that continues to this day.

Turning from the Eucharist to confession, which is not (officially, at least) a sacrament in the Church of England: Anglicans confess publicly and corporately while gathered for prayer and during the Eucharist. After being ordained, I was not accustomed to making or hearing personal confessions, since it was not a practice I had encountered previously. However, I have found that people have wanted to speak with me, and subsequently make confession about such things as adultery or their addiction to pornography. I have witnessed profound levels of restoration and healing through the process of confession and absolution. Key to confession is the art of listening well: as a young person, I was always struck when reading the Bible how Jesus focused on the person in front of him rather than being distracted by the masses. Long before my ordination, I aimed to learn to listen well and took courses in counselling which contributed greatly to the way I live out my vocation then and now. Giving our attention to whoever is in front of us is one of the greatest gifts we can give to others.

Priest as leader

What do ordained leaders do? For Gregory, a principal aspect of the priest's service is to ensure each member of the body of Christ entrusted to his care is flourishing in their relationship with God and working out their own vocation. Each person performs a different function so that the church may fulfil its God-given mission in the world. Thus ordained leadership involves the service of and enabling of others, recalling once more the place and significance of lay vocation. On this, Gregory writes, 'Of this same healing, we who are set over others are the ministers and fellow-labourers.'[43] Being 'set over' others does not mean that priests should lead in ways that suppress or control the body of Christ; leaders are called to work alongside those in our care, since we are all fellow labourers in Christ's service.

When reflecting on the priest as leader, I should note that not all aspects of being a priest are always as positive as those discussed in this chapter. It does become tiresome to be asked what I think about 1 Timothy 2.12, or to present an idea only to have a male colleague repeat it as though it was his own, or to be expected to present an apology for women's ordination, etc. Gregory is of great comfort here, I find, since he spends a good deal of time writing about his own sufferings in being a priest, composing prayers that name his struggles before God. On women priests he is silent, but his views of women in leadership present a challenge to those who believe that women should not lead. In his father's funeral oration, Gregory speaks of his mother as the leader of his father, 'drawing him on by her influence in word and deed'; furthermore, he describes his mother as his father's teacher.[44] This is significant if we bear in mind that Gregory's father was a bishop. He justifies his comments by stressing the importance of virtue and integrity of the person who is leading or teaching. The take-away from this is that women lead.

While he does not make the connection between his views on women leaders and his understanding of the human person, it does not stretch the imagination to understand how Gregory holds his beliefs together. His writing on theological anthropology, albeit a little inconsistent in places, moves readers away from the kind of essentialist thought we see elsewhere in the early church fathers. Rather than presenting 'man' as the image of God, Gregory emphasizes that the image of God does not relate to male or female but should be understood differently.[45] In his poetry, Gregory writes of women not only as images of God but also as images of Christ, leaving his beliefs about women's ability to function as images of God and Christ well defined.[46] He is so utterly convinced of this that he employs the following argument on behalf of equality for women whom he believes are subject to unfair divorce laws:

> There is one maker of man and woman, one sod of clay for both, one image, one law, one death, one resurrection, in the same way we were born from man and woman.[47]

As I cautioned earlier, it is important not to paint idealized portraits of the early church fathers, and I don't intend to do that here; nevertheless, as a woman reading early church texts, one cannot help but be drawn to arguments that do not denigrate women!

As observed earlier, in his second oration on pastoral ministry, Gregory summarizes the goal of those ordained as the deification of the people in their care, that is, 'to make Christ dwell in hearts through the Spirit, and in sum, to deify'.[48] This is no small charge and requires that priest-leaders first attend to their own character and relationship with God. As I argued in the previous section, integrity is crucial; add to this a firm grasp of one's own identity in Christ. If to lead is to keep 'safe that which is according to God's image if it abides', then as I lead others in their vocation to image God more fully, it is crucial that I am attending to my own vocation to be an image of God. Through the power of the Spirit, our vocation as images of Christ is to be deified. Put theologically, Gregory describes this as the 'priority of the Spirit',[49] for we must constantly surrender to the Spirit who purifies and transforms us so that we can participate in the transformation of others.

Further to this, it is essential that leaders are adaptable in their dealings with those in their care, since each person is gifted differently. This brings me back to the importance of listening and attending to the person in front of us, for not everyone requires the same level of support, teaching or advice. As Gregory observes, 'the cowardly and courageous, the wrathful and meek, the successful and failing, do not require the same instruction and encouragement'![50]

The last word on ordained leadership, for now at least, goes to Gregory and is an exhortation from his first oration on pastoral ministry. This reminds us that leadership, whether lay or ordained, is not about empire-building. He encourages the Church to put itself continually at the service of Christ whatever the individual vocations may be, since all vocation is a gift from God; and in receiving a vocation, we are called to offer it back for the glory of our Creator:

But let us bear fruit for the one who died and rose on our behalf. Perhaps you think I speak about gold, or silver, or robes or stones of brilliance and value; earthly stuff which ebbs and flows, remaining below, of which the evil ones and slaves of things below and of the world-ruler have more. Let us bear fruit ourselves, the most honourable possession belonging to God and the nearest to him. Let us give back to the Image that which is according to the image, let us recognise our worth, let us honour the archetype, and let us know the power of the mystery and on whose behalf Christ died.[51]

Conclusion

In reflecting upon aspects of being a priest, I have focused on the priest as theologian, healer and leader, recognizing that these are but a fragment of how I understand the priestly vocation. My experiences have varied enormously with respect to how I have been received by others, since the Church of England has permitted the ordination of women for only a short time in light of its overall history. Sometimes it has proved very costly, but I am not aware of any vocation that does not involve some cost to the person called. While I have encountered some resistance, I have been and continue to be blessed by a greater abundance of wonderful people who have cheered me on, offered wisdom, and at times carried me along the way. I have been enabled to serve in ways I had never imagined and have witnessed people growing closer to God, which brings me great joy.

Let me return to my journey with members of the Orthodox Church. In many ways, being invited to share the gift of my experiences of being a priest is a deeply unsettling experience, since I have many questions around how to offer this gift with integrity. It necessitates much time in prayer, during which I have asked for wisdom and for courage. Once again, reciprocity has come to the fore, since journeying with those from a church which is not my own is both a challenge and blessing for which I am thankful.

As observed at the beginning of this chapter, I am not presenting this reflection as the definitive way to share a gift between different traditions, or indeed one on the life of a priest. Recall that receptive ecumenism is not a strict method, but a way of churches journeying together. Therefore, context matters. While this adventure is bearing fruit, in other contexts it would most likely be apposite to adopt a different approach. Two years after the first conference in which I was invited to share some of my experiences of being ordained, conversations and reflections continue with an expanding group of theologians and practitioners. Recall that receptive ecumenism is not a quick fix but requires a commitment involving a great deal of trust from all involved. Elena Narinskaya, the leader of the Women's Ministries Initiative, and I have edited a book together which includes revised and expanded versions of some of the talks given at the conference along with further explorations in theological anthropology, the diaconate and priesthood, and contemporary practices.[52] Because it includes work by international theologians from diverse theological traditions, we hope that the book will serve as a useful resource for the conversation on women priests, and that our collaboration will stretch the imagination of the church regarding what might be possible through receptive ecumenism.

Notes

1 This chapter draws on my essay 'On Being a Priest in Conversation with St. Gregory Nazianzen' in Gabrielle Thomas and Elena Narinskaya (eds), *Women and Ordination in the Orthodox Church: Explorations and Practice* (Eugene, OR: Cascade, 2020), pp. 187–204. Used with permission.

2 Petertide is the Sunday closest to St Peter's day, which is 29 June.

3 An example from June 2020: On social media, I referred to a book I was co-editing on women and ordination in the Orthodox Church. As a result, even before the book's publication, I was 'trolled' heavily. During this period, I blocked over 92 abusive tweeters who suggested 'burning the book' and 'vomiting on' its editors.

4 Rowan Williams, *Ray of Darkness* (Cambridge, MA: Cowley, 1995), p. 157.

5 See the essays in Thomas Hopko (ed.), *Women and the Priesthood* (Crestwood, NY: St Vladimir's Seminary Press, 1983); Paul Evdokimov, *Women and the Salvation of the World: A Christian Anthropology on*

the Charisms of Women, translated by Anthony P. Gythiel (Crestwood, NY: St Vladimir's Seminary Press, 1994).

6 For early discussions, see Elisabeth Behr-Sigel, 'Keynote' in Constance J. Tarasar and Irina Kirillova (eds), *Orthodox Women: Their Role and Participation in the Orthodox Church. Report on the Consultation of Orthodox Women, September 11–17, 1976, Agapia, Roumania* (Geneva: World Council of Churches, 1977), pp. 17–29; Gennadios Limouris (ed.), *The Place of the Woman in the Orthodox Church and the Question of the Ordination of Women: Interorthodox Symposium, Rhodos, Greece, 30 October–7 November 1988* (Katerini: Tertios, 1992). See, too, Elisabeth Behr-Sigel's foundational book *The Ministry of Women in the Church*, translated by Fr Steven Bigham (Pasadena, CA: Oakwood, 1991), and Kyriaki Karidoyanes FitzGerald, *Women Deacons in the Orthodox Church: Called to Holiness and Ministry* (Brookline, MA: Holy Cross Orthodox Press, 1999). For information online, see http://saintcatherinesvision.org/.

7 Sarah Hinlicky Wilson, *Woman, Women, and the Priesthood in the Trinitarian Theology of Elisabeth Behr-Sigel* (London: Bloomsbury, 2013).

8 Sarah Hinlicky Wilson, 'Elisabeth Behr-Sigel's Trinitarian Case for the Ordination of Women' in Thomas and Narinskaya (eds), *Women and Ordination in the Orthodox Church*, pp. 99–113 (p. 101).

9 The culmination of this work is in Gabrielle Thomas, *The Image of God in the Theology of Gregory of Nazianzus* (Cambridge: Cambridge University Press, 2019).

10 Gregory writes on the Holy Spirit throughout his orations, poems, and letters. In particular, *On the Holy Spirit* is the title given to Oration 31 and Poem 1.1.3. The most recent critical edition is Paul Gallay and Maurice Jourjon, *Grégoire de Nazianze. Discours 27–31. Sources chrétiennes 250* (Paris: Les Éditions du Cerf, 1978). An accessible English translation exists in the Popular Patristics Series: St Gregory of Nazianzus, *On God and Christ: The Five Theological Orations and Two Letters of Cledonius*, translated by Lionel Wickham and Frederick Williams (Crestwood, NY: St Vladimir's Seminary Press, 2002). For a critical edition and translation of Gregory's poem on the Holy Spirit, see Claudio Moreschini and Donald Sykes, *Gregory of Nazianzus: Poemata Arcana* (Oxford: Clarendon Press, 1997). A contemporary English translation of the poem exists in the Popular Patristics Series: Peter Gilbert, *On God and Man: The Theological Poetry of St Gregory of Nazianzus* (Crestwood, NY: St Vladimir's Seminary Press, 2001). Older translations of Gregory's orations are available online; see, for example, www.newadvent.org/fathers/3102.htm.

11 For an essay on Gregory's use and distribution of Scripture in Oration 2, see Ben Fulford, 'Gregory of Nazianzus and Biblical Interpretation' in Christopher A. Beeley (ed.), *Re-Reading Gregory of*

Nazianzus (Washington, DC: Catholic University of America Press, 2012), pp. 31–66.

12 Oration 2.9, in Jean Bernardi, *Grégoire de Nazianze: Discours 1–3*. Sources chrétiennes 247 (Paris: Les Éditions du Cerf, 1978), p. 100. Hereafter, books mentioned more than once in the Sources chrétiennes series will be referenced by 'SC' followed by the series number: for example, SC 247. Translations are my own, unless noted otherwise. A translation of Oration 2 exists online; see www.new advent.org/fathers/310202.htm.

13 Georg Misch, *A History of Autobiography in Antiquity* (London: Routledge, 1950), p. 609.

14 Bradley L. Storin, *Self-Portrait in Three Colors: Gregory of Nazianzus's Epistolary Autobiography* (Oakland, CA: University of California Press, 2019), p. 25.

15 Susanna Elm, *Sons of Hellenism, Fathers of the Church: Emperor Julian, Gregory of Nazianzus, and the Vision of Rome* (Berkeley, CA: University of California Press, 2012), p. 9.

16 I am thankful to Karen O'Donnell, whose work delves into both 'worlds', and who has directed me to resources on the challenges of holding together theology and spirituality, including Elizabeth A. Dreyer, 'Spirituality as a Resource for Theology: The Holy Spirit in Augustine' in Mark S. Burrows and Elizabeth A. Dreyer (eds), *Minding the Spirit* (Baltimore, MD: Johns Hopkins University Press, 2005), pp. 179–99, and Kelly Brown Douglas, *What's Faith Got to Do with It? Black Bodies/Christian Souls* (Maryknoll, NY: Orbis Books, 2005). For a classic essay on this question, see Rowan Williams, 'Theological Integrity', *Cross Currents* 45.3 (1995), pp. 312–25.

17 This is an important debate to which I will return in future work.

18 Oration 28.3, in St Gregory of Nazianzus, *On God and Christ: The Five Theological Orations and Two Letters of Cledonius*, translated by Lionel Wickham and Frederick Williams (Crestwood, NY: St Vladimir's Seminary Press, 2002), p. 39.

19 Oration 28.4; Wickham and Williams, *On God and Christ*, p. 40.

20 Oration 27.3; Wickham and Williams, *On God and Christ*, pp. 26–7 (with amendments).

21 Oration 38.8, in Claudio Moreschini, *Grégoire de Nazianze: Discours 38–41*. Sources chrétiennes 358 (Paris: Les Éditions du Cerf, 1990), p. 118. This oration is also available as a contemporary translation; see St Gregory of Nazianzus, *Festal Orations*, translated by Nonna Verna Harrison (Crestwood, NY: St Vladimir's Seminary Press, 2008).

22 Oration 1.7; SC 247, p. 80. For a contemporary translation of the full-length oration, see St Gregory of Nazianzus, *Festal Orations*.

23 Christopher A. Beeley, *Gregory of Nazianzus on the Trinity and the Knowledge of God: In Your Light We Shall See Light* (Oxford: Oxford University Press, 2008), p. 239.

24 For further reflection on the image of the shepherd, see Chapter 7.

25 Oration 41.9; SC 358, p. 336.

26 Oration 12.2 in Marie-Ange Calvet-Sebasti, *Grégoire de Nazianze. Discours 6–12*. Sources chrétiennes 406 (Paris: Les Éditions du Cerf, 1995), p. 350.

27 Kallistos Ware and Colin Davey (eds), *Anglican–Orthodox Dialogue: The Moscow Statement* (London: SPCK, 1977), p. 91.

28 Poem 1.1.3 in Jacques-Paul Migne, *Patrologia cursus completus, series Graeca*, Vols 35–38 (Paris, 1857–62), Vol. 37, section 402, lines 1–4. Hereafter referenced as 'PG'. Also in Gilbert, *On God and Man*.

29 Oration 20.11, in *St Gregory of Nazianzus: Select Orations*, translated by Martha Pollard Vinson (Washington, DC: Catholic University of America Press, 2003), p. 115.

30 See www.larche.org.uk/news/inquiry-statement. The perpetual problem and causes of abuse in the Church and the academy is beyond the scope of this book.

31 Nicola Slee, *Fragments for Fractured Times: What Feminist Practical Theology Brings to the Table* (London: SCM Press, 2020), p. 39.

32 Sermon 1, in St Gregory of Nyssa, *The Lord's Prayer, The Beatitudes*, translated by Hilda C. Graef (Mahwah, NJ: Paulist Press, 1954), pp. 24–5.

33 Oration 31.33; SC 250, p. 342.

34 Henri J. M. Nouwen, *The Wounded Healer: Ministry in Contemporary Society* (New York: Doubleday, 1979).

35 Oration 2.22; SC 247, p. 118.

36 Oration 38.13; SC 358, p. 132.

37 Oration 40.4; SC 358, p. 204.

38 Oration 40.41–43; SC 358, pp. 292–8.

39 Andrea Sterk, *Renouncing the World Yet Leading the Church: The Monk-Bishop in Late Antiquity* (Cambridge, MA: Harvard University Press, 2004), p. 138.

40 See Oration 2.4; SC 247, pp. 90–2; Oration 25.2, in Justin Mossay, *Grégoire de Nazianze. Discours 24–26*. Sources chrétiennes 284 (Paris: Les Éditions du Cerf, 1981), p. 160.

41 Oration 18.28–29; PG 35, 1017C–1021B. For Gregory's description of his mother's healing, see Oration 18.30; PG 35, 1021B–1024B.

42 Oration 8.18, in *St Gregory Nazianzen and Saint Ambrose: Funeral Orations*, translated by Leo P. McCauley (Washington, DC: Catholic University of America Press, 1953), p. 113.

43 Oration 2.26; SC 247, p. 124.

44 Oration 18.8; PG 35, 993B–996A.

45 On women as images of God, see Thomas, *The Image of God*, pp. 77–86, 99, 145.

46 Poem 1.2.29; PG 37, section 893, lines 125–6.
47 Oration 37.6, in Claudio Moreschini, *Grégoire de Nazianze. Discours 32–37.* Sources chrétiennes 318 (Paris: Les Éditions du Cerf, 1985), p. 284. On this, see John A. McGuckin, *St Gregory of Nazianzus: An Intellectual Biography* (Crestwood, NY: St Vladimir's Seminary Press, 2001), p. 334.
48 Oration 2.22; SC 247, p. 118.
49 Oration 6.1; SC 406, p. 120.
50 Oration 2.28; SC 247, p. 126.
51 Oration 1.4; SC 247, pp. 76–8.
52 Thomas and Narinskaya (eds), *Women and Ordination in the Orthodox Church.*

6

The Gift of Leadership

Receiving the gifts of grace and friendship from Saint Thomas Aquinas to deepen 'mutual flourishing' in the Church of England

The previous chapter explored an example of sharing a gift; this chapter flips the focus of the lens to explore gift reception for the purpose of healing a wound identified by ordained Anglican participants, all of whom lead in the Church of England.[1] I am not suggesting that only ordained people lead, but that this was a particular wound surfacing through the research. The Anglican priests almost univocally specified that the practical outworking of the so-called 'Five Guiding Principles' is a live wound for many ordained women in the Church of England.[2] The principles declare that the three orders of ordained ministry (bishops, priests and deacons) are open to all while recognizing that not everyone is able in good conscience to receive the ministry of women. The fifth principle in particular speaks of 'mutual flourishing' for all in the Church of England, regardless of one's theological convictions on the ordination of women. Against this backdrop, I will explore possible gifts to be received and potential learning for the Church of England with respect to the outworking of the Five Guiding Principles, as specified in the *House of Bishops' Declaration on the Ministry of Bishops and Priests* (2014).[3]

I will begin by describing the conversations in which these concerns arose, and by explaining why the participants express a need for further theological reflection on mutual flourishing. After this, I ask, 'Is there a theological approach that might contribute to the healing of this particular wound?' Responding to this question, I will explore the themes of grace and friendship in the theology of Thomas Aquinas, whose work is one of the many gifts within the Catholic and Anglo-Catholic theological traditions.[4] Thomas's approach to friendship, if received prudently, may serve both as a diagnostic gaze on the wound and a contribution to its healing. The final phase moves on to identify some of the implications of Thomas's theology of friendship for the Church of England, assessing critically how it might be implemented, as stated in the Five Guiding Principles, for mutual flourishing.[5]

While the generation of the Five Guiding Principles was prompted by the admission of women to the episcopate, my focus here is on women who are priests, since the scope of the fieldwork did not extend to bishops. Added to this, note that mutual flourishing is not the only question arising from Five Guiding Principles. Paul Avis addresses the important 'question of the ecclesial integrity of the College of Bishops'.[6] Since the Five Guiding Principles were introduced when women were admitted to the episcopate, Avis focuses on questions that relate directly to the office of the bishop. While I shall focus on the issues that arose during the fieldwork phase of my research, these lie within a broader set of ecclesiological questions addressed appositely by Avis.

The research context

Some 22 Anglican priests attended the focus groups.[7] The Five Guiding Principles were raised as an 'issue', 'wound', or 'fracture' in each of the five focus groups, which indicates that this particular wound is not constrained to a geographical location. That said, the groups did not each spend the same amount of time discussing this concern, and individual women shared different degrees of distress with respect to the Five Guiding Principles, as I shall explain shortly.[8]

Of the 22 participants, 19 agreed with one another that mutual flourishing is a live 'wound' in the Church of England. When the problem was raised, three women reported positively about their roles and experiences with respect to the Five Guiding Principles. Two of the three women explained that they engaged regularly with men from Forward in Faith, who serve as their spiritual directors.[9] As one woman put it: 'I have found this to be an enriching space, which I am really grateful for.' The three women who had not experienced any issues were from different dioceses, again suggesting that geography does not play a strong role here. Interestingly, two of the three who shared positively were in the same dioceses as women who outlined negative experiences. In these instances, the differences exist at deanery levels.[10] This indicates that two women in the same diocese can have a very different experience of mutual flourishing. It is worth emphasizing that this is not necessarily a problem at a diocesan level (although it can be a problem there also), but varies radically from parish to parish, and from deanery to deanery.

Of the 22 women, 12 commented that the women-only focus group which they attended was the first 'safe' opportunity they had been given to say what they thought about the issue and to be honest about the difficulties raised by the Five Guiding Principles. One said, 'This is the first time I have felt safe enough to share what I'm sharing. It's really only in the context of women-only groups that I could say what I've just said.' Seven women commented that they were fearful of raising the issue within their diocese 'in case', as one said, 'I am seen to be disruptive or unsupportive. Because of this I tend to be positive about mutual flourishing in public.' This suggests that dioceses would benefit from creating spaces for 'safe' conversations to take place, albeit it is not an easy task to create spaces that feel wholly safe, exemplified in the process of 'Shared Conversations'.[11]

As the researcher, and as an Anglican priest myself, I listened to several priests with a mixture of shock and horror. I was aware previously of only some of the issues arising with respect to mutual flourishing and had not experienced problems personally. Before exploring the nature of the issues shared by the women, let us briefly set the context in which the phrase arose within the Church of England.

FOR THE GOOD OF THE CHURCH

Mutual flourishing and the Five Guiding Principles

While the phrase bears a particular meaning in the context of the Church of England, generally concepts such as 'human flourishing' conjure up positive images. For example, in a book devoted to 'flourishing', Miroslav Volf describes it as 'the life that is lived well, the life that goes well, and the life that feels good – all three together, inextricably intertwined'.[12] Members of the Yale Center for Faith and Culture engaged in nearly a decade of research relating to human flourishing, observing that it has

> been variously named as 'blessedness,' 'righteousness,' 'abundant life,' 'happiness' and, especially in the 19th and 20th centuries, 'self-fulfillment,' 'self-actualization,' or 'self-realization.' Christian thinkers contend that human flourishing is inseparable from God's active relating to human creatures. Flourishing is thus always a grace that is at least *dependent* on God's assistance – and it may, indeed, be a gift entirely, one that is always contingent on God's ongoing relating to human creatures.[13]

However, for some within the Church of England, 'mutual flourishing' has become a 'catchword'[14] that connotes an 'over reliance on the graciousness of women', as current chair of WATCH (Women and the Church), the Revd Canon Dr Emma Percy, has observed in her article on the Church of England's ambiguous welcome to women.[15] 'Mutual flourishing' appears in the Five Guiding Principles, which were crafted in 2014 because the General Synod of the Church of England voted in favour of admitting women to the episcopate.[16] Since this pronouncement, it is possible for women to be ordained into the three orders of ministry: deacon, priest and bishop. This decision was made after much dispute, and consequently the Five Guiding Principles were given not as a new doctrine but to allow for the continued flourishing of those in the Church of England who do not believe that women should be ordained into these orders.

142

Principles 1 and 2 state that the Church of England has decided that all orders of ministry (deacon, priest and bishop) are open to women. The third principle recognizes the integrity of the universal church and acknowledges that not all Christian traditions agree on ordaining women; for example, the Roman Catholic and Orthodox churches. The fourth principle speaks of the Church of England's commitment to the flourishing of those whose theological convictions prevent them from receiving the ministry of bishops or priests who are women. Lastly, the fifth principle explains that pastoral and sacramental provision will be made for those specified above 'in a way that maintains the highest possible degree of communion and contributes to mutual flourishing across the whole Church of England'.[17]

In 2018, the Faith and Order Commission released a document entitled *A Resource for Study* as a response to the need for further reflection on the content of the Five Guiding Principles.[18] Despite the brevity of this 62-page document, it leads its readers through a penetrating exploration of the Five Guiding Principles, explaining that

> commitment to mutual flourishing does not come without serious costs, and it needs to be acknowledged that in different situations they may be unevenly distributed and fall more heavily on some for reasons not of their own choosing.

The study guide also states, quite rightly, that this is 'a wound in the body'.[19] 'Wound' here does not speak of the experiences of women who are priests, or the experiences of those who do not support the ordination of women; rather, in the document, 'wound' acknowledges the overall pain of a fractured church.

Experiences of flourishing within the Church of England

Speaking of the Five Guiding Principles during the course of the research, many of the Anglican priests raised concerns about their own flourishing. That said, if the research had focused on only this concern, rather than this wound being one of many raised through the practice of receptive ecumenism, the results would have been different. Outside of this research context, I am aware that some of those who do not agree with the ministry of women priests are also experiencing difficulties.

One of the women, despite for the most part describing positive experiences with colleagues who did not agree with her ministry, put it like this: 'I really struggle with that dynamic within the Church of England and how we are dealing with it. I don't think we're dealing with it very well at all.' While listening to the recording of the group's conversation, I could not help but notice the response to her remark from the other Anglican priests. There was a strong sense of recognition which was expressed by snorting sounds and comments such as 'Ha, ha!'; and one woman responded, 'That's got to be the understatement of the decade!'

In a different group, disturbing experiences were shared:

I'm all for mutual flourishing, but is it really that? Or is it simply the flourishing of those I am supposed to seek who do not recognize me as a priest? I don't like sounding cynical, but fellow priests have sent me hate mail. And we are not talking about things which happened twenty years ago; this has happened very recently. It seems to me that the flourishing is one sided.

Other testimonies were equally troubling. One woman spoke about her recent college experience, offering a painful account of an experience ahead of being ordained deacon: 'I'd given out my Ember cards at college, because that's what we all did, and the next day I found two of them torn into little pieces and put back into my pigeon hole.'[20] This had happened to the women not only from when women first began to be ordained during the 1990s, as one might expect, but since 2015. While women are permitted to orders of bishop, priest and deacon, the focus groups have brought to light how painful it can be when women are not recognized as 'real priests', and how it can lead to, as one woman put it, 'bullying'.[21]

In a further group, one woman spoke about the wound of the Five Guiding Principles as they are lived out in the diocese within which she ministers:

> If you asked any women [clergy] in our diocese what they think mutual flourishing is all about, they'd tell you – if they dared, that is – that it means women are expected to be grateful and to keep quiet. It feels like it was an effective way to silence us, and I'm not sure flourishing means silence ... Have you noticed that in the Five Guiding Principles, there's an assumption that women who are ordained are automatically flourishing?

These comments point to an implicit assumption in the Five Guiding Principles, as noted earlier, which implies that the ordination of women equates to women's flourishing; however, this is not necessarily what is experienced in practice.

Several women spoke of their sadness about the gap that often exists between those who hold differing views on the ordination of women to the priesthood. They suggested that it is unhelpful to hold separate Chrism Eucharists and ordination services for those who do not accept the ordained ministry of women.[22] Some reported having sent myriad invitations to groups who do not support the ordination of women and asked, 'How many times do we have to be rejected?' As well as this, those with differing views rarely come together in deanery chapter meetings.[23] Describing this situation, one woman said, 'We are all in our little separate groups, and it's far too easy to avoid one another.'

The report on Wakefield Cathedral in March 2019 demonstrates further this separation. This report is concerned with whether the sex of the priest presiding at a Eucharist should be made public knowledge so that those who do not accept women's ordination can avoid particular services. It was written as a result of a complaint made first to the dean of Wakefield Cathedral, who refused to make public the names of priests presiding at the daily Eucharists. After the dean's refusal to comply, the complaint was made to the bishop, who observed that while it was not within his gift to enforce this, he would like the names to be published for the sake of those who do not want to receive communion from a woman.[24] In this instance, 'mutual flourishing' functions in practice as a euphemism for 'independent flourishing'.[25]

In addition to comments and expressions of 'frustration with the current status quo', one of the women remarked that it did not appear 'at all clear what is actually meant by mutual flourishing, and precisely what kind of theology underpins it'. The study guide from the Faith and Order Commission provides one response to this. It draws on Ephesians 4.13 to suggest that flourishing entails 'growing up to maturity, to the measure of the full stature of Christ'. Much like receptive ecumenism, flourishing 'is likely to mean change and challenge, repentance and deepening conversion'.[26] How this happens when those with opposing views rarely share one another's spaces is not clear. Nor is it evident what repentance looks like in this instance.

Seeking to draw on the theological riches that lie within the Anglo-Catholic tradition, my question is this: 'Is there a way of thinking about this concern theologically which could contribute to the healing of the wound?' I ask this not expecting to cure all souls, but rather to deepen the conversation with respect to how, in the Church of England, we might seek one another's flourishing in a context in which many people are hurting, hold radically diverse opinions, and are in asymmetrical relations with one another.

I will explore this question in conversation with Saint Thomas Aquinas who, I believe, has a great contribution to make to this discussion. It would be remiss, however, to make this move without first recognizing that Thomas has been cited frequently to support the belief that women should not be ordained priests. This is despite the fact that Thomas addresses this question once across his whole corpus – in Book IV of his *Commentary on Sentences*, and only very briefly. The comment is repeated verbatim in the supplement of the *Summa*.[27] Given the vast amount that Thomas has written, one might conclude from this that his comment is overused because he is key to the Western Christian theological tradition, and not because the ordination of women is a prevalent theme in his theological contribution.

That said, even if Thomas's comments on ordaining women have been made to do more work than they should, one could not argue that he is a proponent of women's flourishing particularly. In this, Thomas is representative of the Christian tradition in the Middle Ages.[28] To this end, I do not intend to utilize teaching that denies the full humanity of women, but to engage with Thomas's theology of human flourishing as friendship with God in light of God's grace which can be applied to the flourishing of all human persons.[29] I hope to provoke 'theological imagination to new insight' such that theology might 'flower beyond [the older tradition] as the very consequence of engaging with it'.[30]

Thomas's account of friendship with God as mutual flourishing provides a theological diagnosis of the current stalemate among those who disagree over ordaining women to the priesthood and contributes to a way of moving forward in hope, even if only a little. For Thomas, human flourishing occurs through the incarnation, which occasions a radical gift of friendship in which, through the pure gift of God's grace, human beings respond to God freely as God's friends. According to Thomas, the incarnation makes possible the equality, commonality and benevolence that are required for humans to be friends with God and, through God, friends with one another. This paves a way for the possibility of being friends with people with whom one disagrees, and those with whom power relations are not necessarily balanced equally.

Thomas's theology of grace and friendship

Since it is beyond the scope of this chapter to explore the contentious debates pertaining to Thomas's doctrine of grace I will focus only on that which is most pertinent to my argument, namely, how movement is key to Thomas's understanding of grace.[31] After establishing how grace is dynamic, I shall move on to explore its centrality to Thomas's theology of friendship with God, closing with an analysis of the aspects of Thomas's work on friendship relevant to mutual flourishing.

In an article entitled 'The Sweet Delight of Virtue and Grace in Aquinas's Ethics', Simon Oliver establishes how Thomas weaves together four diverse strands into a cohesive whole to form his theological ethics, namely, grace, virtue, his doctrine of the incarnation, and physics.[32] These four strands also appear in Thomas's theology of friendship, albeit with differing emphases. Oliver's overall thesis supports our aim here and makes an important point about how for Thomas motion occurs. While it is generally agreed that Thomas draws on Aristotle's understanding of motion, commentators do not always appreciate the extent to which Aristotle's view of motion extends throughout Thomas's thought on virtue. Two aspects of Aristotle's understanding of motion are pertinent here. First, motion takes place between contraries, that is, an object might move from cold to hot, or someone who is learning might move from ignorance to knowledge. These contraries consist of potency and act. This works in such a way that if something is cold, it must possess the potency to become hot and must be acted upon by something hot in order to move from one to the other.[33] Second, following on from the previous statement, a mover must exist for movement to take place. Note that for Aristotle, and then for Thomas, this is not straightforward and relates directly to teleology: 'in any motion, there is something in act which moves another towards its *telos*'.[34]

In order for humans to reach their *telos*, Thomas speaks of them needing a 'two-fold help'. He locates this help in two kinds of grace – habitual grace (*habitudo*) and *auxilium* – and movement is embedded within his development of each of these. The gift of the second kind of grace, *auxilium*, assumes that every human person 'needs the help of grace in order to be moved by God to act'.[35] Thus *auxilium* concerns the creature being moved by divine activity to new knowledge or to a specific activity.[36]

The gift of habitual grace describes the movement from 'corrupted human nature' towards wholeness. After human nature is healed, it is 'lifted up so as to work deeds meritoriously of everlasting life'.[37] Habitual grace is able to work as a formal cause because it is infused as a quality in the soul in such a way that the soul can move itself towards God and good acts. According to Thomas, the soul is 'naturally capable of grace because it is made according to the likeness of God, and thus is fit to receive God's grace'.[38] In other words, the soul is created to be 'porous' to grace. In receiving grace, the soul moves dynamically towards good:

> Certain forms and powers, which are the principles of acts, in order that they may of themselves be inclined to these movements, and thus the movements whereby they are moved by God become natural and easy to creatures … Much more therefore does God infuse into such as God moves towards the acquisition of supernatural good, certain forms or supernatural qualities, whereby they may be moved by God sweetly and promptly to acquire eternal good.[39]

Thus for Thomas, 'supernatural qualities' – or, put another way, 'supernatural virtues' – depend upon the human soul being porous to grace and its being created with the capacity to move towards God and participate in the life of God, and therefore with the supernatural virtues.[40] Of these virtues, charity relates directly to Thomas's theology of friendship with God; as Thomas explains:

> Charity is an *amicitia* of people for God, founded upon the fellowship of everlasting happiness. Now this fellowship is in respect, not of natural but of gratuitous gifts … so charity surpasses out of natural faculties. Now that which surpasses

the faculty of nature cannot be natural or acquired by natural powers since a natural effect does not transcend its cause. Therefore charity can be in us neither natural, nor through acquisition by the natural powers, but by the infusion of the Holy Spirit, who is the love of the Father and the Son, and the participation of whom in us is created charity.[41]

Here Thomas weaves together the soul's porosity to God with the virtue of charity, since charity is only possible through 'the infusion of the Holy Spirit'. While Thomas is not the first theologian to explore friendship with God, he is the first to define charity in terms of friendship.[42] His treatise on charity is longer than any other discussion of the theological virtues, consisting of 24 questions.[43] Thomas considers charity to be the greatest of all virtues because it unites 'in will the lover and the beloved: God is loved as God should be, for God's own sake and as God is'.[44] God loves first, and the recipient of God's love is able to love God in return with the aid of grace. Following Augustine's *De doctrina Christiana*, Thomas lists four objects of charity. These are God, the neighbour, oneself and one's body. One is able to love one's neighbour because she is 'made by and for God as end'.[45] It is particularly Thomas's thought on love of God and neighbour with which we are concerned here.

Before moving on, it is important to note that, as Alasdair MacIntyre and others have argued, through modernity friendship has been relegated for the most part to the private life. Ancient models of friendship, such as the Aristotelian tradition of sharing a common goal, are often viewed as 'alien to the modern conception of friendship'.[46] The rise of individualism has resulted in political community no longer being rooted in a common project and instead friendship is generally the place in which human beings seek refuge from the world rather than engaging in friendship within the public space. Moreover, '"friendship" has become for the most part the name of a type of emotional state rather than of a type of social relationship'.[47] When exploring Thomas's approach to friendship, we should bear in mind that it is a radically different view of friendship than the one that developed through modernity and has more in common with Aristotelian thought, although as we shall see shortly Thomas's model transcends that of the philosopher. Aristotle's model of friendship is concerned with relationships between persons of virtue. In Books 8 and 9 of his *Nicomachean Ethics*, Aristotle argues that friendship is a virtue necessary for each person's happiness.[48] For Aristotle, it is not possible for human beings to be friends with the gods because he constructs a model in which friendship exists only among those who are equals and those who have something in common. Aristotle's reasoning for this necessitates that those who are friends must share either an activity, an exchange of goods, and possess direct benevolence towards the other. Thomas agrees with this and argues that friendship must include benevolence. For example, wine is not our friend because we do not wish wine well, even if we like it for our own sakes. Furthermore, Thomas responds by arguing that friendship is more than simply having benevolent feelings towards someone and, following Aristotle, argues that it is based on some kind of equality and reciprocity.[49]

Departing from Aristotle, Thomas focuses first on the friendship between God and creatures, despite having agreed with Aristotle that some kind of equality needs to exist between those who are friends.[50] In response to this, we might ask, 'How then is human friendship with God possible since human beings are not equal, in any sense, to God?'[51] The answer to this is 'Jesus Christ', since friendship, Thomas argues, is possible through the incarnation:

> Since friendship consists in a certain equality, things greatly unequal seem unable to be coupled in friendship. Therefore, to get greater familiarity in friendship between humans and God it was helpful for humans that God became a human, since even by nature a human is a human's friend.[52]

Thomas's discussion on human friendship with God is rooted in his interpretation of Scripture. He explores the words of Jesus to his disciples, as written in the Gospel according to Saint John: 'It is written ... *I will not now call you servants*

... *but My friends.* Now this was said to them by reason of nothing else than charity. Therefore charity is friendship.'[53] Furthermore, true friendship is only possible if it is accompanied by the free choice of the other which is demonstrated in the incarnation.

The incarnation, then, establishes a kind of equality between human beings and God, which is only possible through the supernatural virtue charity. Moreover, Thomas draws once more on the Aristotelian model to establish a sense of commonality between humans and God, again made possible through the incarnation. Thomas makes this move by bringing Aristotle's belief that friends need something in common into conversation with Paul's teaching on fellowship (*koinonia*). Drawing on Saint Paul's first letter to the Corinthians, Thomas explains that commonality between God and humans is possible through the fellowship (*koinonia*) of the Son:[54]

> Accordingly, since there is a communication [*communicatio*] between humans and God, inasmuch as [God] communicates [God's] happiness to us, some kind of friendship must needs be based on this same communication, of which it is written (1 Cor. i. 9): *God is faithful: by Whom you are called unto the fellowship of* [the] *Son.*[55]

This commonality is none other than God's own happiness (beatitude), which is incomplete on earth but experienced more completely in heaven: 'Charity is friendship of humans for God, founded upon the fellowship of ever-lasting happiness.'[56] In this, Thomas transcends the possibilities for friendship as outlined by the philosopher.

Having discussed how God and human beings are able to be friends, Thomas moves on to reflect upon human friendship with other humans. Since charity originates with God, we love others through God: 'Love ... tends to God first, and flows on from him to other things, and in this sense charity loves God immediately, and other things through God.'[57] A little later, Thomas puts it this way: 'We love all our neighbours with the same love of charity, in so far as they are referred to one good common to them all, which is God.'[58] In this way, we are able to love our enemies – insofar as God is the 'only reason for loving one's enemy'.[59] Thomas goes further than this and explains precisely how we are able to love those who are unfriendly to us; this can happen if they are in some way related to those whom we love already:

> That a person should actually do so, and love their enemy for God's sake, without it being necessary for them to do so, belongs to the perfection of charity. For since a person loves their neighbour, out of charity, for God's sake, the more they love God, the more do they put enmities aside and show love towards their neighbour: thus if we loved a certain person very much, we would love their children though they were unfriendly towards us.[60]

Therefore those who love God and whom God loves are able, with the help of the virtue of charity, to love God's children. Or, put another way, sons and daughters of God are able to move in friendship towards those who are unfriendly to them precisely through the grace of charity.

In the same way that Thomas crafts a way of humans moving in friendship towards those who are not disposed to be friends with them, he also paves a way for sharing friendship with those with whom we disagree. Precisely because his view of charity is theocentric, persons are able to move in friendship towards those with whom they do not share the same opinion:

> As the Philosopher says (*Ethic.* ix. 6) friends need not agree in opinion, but only upon such goods as conduce to life, and especially upon such as are important; because dissension in small matters is scarcely accounted dissension. Hence nothing hinders those who have charity from holding different opinions.[61]

Thomas here does not give an example of what counts as a 'small matter' when arguing that friends need not agree on everything. However, this suggests that agreement between persons is not a necessary prerequisite to human friendship because friendship is rooted in charity, a supernatural virtue that belongs first to God. Thus love for friends and enemies alike is possible only through God.

One could not describe the current situation within the Church of England as simply the holding of different opinions. For many, ordaining women as priests is not adiaphorous; some argue that the gender of the priest is a first-order issue and a matter of salvation. On the other hand, the Church of England has 'made a clear decision'[62] and 'holds that those whom it has duly ordained and appointed to office are the true and lawful holders of the office which they occupy'.[63] Whatever the view on this issue, the Church of England has committed to holding the two integrities together for the foreseeable future and its members must find a way of living and flourishing within the tension that this creates.

Thomas on the formation of habit

Before exploring ways in which Thomas's theology of friendship might be appropriated in the Church of England, I must make a further observation that relates to Thomas's views on the formation of habit, and that will help to move beyond the current impasse because of the way it relates to the mutuality aspect of 'mutual flourishing'.

First, for Thomas, habit and human will go hand in hand. With respect to the will, Thomas does not understand human choice as a collection of individual decisions. So, for example, if I want to be a 'good' friend this will not happen by discrete movements of my will, following some kind of utilitarian ethic. Human acts instead form a 'continuous motion towards the universal end in being, truth and goodness'.[64] As far as Thomas is concerned, this is possible through the cultivation of habits, which he understands as implying 'a disposition in relation to a thing's nature, and to its operation or end, by reason of which disposition a thing is well or ill disposed towards its end'.[65] Or, put another way, 'a habit determines the motion of a being towards fulfilment in its *telos* or away from such fulfilment towards the demise of its being'.[66] A habit is different from other kinds of qualities because it determines the very manner in which humans fulfil (or not) their nature. How, then, is a habit acquired? Thomas's response to this follows the logic of his overall argument: a habit is acquired through practice, training and repetition.[67] However, this is not to suggest that the journey of good habits is arduous:

> In contrast to much modern ethical theory, the genuinely good life, for Aquinas, looks 'natural' and easy. It appears spontaneous and swift, because good actions spring from good habits which are infused into and define our nature, just as the motions of natural bodies appear swift and easy as bodies move towards their *telos*.[68]

The cultivation of habit, according to Thomas, is key to the journey of mutual flourishing because it highlights the importance of both individual and communal practices and habits. A continuous flow of action is required which points to a high level of commitment from all involved. It also reminds those of us in the Church of England that the conversation about mutual flourishing lies within the broader teleology of a holy life of friendship.

How does Thomas's theology of friendship contribute to mutual flourishing in the Church of England?

It is well known that, even without the particular issues flowing from disagreement over the ordination of women priests, 'friendship is complex, fraught with risk, exposure, and moral challenge'.[69] I do not suggest that Thomas's theology of friendship is the sum of the reflection needed on mutual flourishing, nor do I expect it to resolve quickly long-standing disputes. However, Thomas's approach to friendship with God as human flourishing serves as a diagnostic gaze upon the wound that many in the Church of England are experiencing with respect to the outworking of the Five Guiding Principles. Furthermore, Thomas's reflection on friendship informs on how we might reflect further on mutual flourishing in the current context.

In Thomas's thought, human flourishing as friendship with God is theocentric and cosmically oriented. His approach de-sentimentalizes friendship so that we locate it as a virtue in the broader economy of God's grace given to human beings in the incarnation. For Thomas, the human response to the incarnation means that humans respond freely to God as God's friends. It renders possible the equality, commonality and benevolence that is required for humans to be friends with God and, through God, friends with one another. This paves a way for the possibility of being friends with those who hold beliefs with which one does not agree, and with those with whom power relations are not necessarily balanced equally.

First, then, mutual flourishing is friendship with God. It does not imply that everyone needs to have the same opinion on ordaining women priests. Mutuality is located first in our shared friendship with God, and only through God is friendship possible with one another.

Thomas's theology of friendship also creates a space in which to explore how we might discuss honestly the effect of asymmetrical relations when thinking about mutual flourishing. Thomas does not avoid Aristotle's challenge that friendship needs to be between those who are equal to one another. He tackles this by exploring the incarnation, which brings about some kind of equality between humans and God. If human friendship with God is possible, then it is also possible, through the same virtue of charity, between those who are not equal to one another. However, in the same way that God is charitable towards humankind, humans must behave likewise if they are to share in the same virtue of charity. Being in friendship with people who commit vindictive acts intentionally does not imply that those on the receiving end should simply turn the other cheek. Thomas makes clear that to 'correct' the brother or sister who sins against a person is an act of charity.[70] Malicious behaviour should be called to account.

Second, as I have discussed, Thomas's analysis of charity as friendship incorporates by necessity movement towards God which is dependent entirely upon grace. Through the Holy Spirit, the soul is infused with the grace of charity, which renders movement towards God possible. This relates directly to the work of philosopher Charles Taylor, who argues that through modernity and the rise of humanism, the human person's understanding of herself has grown increasingly disenchanted and disengaged, which Taylor characterizes as the 'buffered self'. The move towards the buffered self causes problems with friendship because embedded within it is a 'very different existential condition' from the pre-modern self-understanding: 'For the modern, buffered self the possibility exists of taking a distance from, disengaging from everything outside the mind.'[71] This notion of the buffered self contrasts radically with the pre-modern view held by Thomas, who, to borrow from Taylor, understands the self as 'porous'.[72] The porous self is open and porous to God, which for Thomas means that 'the charity by which we love the neighbour is a participation of Divine charity'.[73]

This calls into question current practices in the Church of England which create a buffer for those with differing beliefs by providing separate ordination services, separate Chrism Eucharists, the public naming of priests who preside at the Eucharist, etc. Through many different practices and structures, those in the Church are buffering themselves and choosing to disengage with one another. While obviously there are exceptions to this, the structures more often support a buffered stance than a porous stance.[74] If we are to take Thomas's model of friendship, movement towards and engagement with one another is necessary for any notion of mutual flourishing. This necessitates a choice. We will need to choose to cross boundaries and risk an 'unbuffered' stance by moving into one another's spaces. However, we must bear in mind Thomas's theology of habit. When I speak of 'choosing', I do not imagine a scenario in which Anglican priests, whichever view they might hold, arduously choose to attend a deanery meeting, or indeed a Chrism Eucharist, in which they will find themselves in conversation with those who hold differing opinions. The kind of choice I envisage here is the choice of cultivating good habits which lead us towards God and towards one another. One of these habits could be having productive and prayerful conversations with those who are opposed to one another's beliefs, conversations that do not shame those who disagree, and that allow for deep engagement, rather than the current pattern of life in the Church of England.

While for reasons already stated it would be difficult to begin by sharing the Eucharist, nevertheless it would be possible to come together for daily offices to pray with one another. Since, as Thomas has identified, friendship is not simply possible by human effort but needs divine help, it is imperative that we learn to pray with one another and share one another's sacred spaces. The collect for Quinquagesima in *The Book of Common Prayer* provides the words with which to begin:

> O Lord, who hast taught us that all our doings without charity are nothing worth: Send thy Holy Ghost, and pour into our hearts that most excellent gift of charity, the very bond of peace and of all virtues, without which whosoever liveth is counted dead before thee.[75]

By re-envisioning mutual flourishing in light of Thomas's theology of grace-infused friendship, it would be possible to create a culture in the Church of England in which it is unacceptable to send hate mail and rip up another's Ember cards – or worse. Instead, inspired by Thomas, energy would be better spent on cultivating practices of friendship, since, as Thomas writes, 'the one who possesses the more charity, will see God more perfectly, and will be more beatified'.[76]

Conclusion

When embarking upon this research, I did not anticipate the kinds of wounds that would be revealed, and I was not alone in this; women from all kinds of churches reacted with astonishment at the painful testimonies relating to the Five

Guiding Principles. One of the Catholic women present in a focus group explained that she had assumed 'when a woman is in a church which ordains women to the priesthood – then all glass ceilings are smashed'. Receptive ecumenism proved to be an effective way of facilitating a space in which deeper learning could take place among women from radically diverse churches. By creating a space in which women felt safe to speak honestly about their experiences, both positive and negative, it was evident that not all women leading as deacons, priests and bishops are flourishing currently within the Church of England. As one response to reflecting further on mutual flourishing (while recognizing the good work already done), I have offered an iteration of receptive ecumenism by turning to receive from Saint Thomas, whose theology is a rich treasure. While Thomas's approach to friendship is not a definitive answer to the challenge of mutual flourishing, it provides hope for ongoing and deeper engagement between those with differing views on the ordination of women to all orders of ministry holding positions of ordained leadership in the Church of England.

Notes

1 This chapter draws on an earlier article: Gabrielle Thomas, '"Mutual Flourishing" in the Church of England: Learning Receptively from Saint Thomas Aquinas', *Ecclesiology: The Journal of Ministry, Mission and Unity* 15.2 (2019), pp. 302–21. Used with permission.

2 This is not to suggest that only women find the current practices challenging; to explore this further is beyond the scope of the chapter.

3 GS Misc 1076 [*House of Bishops' Declaration on the Ministry of Bishops and Priests*], available at www.churchofengland.org/sites/default/files/2017-11/GS%20Misc%201076%20Women%20in%20the%20Episcopate.pdf.

4 I am indebted to my colleague Dr Rik Van Nieuwenhove who listened to and critiqued my reading of Thomas and who pointed me in the direction of excellent primary and secondary reading.

5 A resource that reflects on the Five Guiding Principles is available from the Faith and Order Commission: *The Five Guiding Principles: A Resource for Study* (2018), available at www.churchofengland.org/sites/default/files/2018-02/5%20Guiding%20Principles.pdf.

6 Paul Avis, 'Bishops in Communion? The Unity of the Episcopate, the Unity of the Diocese and the Unity of the Church', *Ecclesiology* 13.3 (2017), pp. 299–323 (p. 299).

7 Recall that this research does not claim to represent the view of all ordained Anglican women, but rather the views of those who participated in the research.

8 Note that while I am an ordained woman in the Church of England, I did not personally raise this as an issue during the research.

9 For details on Forward in Faith, see www.forwardinfaith.com/.

10 In the Church of England, parishes are grouped together on the basis of a geographical location to form a 'deanery'. These are supported pastorally and administratively by a rural or area dean.

11 'Shared Conversations' refers to the process of facilitated conversations undertaken across three groups in the Church of England: the College of Bishops, regionally, and with members of General Synod. The conversations took place during 2014 and 2015 and asked: 'Given the significant changes in our culture in relation to human sexuality, how should the Church respond?' For the official website on 'Shared Conversations', see www.sharedconversations.org/. For feedback, see the *Church Times* website: www.churchtimes.co.uk/articles/2016/11-march/news/uk/shared-conversations-come-to-an-end.

12 Miroslav Volf, *Flourishing: Why We Need Religion in a Globalized World* (New Haven, CT: Yale University Press, 2016), p. ix.

13 See https://faith.yale.edu/.

14 Emma Percy, 'Women, Ordination and the Church of England: An Ambiguous Welcome', *Feminist Theology* 26.1 (2017), pp. 90–100 (p. 97). WATCH website: https://womenandthechurch.org. *A Report on the Developments in Women's Ministry in 2019* is available at https://womenandthechurch.org/resources/a-report-on-the-developments-in-womens-ministry-in-2019/. See also the Church of England's *Living Ministry* research (wave 1), led by Liz Gaveling, available at www.churchofengland.org/sites/default/files/2018-10/Living%20Ministry%20Qualitative%20Panel%20Study%20Wave%201%20Report.pdf. The Church of England's ministry statistics show that in 2019 more women than men were ordained as deacons, although many of these women will be working in unpaid capacities, since only a third of the stipends are given to women; see www.churchofengland.org/sites/default/files/2020-06/Ministry%20Statistics%202019%20report%20FINAL.pdf.

15 Percy, 'Women, Ordination and the Church of England', p. 91.

16 Percy provides a clear and concise sequence of events that led to the Five Guiding Principles; see 'Women, Ordination and the Church of England', pp. 91–8.

17 GS Misc 1076, pp. 1–2.

18 The Faith and Order Commission of the Church of England, *The*

Five Guiding Principles: A Resource for Study (London: Church House Publishing, 2018).

19 *Five Guiding Principles*, p. 37.

20 Traditionally, those being ordained in the Anglican Church send Ember cards to ask people to pray for them.

21 'Women Describe Pitfalls on Path to Priesthood', an article by Maddy Fry in the *Church Times* (3 July 2020), speaks to broader issues with respect to women training for the priesthood in the Church of England. Like the participants in this research, the interviewees raise issues of maternity leave and income; see www.churchtimes.co.uk/articles/2020/3-july/news/uk/women-describe-pitfalls-on-path-to-priesthood.

22 The Chrism Eucharist is a service at which ordained clergy gather to receive oil, blessed by the bishop, to use to anoint people being baptized, confirmed and ordained, or people who receive the last rites. Added to this, ordination vows are renewed at these services.

23 Some priests who forgo the deanery chapter meetings have also noted that they feel unwelcome because they do not support women being ordained as priests or bishops. While this is beyond the scope of this particular research, it is clear that the pain is widespread and not confined to women.

24 'House of Bishops Declaration on the Ministry of Bishops and Priests: Wakefield Cathedral – Report of the Independent Reviewer', available at www.churchofengland.org/sites/default/files/2019-03/wakefield_cathedral_independent_reviewer_report_0.pdf.

25 I am thankful to Karen Kilby who, while I worked at Durham University, served as an inspirational conversation partner; this particular insight is hers.

26 *Five Guiding Principles*, p. 30.

27 Thomas Aquinas, *Commentary on Sentences*, Book IV.d25 q.2 art. 1. Also see the supplement to *ST* 39.1. Thomas's main point is that women have a 'state of subjection', but it is not wholly clear whether he is referring to this as pre- or postlapsarian; see John Hilary Martin, 'The Injustice of Not Ordaining Women: A Problem for Medieval Theologians', *Theological Studies* 48 (1987), pp. 303–16. Citations of *Summa Theologiae* give Part, question, article, part of article. For example, *ST* I.1.10 *ad* 1 = ST Part One, question 1, article 10, the response to the first objection. Latin citations are from *Summa theologiae*, 5 vols (Ottowa: impensis Studii generalis OP, 1941–5). English translations, with my own minor amendments, are taken from St Thomas Aquinas, *Summa Theologica*. Translated by the Fathers of the English Dominican Province (New York: Benzinger, 1947).

28 For the views on women in medieval theology, see Christianne Klapisch-Zuber (ed.), *A History of Women in the West: Silences of the Middle Ages* 2 (Cambridge, MA: Belknap Press, 1994). While Thomas

indicates on more than one occasion that he believes women to be inferior to men, he also stipulates that they can be better than men with respect to their souls (*Commentary on Sentences*, Book IV.d25 q.2 re to ob. 1), suggesting a more nuanced position than is often suggested.

29 On the ethics of engaging with retrieval, see Simeon Zahl, 'Tradition and its "Use": The Ethics of Theological Retrieval', *Scottish Journal of Theology* 71.3 (2018), pp. 308–23.

30 A. N. Williams, 'The Future of the Past: The Contemporary Significance of the Nouvelle Theologie', *International Journal of Systematic Theology* 7 (2005), pp. 347–61 (p. 351).

31 Thomas's doctrine of grace is highly developed and much debated. Foundational studies include Henri Bouillard, *Conversion et grace chez S. Thomas d'Aquin* (Paris: Aubier, 1944), and Bernard J. F. Lonergan, *Grace and Freedom: Operative Grace in the Thought of St Thomas Aquinas*, edited by James Patout Burns (London: Darton, Longman and Todd, 1971).

32 Simon Oliver, 'The Sweet Delight of Virtue and Grace in Aquinas's Ethics', *International Journal of Systematic Theology* 7.1 (2005), pp. 52–71.

33 Oliver, 'Sweet Delight', p. 54; Aristotle, *Physics*, III.1.201a. For further discussion, see L. A. Kosman, 'Aristotle's Definition of Motion', *Phronesis* 14 (1969), pp. 40–62; William D. Ross, *Aristotle's Physics* (Oxford: Oxford University Press, 1936), p. 537.

34 Oliver, 'Sweet Delight', p. 56.

35 *ST* I-II.109.9.

36 *ST* I-II.109.9.

37 *ST* I-II.109.9.

38 *ST* I-II.113.10.

39 *ST* I-II.110.2.

40 Brian Davies, *The Thought of Thomas Aquinas* (Oxford: Clarendon Press, 1992), p. 292.

41 *ST* II-II.24.2.

42 For example, Aelred of Rievaulx composed an extended reflection on spiritual friendship.

43 On the originality of Thomas's theology of friendship, see Jean-Pierre Torrell, *Christ and Spirituality in St Thomas Aquinas* (Washington, DC: Catholic University of America Press, 2011), p. 45; Rik Van Nieuwenhove, *An Introduction to Medieval Theology* (Cambridge: Cambridge University Press, 2012), p. 194.

44 Joseph Wawrykow, 'The Theological Virtues' in Rik Van Nieuwenhove and Joseph Wawrykow (eds), *The Theology of Thomas Aquinas* (Notre Dame, IN: University of Notre Dame Press, 2005), pp. 287–307 (p. 296).

45 Wawrykow, 'The Theological Virtues', p. 296.

46 Daniel Schwartz, *Aquinas on Friendship* (Oxford: Oxford University Press, 2007), pp. 2–3.

47 Alasdair MacIntyre, *After Virtue* (London: Duckworth, 1985), p. 156.

48 The nuances of Aristotle's views are beyond the scope of this chapter.

49 *ST* II-II.23.1.

50 *ST* II-II.23.1.

51 For a succinct summary of friendship with God, see Maggie T. Farrell, 'Thomas Aquinas and Friendship with God', *Irish Theological Quarterly* 61.3–4 (1995), pp. 212–18.

52 *Summa contra gentiles* IV.54.6, translated by Charles J. O'Neil (Notre Dame, IN: University of Notre Dame Press, 1975). With amendments.

53 *ST* II-II.23.1.

54 Van Nieuwenhove, *An Introduction to Medieval Theology*, p. 195.

55 *ST* II-II.23.1.

56 *ST* II-II.24.2.

57 *ST* II-II.27.4.

58 *ST* II-II.25.2.

59 *ST* II-II.27.7.

60 *ST* II-II.25.8.

61 *ST* II-II.29.3. *ad* 2.

62 Principle 2.

63 Principle 1.

64 Oliver, 'Sweet Delight', p. 58.

65 *ST* I-II.49.4 *responsio*. See Aristotle, *Nicomachean Ethics*, II.4.

66 Oliver, 'Sweet Delight', p. 58.

67 *ST* I-II.51.3 *sed contra* and *responsio*.

68 Oliver, 'Sweet Delight', p. 60.

69 Lorraine Cuddeback, 'Becoming Friends: Ethics in Friendship and in Doing Theology', *Journal of Moral Theology* 6.2 (2017), pp. 158–79 (p. 159).

70 *ST*.II-II.33.1.

71 Charles Taylor, *A Secular Age* (Cambridge, MA: Harvard University Press, 2007), p. 38.

72 Taylor, *A Secular Age*, p. 27.

73 *ST* II–II.23.2 *ad* 1.

74 In light of some of the reports of bullying in the focus groups, it is important to recognize that some kinds of buffering are necessary at this stage of the implementation of the Five Guiding Principles.

75 Church of England, *The Book of Common Prayer*, 1662 (Cambridge: Cambridge University Press, 1960).

76 *ST* I.12.6.

7

The Gift of Power

Reflections on power bubbled under the surface of the women's exchanges and often became the focus of conversation, as demonstrated in Chapter 3. Whether the women were talking about vocation, hospitality or leadership, power emerged as an accompanying theme while also being discussed on its own. Conversations revolved around aspirations of possessing power, the seduction of power, uses and abuses of power, structures of power and men in positions of power. While reading through the transcripts, I highlighted 'power' with a luminous green marker which left a colourful reminder of the prevalence of the women's concerns: thoughts on power ranged widely, but the most frequent wound that the women identified in their churches relates to the hierarchical structures that enable leaders to use power negatively for their own ends. Comments on this theme came from women working in churches as diverse as Baptist, Anglican, Catholic, Eastern Orthodox, Independent Evangelical, Independent Pentecostal, and the Assemblies of God. Conversations about power focused mostly on power used badly, which accounts for why women fell silent on hearing this:

> Methodism is a safe place for women to be women. (Methodist, 52)

I was struck by this comment, slipped into conversation almost as an afterthought while a woman summarized over two decades of working as a Methodist presbyter. Listening to her, it seemed to me that she had revealed something important, both with respect to the culture within Methodism, and also about the broader ecumenical context.[1] I asked in response, 'If it is safe to be a woman within Methodism, do you mean that it is not safe to be a woman elsewhere?' 'Absolutely', she replied.

> It's not as safe in churches where structures and accountability allow for abuse, and where power is held badly as a result. I'm not saying that the Methodist Church is perfect – of course it's not – but, personally, I've experienced greater challenges through ecumenical work.

Her reflection identifies the same issue highlighted by other Methodists, as discussed in Chapter 3. It is the woman's comment about Methodism being 'safe for women' that forms the basis for this chapter's central question: 'Which gifts exist within Methodism promote the positive exercise of power?'

Participants outside of Methodism identified the Methodist Quadrilateral and Connexion as gifts that they would like to explore further. Before delving into these gifts, I will first frame 'power' to reflect as much as possible the women's descriptions. Drawing on their testimonies, I will identify the ways in which power is used to discriminate against women who want to take on leadership roles, highlighting how the distribution of power is a wound across diverse traditions. Turning to the gifts of Methodism identified by participants, I will argue that, along with Methodism's pneumatology and theology of power, these gifts critique the distributions of power within many of the churches in England.

What do we mean by 'power'?[2]

In his biography of US president Lyndon Baines Johnson, Robert Caro shares a key insight relating to power:

> But although the cliché says that power always corrupts, what is seldom said, but what is equally true, is that power always *reveals*. When a man is climbing, trying to persuade

others to give him power, concealment is necessary: to hide traits that might make others reluctant to give him power, to hide also what he wants to do with that power.[3]

With echoes of this insight, women told stories of times when those who held senior leadership positions in their churches did not make good use of their power. One Catholic woman commented that power shows 'what kind of person a priest really is', before moving on to share a harrowing experience of being sexually abused by her priest as a young child. Listening to this and to other disturbing accounts, the women in one of the focus groups agreed that 'generally, it does not do well for one person to hold all the power, particularly when that person is a man with a history of sexually abusing children. The most moral thing to do is spread power widely.'[4] Such conversations about gender and power should not be surprising. Jantine Oldersma and Kathy Davis, in the introduction to their book *The Gender of Power*, observe that 'it is hardly possible to open a book on gender relations without power being an essential, if implicit, part of the story'.[5] Despite radical shifts in theories on gender since their book was published, many women working in churches in England continue to narrate their stories against the backdrop of power and gender.

Bearing in mind that 'power is a feature of every human interaction',[6] I did not ask the women themselves to define power because this would have taken conversations in a different direction and prevented the stream of testimonies. Janet Trisk, a South African Anglican priest and theologian, comments on her work in the Anglican Communion, observing 'power can mean very different things'.[7] Likewise, Steven Lukes, in his edited collection *Power*, advises against attempting to define power on the basis that interests in power are so broad and motivations so complex, it is impossible to do more than critique how it is used or account for how we think it should be used.[8] Further to this, the postcolonial critic Gayatri Spivak argues that there are at least two senses of power, the general (neutral or descriptive) and the specific (pejorative). Her work highlights the importance of recognizing the ambiguity of the two senses and also the way in which they do not remain distinct from each other.[9] These comments reflect the ways in which the women spoke of 'power'. They applied power broadly, more often negatively than neutrally, and regularly conflated 'power' with 'authority'. In an attempt to honour the women's usage, I shall characterize power here loosely as 'the ability to effect control'.[10]

Identifying the wound(s)

Let us turn to focus on the wounds that relate to the use and abuse of power. Participants from the Assemblies of God, Independent Evangelical, Independent Pentecostal, Anglican, Eastern Orthodox, Catholic and Baptist traditions gave accounts of the ways in which their churches both discriminate against and prevent women from assuming positions of authority through their diverse structures, as recorded in Chapter 3. Since Chapters 4, 5 and 6 focused on the Catholic Church, the Eastern Orthodox Church and the Church of England respectively, next we will turn to Baptist congregations while recognizing the misuse of power is not a problem peculiar to Baptists. Roughly 80 per cent of Baptist women participating in the receptive ecumenism research said that they were not supported in vocations to preach or in vocations to become ministers, precisely because they were women. Some 20 per cent were content in their vocation and described themselves as 'fortunate', 'blessed' and 'without complaint'. The following comment by a Baptist minister encapsulates what the majority of the other Baptist women were saying:

We were one of the first denominations to ordain women. At one time we were ahead of the times ordaining women! Now it's over 100 years of ordaining women, and yet only between 13 and 16 per cent of women are in full-time paid ministerial roles. We are losing them. They are either in chaplaincy or someplace else. There's a latent sexism. For example, the church I work in would never have called me if it were not

FOR THE GOOD OF THE CHURCH

for the fact that I was applying for an associate role. They would never appoint a senior female. The structure of the Baptist denomination means that there is nothing I can do about that. If they don't want to engage with a woman, then no one can challenge it structurally. I've been a minister for 25 years now and I have seen no change. When I have taken up the cause, I'm labelled as the gobby woman or the feminist – but how else do we do it? Otherwise, if we stay silent, then issues never get raised. It's a real problem and, if I'm really honest, I'm exhausted by it.

In a different group, while the women were discussing who did (or did not) empower them in pursuing a call to ordained leadership, another Baptist commented with tears in her eyes:

> I spent ten years, ten whole years, in my church thinking I had a call to preach, but believing I must be wrong. It never entered my head that women could really preach or be ordained because my [Baptist] minister said we couldn't. I moved to a different job and area which meant moving churches, and only then did I find out that as a Baptist, I could be ordained and preach despite being a woman.

As the women who were sat in the room continued to listen to her, many were visibly shocked. There were audible gasps, shaking heads, and supportive comments coming through in hushed tones because no one wanted to interrupt her. When she had finished speaking, the women paused and discussed what she had said, agreeing with one another that this kind of deceit is an abuse of power and authority. Two Baptist participants responded: 'I am not at all surprised this kind of thing could happen to women in our church', and 'I wish I was surprised to hear this, but I'm not. It's what I would expect'.

Sadly, these kinds of experiences are all too common. In 1996, the Baptist Union Council established the Women's Justice Committee, which in 2008 undertook a survey of the Baptist Assembly.[11] Extracts from this report are found in the 2011 document published by the Baptist Union, *Women in*

Ministry: A Reader Exploring the Story of Women in Leadership and Ministry within the Baptist Union of Great Britain.[12] In a section entitled 'Authority and Power', interviewees make candid remarks concerning 'men in suits', as witnessed at the Baptist Assembly. Some women at the Assembly believed this to be a form of 'power-dressing' through which men on the main stage convey power and authority. Further commentators noted that power dynamics were unbalanced: men were interviewing women and men were praying for women; in short, despite also being Baptist ministers, women generally assumed passive roles.[13]

The authors of the *Reader* observe that women's ministry is fraught with complexities and acknowledge that there is a

vast wealth of ecumenical material which could be drawn on in helping to frame discussion within the Baptist family. In terms of the big picture, this is clearly an issue we face in common with other denominations and it may be that ecumenical resources should inform our own journey.[14]

The *Reader* makes explicit the support for women's ministry by the Baptist Union of Great Britain. However, congregations can reject this advice. Baptist ministers who are women are supported by the Baptist Union, while local Baptist churches are permitted to refuse to call a minister who is a woman. As outlined on the Baptist Union website:

Baptists are grass roots people, with a particular emphasis on the local church. These local churches are self-governing and self-supporting, ranging in size from twenty or so members to many hundreds.[15]

Most recently, insights in the Spring 2019 issue of *Baptists Together* (the magazine published for the Baptist Union of Great Britain) confirm further the particular challenges for women who work in Baptist churches. The issue 'Celebrating, Surviving, Thriving: A Focus on Women in Baptist Ministry' provides a historical and contemporary analysis of women in Baptist ministry today. Exploring the fruitful ministries of Baptist women, it recounts the arguments against women in ministry to demonstrate what women face when they explore vocations to ordained Baptist ministry.[16] The Revd Lynn Green, General Secretary of the Baptist Union of Great Britain, writes, 'Looking back over the last hundred years it seems that the affirmation of women's ordination has been a slow and painful unfolding.'[17] Likewise, Baptist minister and academic theologian Ruth Gouldbourne observes, 'It is very possible to spend a lifetime in Baptist churches and not come across a woman in ministry ... and there remain a significant number of churches in which the ministry of women is not recognised or encouraged.'[18]

Having outlined this wound, let me draw attention to the positive changes at the time of writing. In September 2019, the Revd Jane Day was appointed by the Baptist Union to the post of 'Centenary Enabler'. This role was created both to commemorate the centenary of women being ordained for Baptist ministry, and to research the significant challenges for Baptist women, recognizing that the Baptist church is 'lagging in equality within some of our practices and structures'.[19] The Baptist women participating in the focus groups commented that they hoped the testimonies recorded in this book would contribute to possible ways forward, observing that 'conversations with the Methodists were helpful' and that 'gifts in Methodism could prove fruitful'.

Experiences of Methodist women

Before exploring the gifts of Methodism's theology of power, it is important to clarify that the women did not present their experiences of working in the Methodist Church as a utopian dream. They presented their gifts accompanied by critiques and with the clarification that there is 'room for improvement when it comes to the structuring of the Methodist Church'.[20] In its Notices of Motion, the Methodist Conference in 2020 voted to conduct an extensive review to simplify the structures of the Church for the purpose of doing mission and ministry with greater efficiency. The Notices of Motion state that the review will 'provide the ideal opportunity for identifying some of the systemic failures within our structures that prevents some people from being encouraged to take up positions within the church', recognizing that 'the women of the church are less likely to be seen in positions of responsibility within the church, despite our long history of commitment to the inclusion of all people'.[21]

As established in Chapter 3, along with women from other churches, Methodists recounted tales of sexism, racism and sexual harassment, and shared challenges around being single and/or being mothers, etc. For example, a Methodist lay worker in her thirties explained that she is juggling childcare with work. Both she and her husband trained together as worship leaders, but after she had given birth to their first child some of those in authority expected her to be too busy with childcare to continue training. Because of this, she was not invited to train as a local preacher at the same time as her husband. This is a simple example of how assumptions persist concerning 'women's duties', even in a church where women may flourish. In this instance, a senior leader stepped in to suggest ways forward with childcare so that both husband and wife could train as local preachers.

Other Methodist women, while discussing difficult experiences, observed that the challenges related to women generally and were not trials specific to Methodism as an institution. One commented:

As with many institutions and companies, if you occupy one of the more senior roles as a woman you're always in a minority. That's never consciously worried me, but I think there are differences in approach and style. And sometimes I find that some of the conversations I can't contribute to because the men will get together in the pub and not think to invite me. I don't think they are being nasty; it's more that they just would not think of it.[22]

Further challenges lay in fulfilling vocation. Two Methodist participants identified themselves as 'missional' but described themselves as 'constrained', in part because they were expected to take on a greater amount of 'inside' work than their male counterparts. One deacon said, 'I'm missional – that's why I was ordained deacon; yet I find myself constantly squeezed into roles inside the church. I find it so frustrating.' Another was expected to set up a mother and toddler group for church members, which she explained 'is neither my gift, nor my call'.

Other critiques from Methodists were made in response to the language used for job advertisements. One observed:

Something we are seeing creep in now is a request for 'strong' leadership. Loosely translated, this means that the congregation would like a male leader. Of course, it's just a stereotype, as there are plenty of men who don't set out to lead as a *strong* leader.[23]

I include these comments in order to present a non-idealized picture of the women's experiences of working in the Methodist Church. While speaking of difficult experiences, they also shared significant gifts which result in the admission of women into all forms of leadership in the Methodist Church. Some Methodist churches may not want a woman's ministry or authority; however, structurally Methodism does not obstruct women from adopting leadership roles, unlike so many other traditions in England.

Gifts in Methodism

When I contacted Methodists with an invitation to participate in this research, each one responded with a decisive 'yes'. Impressed and curious by their willingness to be involved, I asked them why they thought Methodists were keen to participate. The answers revealed much about the Methodist Church's culture: 'we are ecumenically minded'; 'Methodist women know we have things to say'; 'women in Methodism are used to having a voice'; and 'we are a "let's get on with it" kind of denomination'.[24]

What is it about Methodism that empowers many of its women so that they expect their voices to be heard? During the course of the research, women from other churches were keen to understand more about the way the Methodist Church distributes power and the way in which this impacts the empowerment of women.[25] Whether a participant was serving as a deacon, presbyter, local preacher, worship leader, chaplain, circuit superintendent, theological educator or youth worker, they mentioned particular gifts in Methodism relating to the positive use of power: the 'Methodist Quadrilateral' and 'Connexion'.

The Methodist Quadrilateral

Commenting on her 15 years as an ordained woman, one Methodist said, 'I think that unlike other churches, Methodism lets the women shape and shift the culture. It's because of the way we think about the Quadrilateral and Connexion – it's really important to us.'

The Methodist – also called Wesleyan – Quadrilateral draws together interpretation of Scripture, tradition, reason and experience. It facilitates the people of God to do their theological reflection creatively, both with an openness to the work of the Spirit, and with a recognition of their interdependence with other churches. Due to the scope of this chapter, I will focus on experience.

In his foundational work on Methodism, Henry Bett observes, 'Experience is the governing principle with Methodism all the way through.'[26] In the history of 'its spirituality and its largely implicit theology there is no escaping the *religious* nature of Methodism's primary appeal to experience ... nor can there be avoidance of the deeply felt nature of that experience'.[27] However, it is not immediately apparent what constitutes experience. Engaging with Bett's work, Clive Marsh observes that the appeal to experience is actually about *Christian* experience, namely, 'the experience of the redeemed, or know-ing oneself to be forgiven'.[28] It is not experience in the sense of daily living, nor 'simply an emotion', nor is it a starting place for theological method, although it has been interpreted as such by some. Rather, it is the experience of redemption and partici-pation in Christ, which functions as shorthand for the 'whole of the Christian life', where 'in Christ' suggests 'dependence, corporateness and empowerment ... Christians are dependent on God's saving action in Christ for their contemporary sense of well-being ... the dependence is empowering and energiz-ing'.[29] Here 'participation in Christ' includes the work of the Spirit, since 'experience is at root spiritual experience and thus experience of the Spirit'.[30]

Richard Clutterbuck's analysis of how British Methodists do theology draws similar conclusions with respect to the experi-ence of the Spirit. First, he argues that theology is done through dialogue and encounter with other churches and people of other faiths; second, through being sensitive to the 'work of the Spirit in the world'; and third, through storytelling.[31] On the latter point, the Methodist participants recognized that they are used to hearing and telling stories that reflect the work of God in their lives and in the church.

How does sensitivity to the Christian experience, the work of the Spirit in the world, and telling stories contribute to the empowerment of women? Methodist academics offer nuanced responses to this. In her essay on 'Methodism and Women', Margaret Jones argues that women have always been part of the story that Methodists have told about themselves because they attend to 'experience', which includes the work of the Spirit in giving preaching gifts to women.[32] Diane LeClerc also observes that women in Methodism in the eighteenth century were given more opportunities than women elsewhere,[33] featur-ing in printed media of the time because John Wesley was keen to publish the writings of the women with whom he was in fellowship.[34] Continuing to reflect on the place of experience in Methodism, Jane Craske observes:

There are strands in Wesleyan theologies that have empha-
sized experience, even if that now tends to be reinterpreted to
mean something much broader than the religious experience
that Wesley would have meant by it; those strands offer space
for the experiential and praxis approach of all liberation theologies. Wesleyan theology has offered hope of sanctification
– whole-life transformation – which is conducive to the trans-
formation-seeking of many radical theologies.[35]

Womanist theologian Elaine Crawford confirms this, arguing,
'As I study Wesleyan theology, I see some convergence with
the basic tenets of Womanist theology.'[36] She explores questions asked by groundbreaking theologian Delores Williams,
who writes about theologies of the cross. Williams argues
that against the backdrop of the particular suffering of black
women, certain theologies of the cross are inappropriate.[37]
Resonating with this, Crawford underscores that 'the cross
does not sacralize abuse but is an example of it. The cross rep-
resents what God was willing to sacrifice so that no others
would be sacrificed.'[38] In conversation with Williams's observa-
tions, she concludes that Wesley provides a theology in which
God's sanctifying grace is for everyone, and that it lends itself
to those whose voices have not been heard.

In light of these themes, it should be no surprise that Ghana-
ian Methodist theologian Mercy Amba Oduyoye has been
described as 'the foremost African feminist theologian and out-
standing leader in the ecumenical movement'.[39] Among other
ecumenical work, Oduyoye worked at the World Council of
Churches (WCC), making significant contributions to how
churches engage with women. During her time working at the
WCC, she wrote 'Who Will Roll the Stone Away?' in response
to the WCC's 'Ecumenical Decade of the Churches in Solidarity
with Women'.[40] In her book, Oduyoye observes that churches
are often supportive of engaging in work that promotes justice
for women globally, but are rarely as keen theologically to interrogate issues 'closer to home', such as the ordination of women.
She argues, quite rightly, that churches should not view themselves as separate from the world with respect to questions of

sexism.[41] The non-hierarchical structures of Methodism inhibit this particular manifestation of sexism, which has contributed to empowering Oduyoye in her work for women in the church.

Thus far, I have argued that experience is at the heart of Methodism, albeit interpreted differently by Methodists themselves, and that this core strand of the Methodist Quadrilateral creates space for exploring women's roles positively in the Methodist Church. Turning to Connexion, I will explore similar themes with respect to the empowerment of women.

Connexion

When asked to speak about their tradition's greatest gift, the Methodist women referred most often to Connexion, observing that being connected enables collaboration; at the same time, they were honest about the limitations of the lived reality of this: 'For Methodists, being connected is really important. So, it's the sense, which may not always be strongly felt by everybody, of all being connected right across Britain and therefore of seeking to share resources.'[42]

The Conference is at the heart of the Connexion which began with John Wesley's preachers and helpers, who were 'in connexion with Mr Wesley' and with one another.[43] These people met with Wesley in 'Conferences', during which they sought to discern the movement and leading of the Spirit, among other business. When Wesley died he was succeeded not by another man, but by a group that developed over a period of time into the formal body of the Conference.[44] The Methodist theology of 'conferring' means that the Conference itself functions like a presiding bishop, rendering the role of the bishop unnecessary with respect to a single person. The emphasis is placed on the doctrine of the priesthood of all believers while holding a tension between 'authority and accountability' in the Connexional system.[45] The oversight is first corporate (at least, since Wesley's death) and, second, finds a focus in lay and ordained individuals and groups: 'At the heart of oversight in the Connexion is the Conference which in turn authorises people and groups to embody and share in its oversight in the rest of the Connexion.'[46] Power, as such, is dispersed. The theological principle for a Connexional way of being church is grounded in and witnesses to a 'mutuality and interdependence which derive from the participation of all Christians through Christ in the very life of God'.[47] Colossians 2 forms the biblical imagination for the theology that supports and weaves through the image of connectedness, depicting the body and the links between the various parts of a body, held by the head, which is Christ (Col. 1.18).

When Conference makes a decision it is final, unlike congregation polities, which is one of the most prominent differences with respect to the Baptist denomination regarding support of women's ministry. It negates congregational autonomy from below and likewise from above, so that churches and circuits receive and accept the decisions of the Conference. The implications for women's ministry are obvious: in the early 1970s, when Conference agreed that women should be permitted to exercise all forms of ministry, no church or circuit could formally and explicitly reject women from serving as presbyters, superintendents, etc. As one Methodist put it:

> The power to validate or invalidate women does not lie in one or two individuals. With Methodism, power lies in the Conference. The Conference ordains, makes decisions, stations ministers, and contains representatives from across the Methodist Church.

Methodism's theology of power

The report from the 2005 Conference 'The Nature of Oversight: Leadership, Management and Governance in the Methodist Church in Great Britain' analyses the Methodist theology of power, which emerges from reflections on oversight, leadership and authority. While the report provides concise definitions of key terms such as 'oversight', 'leadership', 'governance', etc. (1.4–1.14), I will concentrate on section 4, which focuses on power. That said, I recommend reading the document in its entirety, since it offers critical thinking on numerous relevant issues relating to governance and leadership.

Recall the power-related wounds identified by the participants. For the most part the women were 'suspicious of power', speaking of those in positions of authority as 'misusing their power'. This resulted in a view of power as destructive. For example:

> I suppose any group in which one gender dominates will always be at risk of dysfunction, especially if gender exclusiveness is aligned with power. (Catholic, 46)

> Pastors have power: an enabling power and a restricting power. What's sad is that I seem to have experienced the restricting power more often than the enabling one. (Independent Evangelical, 53)

> Collaboration is sometimes tricky because not all Baptist leaders want to collaborate, especially with women. You could say that they misuse their power. (Baptist, 62)

Keeping in mind these comments and those throughout the book, let us turn to the 2005 Conference report, which delineates a positive theology of power. It does this, not with an idealistic vision of power's consistent goodness, but rather with a nuanced recognition that God's power alone is wholly good. Section 1.14.6 characterizes power as

> the capacity to act in ways which have significant effects on others and which ensure that a particular set of interests are maintained or achieved. It can be characterized as 'power-over',[48] 'power-within' and 'power-with'.[49] 'Power-over' is closely allied to 'authority' when one party is able to require that another act in a particular way. 'Power-within' is related to an individual's personal qualities and charisma. A person with a high level of such charisma can exercise 'power-over' others by virtue of inspiring them but may have no formal

authority as such. 'Power-with' operates when there are bonds of solidarity between people, whether or not any of the parties involved exercise formal authority.

'Power-over' aligns closely with the women's ways of describing abuses of power, as recounted above and in Chapter 3. Conversely, the report itself embodies 'power-with', evident from the description below which summarizes the Methodist approach to the discernment of doctrine:

> The whole Christian church is engaged in a constant interpretative task as it seeks by the Spirit to discover more about God as known in Christ, and to discern how the developing, collective wisdom it carries with it should issue in forms of social organisation and human conduct. Different emphases and different aspects of God are, furthermore, brought to the fore in different generations. (4.0.2)

The report begins by claiming, quite rightly, 'All power derives from God' (4.1.5). When we speak of power as 'in God' and deriving 'from God', we hold a space in which power is wholly good and best 'understood as a gift, to be received, treasured and used accordingly' (4.1.5). As Catherine Keller has argued, 'God's power, rightly understood, grounds rather than subverts good human power.'[50] Her description of good power as 'an indispensable condition of the good' determines power as good precisely because it empowers the good.[51] This places divine power as that which is non-coercive and co-operative in such a way that it works 'to shift the elemental forces to the good'.[52]

If we were to look to the images existing within the Christian tradition that might help with conceptualizing good power as that which empowers, we might turn to the Good Shepherd. This is a strong image which encapsulates the nature of good divine power, albeit easily misunderstood. Reclaiming this image, Kathryn Tanner argues:

This power of the shepherd, or the power relation set up between shepherd and flock, is good in virtue of its beneficence; the power of the shepherd is a power of caring for the sheep, attending to their every need, ensuring their wellbeing, vigilant to every danger they might face. The shepherd's power is good power, in short, because it is one completely devoted to their good; the shepherd is not, say, fattening these sheep simply for the slaughter.[53]

Tanner maintains that like the image of the shepherd God's power is wholly good. It has 'significant effects', which could be summarized as 'the goods of creation (existence) and salvation (wellbeing), and the overcoming of dangers to both (sin and suffering, for example)'.[54] Furthermore,

God's power is good because it is productive of the good for others and because it works continually, in a potentially radically transformative way, to sustain and increase that good against all impediments.[55]

The image of the shepherd is apposite precisely because it embodies 'pastoral power', which works for the unmitigated good of all through a relationship encapsulated by love. This is radically different from the kind of pastoral power brought into focus by Foucault, who writes prolifically on power. For him, the pastoral power 'designates a very special form of power'[56] because it suggests that 'there is no salvation outside of the church'.[57] Understood this way, 'the exercise of power is not simply a relationship between partners, individual or collective; it is a way in which certain actions modify others'.[58] Conversely, God's power is good because like the shepherd it committedly pursues every sheep which strays from the fold, seeking the safety and wellbeing of the flock.

Excursus on Methodism's pneumatology

When exploring how God's power relates to human power, Methodism's pneumatology contributes to a positive construction of power in relation to the Church. Wesley's interpretation of Scripture, along with his personal experience of God, results in a strong tradition of understanding power in relation to the Holy Spirit.[59] Methodist hymns, liturgies and doctrines all serve as signposts to the work of the Spirit and to the human experience of the Spirit's transforming power. For example, one such hymn begins by recognizing God as the 'Maker, in whom we live, in whom we are and move', before moving on to proclaim that the saints adore the 'sacred energy' of the 'Spirit of holiness', and bless the Spirit's 'heart-renewing power'.[60] These lyrics serve to remind those singing that power belongs to the Spirit and that humans receive this gift of power for the glory of God. Confession of the Spirit's power extends even to the 1952 Minutes of the Methodist Conference and Directory, which states 'we can only do God's will by the power of the Holy Spirit whom he gives us'.[61]

The Spirit transforms the heart of each person, which is why Methodist congregations in England confess to 'Holy Spirit, Lord of life'.[62] One cannot help but note that by addressing the Holy Spirit directly, Methodists cultivate a strong familiarity with the Spirit; likewise in the Church of the Nazarene, which is the largest denomination in the classical Wesleyan-Holiness tradition. Many Methodists and members of the Church of the Nazarene understand Methodism as a Holiness/Pentecostal movement; this also accounts for Methodism's emphasis on the Spirit.[63]

Phoebe Palmer, 'mother of the holiness movement',[64] explains that 'holiness is power'[65] in *Promise of the Father*, in which she examines the Spirit pouring out the gift of power on the church on the day of Pentecost.[66] Her argument is that the Spirit gives gifts of power to all the church, which includes women. Together with the image of the Good Shepherd, a focus on the Spirit emphasizes that power can be understood positively when it is received as gift, distributed well, and used for the flourishing of those working in churches. All too often, the call to divestment of power is heard by women as yet another reason why they should not lead.[67] Contrary to this, attention to the Spirit's gift of power leads to empowerment, as observed through the work of Mercy Amba Oduyoye, Elaine Crawford, and many other Methodist women.[68]

As with all doctrines, however, this comes with a caution. Angela Shier-Jones, in her work on the Spirit in Methodism, warns against confining descriptions of the Spirit to actions only, since this may lead to a distorted trinitarian doctrine. She observes that Wesley does not fall into error on this because he attributes consistently the Spirit's equality to the Father and the Son and she argues that the Spirit is indeed able to perfect and assure precisely because the Spirit is God. The 2005 Methodist Conference report is likewise explicit in its recognition of the Spirit's equality with the Father and the Son while arguing that the Trinity is not a blueprint for how we might understand power relations and power dynamics: 'No form of trinitarian thinking translates easily into a clear picture of how human communities can be structured socially or politically' (4.7.3). That said, 'it does challenge all organisations to declare how their structures enable all to flourish in the context of empowering relationships, whatever roles and positions people hold and occupy' (4.7.4).[69]

Human power

How does all this relate to human power? 'The proper human exercise of power, in Christian understanding, is to be understood as participation in the redemptive work of God' (4.1.6). In sum, Christians participate in the work of the Good Shepherd in a 'Spirit-driven movement'.[70]

So far, so good. However, human shepherding rarely (or, rather, never) lives up to the Good Shepherd's shepherding. What Christian tradition does not fall short in its reception of God's gift of power to the extent that it could be said to be wholly healthy? As Catholic theologian Karl Rahner argues, we understand power first as a 'good gift' coming from God, but when this power equates to brute force, sin is present.[71] Similarly, with respect to Christian theological ethics, Harvey Cox writes, '[It] has often made the mistake of assuming that any exercise of power was sinful, but sin has more to do with how power is exercised.'[72] The 2005 Conference report likewise recognizes that sin obstructs a wholly good use of power. Sin reveals itself in many ways, one of which is to refuse power as the gift of God:

> Where [power] is not understood as gift, where it is used to demean others, and where no attempt is made to clarify how it can be shared, then power is abused and God, as the source of all power, is dishonoured. (4.1.5)

Power operates within broken systems. Human will all too easily relates in ways that mean that the exercise of power is akin to domination (4.6.1). Oversight is 'fraught with difficulty' (4.6.2), since it functions within structures and institutions interwoven with sin. The recognition of this is crucial, since 'as long as there is power (and this is always), and as long as one is not aware of this power, there is always a risk of the abuse of power'.[73] Women participating in the research testified to the truth of this claim.

How, then, are Methodism's structures enabling the best possible use of power for the flourishing of its people? At the beginning of this chapter, I reported one woman's observation that 'it does not do well for one person to hold all the power'. Recognizing this, Methodism spreads power as widely as possible, both vertically and horizontally, with considered structures of accountability:

> At their best, good accountability structures, and the refusal of organisations to rely too much on individuals, protects people, by acknowledging fallibility. Individuals receive the support of groups, and have their visions and ideas checked out by others. Groups in turn can generate more (initiatives, encouragement, inspiration, resources) than individuals. (4.6.2)

The report does not suggest that Methodism spreads its power widely because the Church is broken and operates in a fallen world; nor, as I observed earlier, does it suggest that the Trinity should function as a kind of archetypal blueprint for how churches hold or use power. These structures represent a belief in a Spirit who empowers individuals within a wider gathering of connected people while pragmatically safeguarding against, where possible, one or two individuals holding all the power.

Receiving gifts such as these

This chapter began by identifying (a) the distribution of power as a wound in diverse traditions, and (b) the ways in which power is used to discriminate against women who want to take on leadership roles. Following on from Chapter 3 in which participants shared experiences of church leaders misusing power, I drew on the testimonies of women who work in Baptist churches while recognizing that the misuse of power is not a problem peculiar to Baptists. The women shared experiences of being blocked by ministers who believe that women should not be ordained, despite the Baptist Union in Great Britain recognizing women's ordination. Along with the *Reader* emerging from the Women's Justice Committee's 2008 Report and the Spring 2019 issue of *Baptists Together*, the testimonies documented the struggles of women who longed for the opportunity to explore vocations to leadership and other ministries such as preaching and teaching.

Following the way of receptive ecumenism, I turned to explore possible gifts from a different tradition, namely, Methodism. I made this move because during the focus groups and research conversations, the following gifts were shared: the Methodist Quadrilateral and Connexion, woven through which are Methodism's pneumatology and its theology of power. Other voices, such as womanist and feminist theologians, have also argued that Methodism makes room for creative theologies and for the flourishing of women. These gifts critique current practices of the Baptist congregations, as well as many other traditions, and provide the potential for churches to transform the way that power is held, especially with respect to women's flourishing in leadership.

The 2005 Methodist Conference report, together with perspectives on the theology of power from Catherine Keller and Kathryn Tanner, outlines a way of conceiving power positively. This is important in light of the participants' myriad testimonies and reflections on destructive experiences of power used badly. The image of the Good Shepherd helps us here, evoking God's power as relentless love which pursues humankind and is wholly devoted to the good of all creation. Methodism's focus on the Holy Spirit's transforming power, which is key to the Quadrilateral's attention to Christian experience, thickens its theology of power, since it is the Spirit who transforms human hearts non-coercively. Methodist hymns, doctrines and liturgy embody this, along with the practice of confessing to the Holy Spirit directly.

Methodism approaches a theology of power by both exploring the Spirit's transforming power positively while also attending to the broken systems in which power is distributed, the result of which is that power is distributed widely in the Methodist Church. I cannot overstate the positive result of this distribution of power since it means that women cannot be blocked from leadership structurally. While they may encounter (and indeed have testified to encountering) all kinds of other challenges because they are women, they are permitted to explore vocation, to lead and to minister. This differs from Baptist churches, which do not adopt Baptist Union policies unilaterally; it differs from the Church of England, which operates with a system in which parishes may choose to exclude women from leadership; and more obviously, it differs radically from Catholic and Eastern Orthodox churches, in which women's voices are limited at the formal levels of authority and decision-making.

While I have drawn out the positive aspects of Methodist structures, there are, of course, weaknesses to this way of being church, as mentioned in the papers from the 2020 Methodist Conference found earlier in the chapter. The Methodists participating in the research were also unanimous on this point: 'it takes for ever to make any changes and to get anything done'. Indeed, the spread of power may not be immediately appealing to those who like to move quickly, nor to those who lean towards world domination – these people are probably not going to be happy as Methodists!

I am not suggesting that churches simply adopt a Methodist structure because, even if it were flawless, this would be an ecclesiological impossibility. Added to this, the Methodists themselves are reviewing their own structures in an extensive review process over the next five years. Nevertheless, through Methodism's theology of power, its focus on the Spirit, the Methodist Quadrilateral and Connexion, churches are confronted with the way in which their structures and theologies might disempower women. While it may not be possible or preferable for other churches to flatten their structures, I hope that the gifts of Methodism provoke churches to explore stronger systems of accountability, to re-evaluate their theologies of power, and to pursue governance structures that not only limit abuses of power but also draw on the gifts of the Spirit – resources of wisdom and insight – as widely as possible.

Notes

1 On definitions of 'Methodism', see Jane Craske who, in an essay on feminisms and Methodism, argues, 'I do not believe trying to establish the strongest and most exclusive of definitions of what is "Methodist" or not is possible or fruitful'; see 'Methodism and Feminism' in James E. Kirby and William J. Abraham (eds), *The Oxford Handbook of Methodist Studies* (Oxford: Oxford University Press, 2011), pp. 664–79 (p. 663).

2 Debates over the meaning of power reach across disciplines such as philosophy, theology and sociology. For a succinct summary of the debates, see Sarah Coakley, *Powers and Submissions: Spirituality, Philosophy and Gender* (Oxford: Blackwell, 2002), pp. xii–xx; Martyn Percy, *Power and the Church: Ecclesiology in an Age of Transition* (London: Cassell, 1998), pp. 1–19.

3 Robert A. Caro, *The Years of Lyndon Johnson: The Passage of Power* (New York: Alfred A. Knopf, 2012), p. xiv. Thanks to Rachel Muers for drawing my attention to this. Power also 'forms'; see Judith

Butler, *The Psychic Life of Power: Theories in Subjection* (Stanford: Stanford University Press, 1997), p. 13.

4 This is not to suggest that women who work in churches are not also capable of committing crimes against children; nevertheless, throughout this research, women gave no accounts of being sexually abused by other women.

5 Jantine Oldersma and Kathy Davis, 'Introduction' in Kathy Davis, Monique Leijenaar and Jantine Oldersma (eds), *The Gender of Power* (London: Sage, 1991), pp. 1–18 (p. 13).

6 Anthony Giddens, *New Rules of Sociological Method: A Positive Critique of Interpretative Sociologies*, second edition (Stanford, CA: Stanford University Press, 1993), p. 118.

7 Janet Trisk, 'Authority, Theology and Power' in Mark D. Chapman, Sathianathan Clarke and Martyn Percy (eds), *Oxford Handbook of Anglican Studies* (Oxford: Oxford University Press, 2015), pp. 608–19 (p. 608).

8 Steven Lukes (ed.), *Power* (New York: Red Globe Press, 2005), pp. 4–7.

9 Gayatri Chakravorty Spivak, *Outside in the Teaching Machine* (New York and London: Routledge, 1993), p. 28.

10 In her monograph on the apostle Paul's discourse on power, Sandra Hack Polaski observes that women 'may possess no authority, and authority may not be available to them, but this situation does not mean that they are completely without power, and the power they possess influences social interaction'; see *Paul and the Discourse of Power* (Sheffield: Sheffield Academic Press, 1999), p. 35.

11 The Baptist Assembly is the annual gathering of churches affiliated with the Baptist Union of Great Britain; see www.baptist.org.uk/Groups/247895/The_Baptist_Assembly.aspx.

12 Baptist Union of Great Britain, *Women in Ministry: A Reader Exploring the Story of Women in Leadership and Ministry within the Baptist Union of Great Britain* (Didcot: Baptist Union of Great Britain, 2011). The document, written by Simon Woodman and Graham Sparkes, has an excellent list of resources on women with respect to historical, biblical, theological and sociological questions related to Baptist ministries.

13 *Women in Ministry: A Reader*, p. 48.

14 *Women in Ministry: A Reader*, p. 53.

15 See www.baptist.org.uk/Groups/220484/Who_are_Baptists.aspx.

16 *Baptists Together* (Spring 2019), p. 18, available at www.baptist.org.uk/Publisher/File.aspx?ID=220932&view=browser.

17 *Baptists Together* (Spring 2019), p. 5.

18 Ruth Gouldbourne, 'Baptists, Women and Ministry', *Feminist Theology* 26.1 (2017), pp. 59–68 (p. 62).

19 See www.baptist.org.uk/Articles/554164/Jane_Day_appointed. aspx.

20 Jane Craske observes, 'Methodism, historically and today, is an ambiguous environment for feminisms.' She explains that there are strands in the tradition which do not raise up or encourage women; see 'Methodism and Feminism', p. 674.

21 'Notice of Motion 2020/108: Report 25. Reaffirming Our Calling: Oversight and Trusteeship', available at www.methodist.org.uk/media/17862/conf-2020-notices-of-motion.pdf, pp. 7–9.

22 This may be true for academic studies of Methodism also. It is notable that women make up roughly 20 per cent, or less, of the total contributions to edited collections on Methodism, as in the case of the *T&T Clark Companion to Methodism*, edited by Charles Yrigoyen Jr (London and New York: T&T Clark, 2010).

23 One of the sensitive aspects of current calls is also that 'strong leadership' can be implicitly or explicitly appealing to the patriarchy associated with certain kinds of Evangelical/Pentecostal leadership. This remains for further research in which engagement in receptive ecumenism could prove fruitful.

24 The Methodist inclination towards ecumenical work is evident through the extensive involvement of Methodist churches in Local Ecumenical Partnerships; see Richard Clutterbuck, 'Theology as Interaction: Ecumenism and the World Church' in Clive Marsh, Brian Beck, Angela Shier-Jones and Helen Waring (eds), *Unmasking Methodist Theology* (New York and London: Continuum, 2004), pp. 59–69.

25 It is notable that over two decades ago, the Anglican priest Elizabeth Carnelley argued that the Church of England could learn from the Methodists with regards to the equal participation of women. See 'The Future of British Methodism: An Anglican Perspective' in Jane Craske and Clive Marsh (eds), *Methodism and the Future: Facing the Challenge* (London: Cassell, 1999), pp. 161–70 (pp. 166–7).

26 Henry Bett, *The Spirit of Methodism* (London: Epworth Press, 1937), p. 125.

27 Clive Marsh, 'Appealing to "Experience": What does it Mean?' in Marsh, Beck, Shier-Jones and Waring (eds), *Unmasking Methodist Theology*, pp. 118–30 (p. 119).

28 Marsh, 'Appealing to "Experience"', p. 119.

29 Marsh, 'Appealing to "Experience"', p. 125.

30 Marsh, 'Appealing to "Experience"', p. 127.

31 In light of this, it is not surprising that Methodists lead the way ecumenically; see Clutterbuck, 'Theology as Interaction', p. 68.

32 Margaret Jones, 'Methodism and Women' in William Gibson, Peter Forsaith and Martin Wellings (eds), *The Ashgate Research Companion to World Methodism* (Surrey: Ashgate), pp. 157–75 (p. 157).

33 Diane LeClerc outlines that women were part of Wesley's inner

circle and that he deemed them to be confidants; see *Singleness of Heart: Gender, Sin, and Holiness in Historical Perspective* (Lanham, MD, and London: Scarecrow Press, 2001), pp. 69–70.

34 See also Paul W. Chilcote (ed.), *Her Own Story: Autobiographical Portraits of Early Methodist Women* (Nashville, TN: Kingswood Books, 2001).

35 Craske, 'Methodism and Feminism', p. 674.

36 A. Elaine Crawford, 'Womanist Christology and the Wesleyan Tradition', *Black Theology* 2.2 (2004), pp. 213–20 (p. 214).

37 Delores S. Williams, *Sisters in the Wilderness: The Challenge of Womanist God-Talk* (New York: Orbis Books, 1993), pp. 167–70.

38 Crawford, 'Womanist Christology', pp. 218–19.

39 Elisabeth Schussler Fiorenza, 'Editor's Introduction', *Journal of Feminist Studies in Religion* 1 (2004), p. 1.

40 For the website of the World Council of Churches, see www.oik oumene.org/en/about-us.

41 Mercy Oduyoye, *Who Will Roll the Stone Away? The Ecumenical Decade of the Churches in Solidarity with Women* (Genève: WCC Publications, 1991), p. 3.

42 For more on connection and connectionalism, see Russell E. Richey's chapter of the same name in Kirby and Abraham (eds), *The Oxford Handbook of Methodist Studies*, pp. 211–28 (p. 211).

43 Angela Shier-Jones, 'Being Methodical: Theology Within Church Structures' in Marsh, Beck, Shier-Jones and Waring (eds), *Unmasking Methodist Theology*, pp. 29–40 (p. 36).

44 Jane Craske explains that 'connexion' is a key tenet of Methodism, facilitating relationships and networks of circuits. See 'The Threads with which We Weave: Towards a Holy Church' in Craske and Marsh (eds), *Methodism and the Future*, pp. 171–86 (p. 172).

45 Philip Drake, 'Joining the Dots: Methodist Membership and Connectedness' in Marsh, Beck, Shier-Jones and Waring (eds), *Unmasking Methodist Theology*, pp. 131–41 (p. 135).

46 'The Nature of Oversight: Leadership, Management and Governance in the Methodist Church in Great Britain', 2005 Conference Report, summary, pp. 1–2, available at www.methodist.org.uk/ about-us/the-methodist-conference/conference-reports/conference-reports-2005/.

47 Conference Report, 2005; section 2.1. Section numbers divide the report. For ease of reading, I will indicate sections within the main body of this chapter.

48 In her essay 'Doing Leadership Differently? Women and Senior Leadership in the Church of England', Rosie Ward argues that often within the Church of England, 'masculine power' could be described as 'power over'. In 2008, she called for a move towards 'power to' as a means of enabling others, suggesting that women might contribute

to this. See Ian Jones, Kirsty Thorpe and Janet Wootton (eds), *Women and Ordination in the Christian Churches: International Perspectives* (London: Bloomsbury, 2008), pp. 76–86 (p. 83).

49 See further Martha E. Stortz, 'Naming and Reclaiming Power' in M. R. A. Kanyoro (ed.), *In Search of a Round Table: Gender, Theology and Church Leadership* (Genève: WCC Publications, 1997), pp. 71–81.

50 Catherine Keller, 'Folding Power', p. 21. Paper presented at the Yale Center for Faith and Culture consultation on Good Power – Divine and Human (October 2007).

51 Keller, 'Folding Power', p. 21.

52 Keller, 'Folding Power', p. 21.

53 Kathryn Tanner, 'Power of Love', pp. 3–4. Paper presented at the Yale Center for Faith and Culture consultation on Good Power – Divine and Human (October 2007).

54 Tanner, 'Power of Love', p. 5.

55 Tanner, 'Power of Love', p. 5.

56 Michel Foucault, 'The Subject and Power', *Critical Inquiry* 8.4 (1982), pp. 777–95 (p. 783).

57 Sally Purvis, *Power of the Cross: Foundations for a Christian Feminist Ethic of Community* (Nashville, TN: Abingdon Press, 1993), p. 19.

58 Foucault, 'The Subject and Power', p. 788.

59 Wesley draws upon Romans 8.16 ('it is that very Spirit bearing witness with our spirit that we are children of God'); see Bett, *The Spirit of Methodism*, p. 138. Added to this, the Spirit is at the heart of the doctrines most often associated with Wesley, such as Christian perfection and assurance; see Angela Shier-Jones, *A Work in Progress* (Peterborough: Epworth Press, 2005), pp. 99–101.

60 Charles Wesley, *Methodist Church: Hymns & Psalms*, No. 4 (London: Methodist Publishing House, 1983).

61 MMC 1952, p. 222, cited in Shier-Jones, *A Work in Progress*, p. 99.

62 Methodist Church of Great Britain, *The Methodist Worship Book* (Peterborough: Methodist Publishing House, 1999), pp. 42, 174.

63 The doctrine that distinguishes the Church of the Nazarene and other Wesleyan denominations from most other Christian denominations is that of entire sanctification; see https://nazarene.org/. For the North American discussion about the relationship between Methodism and (various) Holiness movements, see Donald Dayton, 'Methodism and Pentecostalism' in Kirby and Abraham (eds), *The Oxford Handbook of Methodist Studies*, pp. 172–87. Dayton observes that many Methodists would not approve of the use of 'and' in the title.

64 Henry H. Knight III, *Anticipating Heaven Below: Optimism of Grace from Wesley to the Pentecostals* (Eugene, OR: Cascade, 2014), p. xiv. Knight highlights important aspects of Methodism, including

drawing together the themes of holiness and power in the tradition; see pp. 97–118. He also provides an account of Wesley's movement towards women preachers (pp. 97–105).

65 Phoebe Palmer, *Promise of the Father* (Boston, MA: Degen, 1859), p. 206.

66 Palmer, *Promise of the Father*, p. 14.

67 Some theologians have challenged traditional feminist critiques of self-giving; for example, Anna Mercedes, *Power for Feminism and Christ's Self-Giving* (London: T&T Clark, 2011).

68 On the dangers of calling for an acceptance of diminished power, see Karen Kilby, 'The Seductions of Kenosis' in Karen Kilby and Rachel Davies (eds), *Suffering and the Christian Life* (London: T&T Clark, 2019), pp. 163–74 (p. 166).

69 The report implicitly critiques a further contemporary trend known as the 'social Trinity', often employed (especially towards the end of the twentieth century) to justify all sorts of understandings of 'relational' or 'collaborative' (power) structures and forms of leadership. For a foundational critique of these issues, see Karen Kilby, 'Perichoresis and Projection: Problems with Social Doctrines of the Trinity', *New Blackfriars* 81.956 (2000), pp. 432–45.

70 Marsh, 'Appealing to "Experience"', p. 127; also see Rupert Davies, *Methodism* (London: Epworth Press, 1990), p. 11.

71 Karl Rahner, *Theological Investigations, Volume IV*, translated by Kevin Smyth (London: Darton, Longman and Todd, 1966), pp. 391–8.

72 Harvey Cox, 'Power' in James F. Childress and John Macquarrie (eds), *The Westminster Dictionary of Christian Ethics* (Philadelphia, PA: Westminster, 1986), pp. 489–91 (p. 490).

73 Machteld Reynaert, 'A Kenotic Use of Power in Theology: Dangerous or Not?' in Stephen Bullivant, Eric Marcelo O. Genilo, Daniel Franklin Pilario and Agnes M. Brazal (eds), *Theology and Power: International Perspectives* (New York: Paulist Press, 2016), pp. 33–48 (p. 39).

Conclusion

There are, of course, many more stories to tell about women's experiences of working in churches in England. Women's vocations are not the principal hindrance to ecclesial unity, despite being named as such. Women's voices need to be heard not only at grass roots but also within the formal ecumenical movement, encouraging churches to move towards unity with God and with one another: the unity for which Christ prays in John's Gospel. Until women play their part fully, the ecumenical movement will continue as a shadow of the full radiance possible through the power of Christ's love.

Receptive ecumenism has a role in the broader ecumenical movement as keen ecumenists navigate their way through a bleak winter of ecumenism, hoping and believing for the coming spring. My contribution to this wider conversation is (a) to engage constructively with receptive ecumenism, (b) to bring to the fore women's ecumenical work, and (c) to underscore the part women could play within formal ecumenism if churches were to exercise with greater magnitude the power and imagination that the Spirit bestows upon them. At the same time, I want to draw attention to some of the sins and dysfunctions of the churches in England, which result in the wounding of the women who so faithfully work for their good.

I could have filled countless pages, all testifying to ways God is blessing the church through women's gifts: pages that speak of women flourishing, pastoring, encouraging the faith of children and young people, praying, theologizing, creating hospitable spaces, singing, leading and teaching. This list could go on and on. There are myriad positive stories to tell. But there are also disturbing stories: stories that tell of the judgement heaped on women who are mothers and the difficulties they experience in securing an income and maternity leave; stories of the extra burdens borne by those who are single; stories from those who are made to feel as though they are *the* problem because they identify as LBGTQIA+; stories told by women of colour about their experiences of racialized abuse; and stories that give voice to the bullying, sexual harassment, and even sexual assault experienced by women as they work in churches in England. Receptive ecumenism bids the faithful to hear these stories and to examine churches' dysfunctions courageously; to take those old, chipped cups out of their hiding place at the back of the cupboard with a view to asking for insight and wisdom from others.

Receptive ecumenism: continuing the journey

By asking, 'What do we need to learn from another tradition to help us address difficulties in our own?', receptive ecumenism affords churches a way of moving beyond the status quo, offering hope of transformation on a congregational level, on a national level, and within global ecumenism. That said, the receptive journey is both costly and risky, calling for churches to (a) humbly examine themselves, (b) commit for the long haul, and (c) be willing to risk receiving others' gifts; gifts that might usher in that oft-dreaded word, 'change'. It may not be a quick fix to ecclesial unity, but the core commitments of receptive ecumenism enable churches to journey through repentance, hope, and on to healing.

As well as pointing to its established features, this book has extended the conceptual and constructive work on receptive ecumenism by outlining ways in which it witnesses to biblical and philosophical imagination. To this end, Chapter 1 established three threads woven through Scripture which align with the commitments of receptive ecumenism. The first thread resonates with Christ's prayer in John 17, which has become the 'go-to passage' for those who want to invoke Christian unity, and as such is well-known. This prayer reaches into the heart of receptive ecumenism, not as a prayer for Christians to get along better for the sake of evangelism, but for the mystical unity of believers with God and with one another, a unity that celebrates the rich spread of gifts across the churches.

The second thread points to the belief that God has spoken through the prophets and continues to speak today, and that one of the ways God speaks is through the Spirit, who calls the churches to repentance. This is summed up in the Spirit's cry to the churches in Revelation: 'Let the one who has an ear hear what the Spirit says to the churches.' It is not always easy to pause and listen to the Spirit. As we have seen throughout the book, it takes courage and humility for a church to recognize its own weaknesses, but greater wholeness awaits those churches who dare to hear the Spirit's call to repentance.

Lastly, receptive ecumenism celebrates that God lavishes gifts on the churches, diverse gifts that are for the good of the church and for the good of the world. All involved, whether giving or receiving gifts, are brought closer to God and one another through reciprocity. Christ by his own self-definition is gift and encourages his followers to ask God for good gifts, which requires faith. When churches discern which of God's gifts to receive from another, they trust that they will not receive a stone when asking for bread (Matt. 7.7–11).

As well as engaging constructively with receptive ecumenism, this book contributes to ongoing work by establishing some considerations for those practising, or intending to practise, receptive ecumenism. Drawing on the focus groups and research conversations, important learning emerges which helps with smoothing the potentially rocky path of receptive ecumenism. This learning takes the form of three intermingling themes: people, power, and prayer.

When focusing on the conceptual aspects of receptive ecumenism, it is all too easy to forget that, like any other, this way of ecumenical engagement involves actual people. Whether they are academic theologians participating in a formal ecumenical dialogue or churchgoers gathering in someone's front room, receptive ecumenism entails people meeting together across difference, each bringing their own unique set of biases and preferences. In Chapters 2 and 3 I drew readers' attention to how the research on women's experiences of working in churches shines a new light on how some participants in receptive ecumenism prefer to focus only on the positive aspects of their church's life while experiencing difficulty in naming weaknesses in their church. For others, directing attention to gifts is not always easy, especially if they have experienced rejection or abuse. Gathering the faithful to discuss the weaknesses, sins, dysfunctions, or the gifts in their churches elicits very different responses; and even when churches engage in formal dialogues and release reports that speak on behalf of a church, these formal processes still consist of people working together, each with their own bias. Self-awareness and self-management help when journeying according to the way of receptive ecumenism. With this in mind, it would be beneficial to incorporate a time of reflection at the beginning of each gathering for receptive ecumenism. This would create space for participants to reflect on their own biases, especially with respect to whether they prefer to focus on the strengths or the weaknesses of their church. Added to this, whether we speak of 'power dynamics', 'power games' or 'powers that be', those involved in the receptive journey enter into relationships of power. When churches come together to practise receptive ecumenism, an explicit recognition of these factors demonstrates care for the participants, also enabling productive conversation and learning.

Along with considerations of people and power, this research emphasizes the place of prayer in receptive ecumenism. Through prayer, we locate ourselves and our stories in God, and we are reminded that this vision of unity is God's. As Nicola Slee puts it, 'In the end, it is God who is at work praying in us, and God is faithful to God's own loving purposes.'[1] Through prayer, those seeking to give and receive gifts recognize God as the one who gives good gifts; as one participant said, 'Prayer together affirms that it is the Spirit whom we trust to lead us forward into unity. This is Christ's church, not ours.' Nearly every piece of feedback I received from women mentioned the importance and place of prayer: women spoke of the 'beauty of praying with those from quite different churches' or 'enjoying the poetry of liturgy' which they would not normally encounter, whereas others valued the 'opportunity to pray extemporarily for the very first time'. Over half of the participants observed 'the importance of placing potentially difficult conversations into God's hands' and everyone agreed that the receptive journey 'needs to be drenched in prayer'.

For the good of the church

When women engage with one another through receptive ecumenism, we cannot rightly say 'women are flourishing in X church, but not in Y church'. Even when working for the same church, women testify to different experiences. Some say that 'X' church is 'great to work in as a woman', while others experience their work in the same church as 'truly abysmal'. In sum, women's experiences of working in churches in England are as diverse as the women themselves. As one Catholic participant noted:

> I do believe that women bring something distinctive to the table, although what that is would be hard to pin down, I think. For example, from those of us who met to have a go at receptive ecumenism, not all are married, or in partnerships, or mothers. Our skin is not the same colour and we identify in very different ways. Some of us like to chatter and others prefer to listen. What was very evident to me, and this I can say resolutely, is that the church, not to mention much of the Christian theological tradition, is all the poorer for squeezing us into little boxes and then pressing down on the lids.

I hope and pray for the time when women are no longer construed as the principal stumbling blocks to Christian unity, and for the recognition of the role women play as a vital stepping stone to a more flourishing ecumenical conversation. I hope for a time when women who work in the church no longer receive comments on the size and shape of their legs, on how they raise their children, or on how they might choose to clothe themselves. I hope for a time when women of colour do not bear the additional burden of racist abuse. And I hope for a time when women's vocations and voices are received as gifts intended by God for the good of the church.

Note

1 Nicola Slee, *Fragments for Fractured Times: What Feminist Practical Theology Brings to the Table* (London: SCM Press, 2020), p. 45.

Appendix 1

Sample models

If you would like to gather people to explore receptive ecumenism either as an online group or in your local area, the following pages provide suggestions and ideas on how to proceed. The models are aimed at participants with no prior experience of receptive ecumenism. These sessions have been used with women-only groups but could be adapted to incorporate greater diversity. Adapt them to suit your own context and areas of interest, encouraging attendance from diverse traditions to promote learning and fruitful conversations.

Included below:

- Model 1 is based on the focus group research and could run as a single session for 4–6 hours
- Model 2 runs over three sessions, each session lasting 1.5–2 hours
- Sample description of receptive ecumenism
- Facilitator's notes

Model 1: 'Receiving from the other': introducing receptive ecumenism

This model was adapted from the focus groups that met at different locations across England. For online gatherings or for those who are unable to meet for this length of time, I suggest splitting the session across two meetings.

Participants: 4–10 (break into smaller groups, if you have more than ten participants)

Time: approx. 4–6 hours

Suggested themes: work, mission, prayer, liturgy, or any suitable theme

Outline

The following times are approximations and can be lengthened/shortened to suit:

- Welcome and refreshments (30 mins)
- Introduction to the theme and to receptive ecumenism (15 mins)
- Prayer and Bible reading (15 mins)
- Group discussion (70 mins)
- Lunch (30 mins)
- Jotting down gifts and wounds (30 mins)
- Feedback and group discussion (35 mins)
- Prayer and farewell (15 mins)

Resources

- A venue (with disabled access) or online (with adjustments)
- Facilitator(s)
- Seats for participants
- Bibles
- Bowl of water
- Refreshments
- Bring your own lunch
- Flip chart or equivalent with paper
- Markers/felt-tip pens
- Sticky notes or equivalent

Welcome and refreshments (30 mins)

- Begin by including time for refreshments – always. If people do not know one another, this provides an opportunity for them to chat and relax. Never underestimate the reassurance offered by a cup of tea, especially in England! If you are holding this online, you might want to shorten the time – but do encourage everyone to bring their drinks.

Introduction to the theme and to receptive ecumenism (15 mins)

- Introduce receptive ecumenism (for help on how to do this, see the section following Model 2 entitled 'Introducing receptive ecumenism').
- Explain that you hope each person will feel safe and able to share what they think.
- Agree on confidentiality.
- Note that the participants are from different traditions and encourage everyone to be respectful of the others.

Prayer and Bible reading (15 mins)

- You might keep a few minutes' silence for people to offer themselves to God. Invite the Holy Spirit to lead the gathering. Bear in mind that people pray differently (even within the same church).
- One option is to have a bowl of water visible as a reminder of one common baptism amid difference.
- Ask someone prior to the gathering to read John 17.20–26, Jesus's last prayer for his friends, 'that they may be one':

  I ask not only on behalf of these, but also on behalf of those who will believe in me through their word, that they may all be one. As you, Father, are in me and I am in you, may they also be in us so that the world may believe that you have sent me. The glory that you have given me I have given them, so that they may be one, as we are one, I in them and you in me, that they may become completely one, so that the world may know that you have sent me and have loved them even as you have loved me. Father, I desire that those also, whom you have given me, may be with me where I am, to see my glory, which you have given me because you loved me before the foundation of the world. Righteous Father, the world does not know you, but I know you; and these know that you have sent me. I made your name known to them, and I will make it known, so that the love with which you have loved me may be in them, and I in them.

Group discussion (70 mins)

- Use this time for the participants to introduce themselves to one another and invite them to share some of the wounds and gifts of their traditions according to the theme (having explained beforehand that you will do this). For example, if the theme is work, the participants might like to think about how their church encourages them in different kinds of work, or about the gifts and/or wounds they have experienced while working for their churches.
- Be sure to allow time for each person to speak for a maximum of 5–7 minutes – or longer, depending on the size of your group.
- Invite everyone to respond to what they've heard and to explore what their churches might learn and receive from the others.

Lunch (30 mins)

- Break together for lunch and encourage the conversation to continue. Let people know that after lunch you are going to ask them to write a summary of wounds and gifts on sticky notes (if you want to be creative you could accomplish this task in all kinds of ways).

Jotting down gifts and wounds (30 mins)

- Invite the participants to jot down on sticky notes:
  (a) wounds according to their experiences of the theme
  (b) gifts in their own church, according to their experiences of the theme
  (c) gifts in another's church on the basis of the conversations earlier that day

If this session needs to be split into two, the group could gather their responses and return to discuss them at a later date.

Feedback and group discussion (35 mins)

- The facilitator(s) enable a conversation among the participants regarding what they have written down on the sticky notes. Are there any surprises? Are there any differences? Any similarities? Points of interest? What might the group learn/receive? Any prominent gifts or wounds?

Prayer and farewell (15 mins)

- Give the participants the opportunity to spend some time quietly with God.
- Encourage them to ask God to show them how they might continue to receive gifts from those in different churches.
- Play some background music.

Conclude with prayer

You could invite participants to pray for one another or together as a group, or simply close with the following prayer:

> Loving God, Father, Son and Holy Spirit,
> we ask that you would help us to allow your Holy Spirit to work in us and through us.
> Grant us a spirit of generosity to reach out to you and one another in trust.
> Give to us, we pray, the humility to accept that our church is broken.
> Give to us, we pray, the discernment to recognize where we may learn from others.
> Give to us, we pray, the gift of hospitality so that we may receive gifts from others.
> Thank you, gracious God, for all your gifts to us.
> Amen.

Model 2: 'Receiving from the other': being inspired by Scripture

Participants: 3–8
Time: approx. 2 hours per session – any time of day
Number of gatherings: 3

Model 2 works well as a three-week Advent course, particularly if people from different churches want to journey together towards Christmas. It is aimed at small groups, but if there were larger numbers of participants it would work to begin and end each session as a large group, breaking off into smaller groups for discussion time. If this gathering meets through an online platform, such as Zoom, breakout rooms could be arranged prior to meeting.

Outline

- Welcome and refreshments (15 mins)
- Introduction to the theme and receptive ecumenism (10 mins)
- Prayer (5 mins)
- Read the Bible passage for the session (5 mins)
- Time to share (60 mins)
- Time to reflect (15 mins)
- Prayer and farewell (10 mins)

Resources

If the gathering is online, only some of these resources will be required.

- Facilitator(s)
- A venue (with disabled access): online, a church room, someone's home
- Seats for participants
- Refreshments
- Bibles

Welcome and refreshments (15 mins)

- Following Model 1, begin by offering refreshments – always. If people do not know one another, this provides an opportunity for them to chat and relax. Never underestimate the reassurance offered by a cup of tea, especially in England! Even if you are meeting online, include time for this and invite people to bring their own drinks and snacks.

Introduction to the theme and to receptive ecumenism
(10 mins)

- The facilitator(s), or someone who has been invited earlier, should lead this section.
- Introduce receptive ecumenism (for help on how to do this, see the section following Model 2 entitled 'Introducing receptive ecumenism').
- Say that you hope each person will be able to speak openly.
- Encourage confidentiality.
- Note that the participants are from different traditions and encourage everyone to be respectful of the others.

Prayer (5 mins)

- You might keep a few minutes' silence for people to offer themselves to God.
- Invite the Holy Spirit to lead the gathering.
- Be aware that people pray differently even within the same church.

Read the Bible passage for the session followed by
discussion questions (5 mins)

Time to share (60 mins)

- Ask two people in advance to read the passage(s) – not everyone is comfortable with being put on the spot.
- Listen to the passage twice – it can be helpful to hear different voices reading.
- Allow silence between each reading.

Week 1: Jesus's last prayer for his friends, 'that they may be one'

John 17.20–26

I ask not only on behalf of these, but also on behalf of those who will believe in me through their word, that they may all be one. As you, Father, are in me and I am in you, may they also be in us so that the world may believe that you have sent me. The glory that you have given me I have given them, so that they may be one, as we are one, I in them and you in me, that they may become completely one, so that the world may know that you have sent me and have loved them even as you have loved me. Father, I desire that those also, whom you have given me, may be with me where I am, to see my glory, which you have given me because you loved me before the foundation of the world. Righteous Father, the world does not know you, but I know you; and these know that you have sent me. I made your name known to them, and I will make it known, so that the love with which you have loved me may be in them, and I in them.

Discussion questions

- How has Jesus made himself known to you?
- You might like to give thanks for the people in your life through whom you have come closer to God. Who are these?
- What do you feel about unity, and how do you see your own role regarding the unity of your local church and churches more widely?

Week 2: The Spirit's call for churches to transform

Revelation 2.7, 11, 29

Let anyone who has an ear listen to what the Spirit is saying to the churches.

2 Corinthians 3.17–18

Now the Lord is the Spirit, and where the Spirit of the Lord is, there is freedom. And all of us, with unveiled faces, seeing the glory of the Lord as though reflected in a mirror, are being transformed into the same image from one degree of glory to another; for this comes from the Lord, the Spirit.

Discussion questions

- In what areas do you think the Spirit might be calling for your church to be transformed?
- How do you feel about change?
- How might the Spirit be calling you to be part of the work of transformation?

Week 3: God the giver of good gifts

Matthew 7.7–11
Ask, and it will be given to you; search, and you will find; knock, and the door will be opened for you. For everyone who asks receives, and everyone who searches finds, and for everyone who knocks, the door will be opened. Is there anyone among you who, if your child asks for bread, will give a stone? Or if the child asks for a fish, will give a snake? If you then, who are evil, know how to give good gifts to your children, how much more will your Father in heaven give good things to those who ask him!

James 1.17
Every generous act of giving, with every perfect gift, is from above, coming down from the Father of lights, with whom there is no variation or shadow due to change.

Discussion questions

- What gifts do you see in other churches that you would like your church to receive?
- What gifts has God given to you, through which you might bless your church?
- What gift(s) has God given to your church?
- Could these gifts be shared with others?

Time to reflect (15 mins)

- The facilitator(s) will offer some gathering thoughts.
- Give people the opportunity to spend some time quietly with God.
- Encourage them to ask God to show them how they might continue to receive gifts from different churches.
- Depending on your context, you could play some background music to close.

Prayer and farewell (10 mins)

Conclude with this, or some other, suitable prayer:

> Loving God, Father, Son and Holy Spirit,
> we ask that you would help us to allow your Holy Spirit to work in us and through us.
> Grant us a spirit of generosity to reach out to you and one another in trust.
> Give to us, we pray, the humility to accept that our church is broken.
> Give to us, we pray, the discernment to recognize where we may learn from others.
> Give to us, we pray, the gift of hospitality so that we may receive gifts from others.
> Thank you, gracious God, for all your gifts to us.
> Amen.

Introducing receptive ecumenism

The following section includes different ways of introducing people to receptive ecumenism.

Ask: 'What do we need to learn from another tradition to help us address difficulties in our own?'

APPENDIX I

Receptive ecumenism as an English afternoon tea

One way of thinking about receptive ecumenism is to imagine an English afternoon tea. This tradition involves the hosts bringing out the finest bone china, covered with delicate sandwiches, scones, and a selection of sweet delights (you could show a picture of this). On these occasions, the convention is to use only the very best china and crockery, preferably a matching set. If the host owns broken or chipped cups, then these must be kept hidden at the back of a cupboard, well out of the sight of any guests (you might want to show a picture of some chipped crockery). When churches come together ecumenically it can be a little like an English afternoon tea in which we share only the best of ourselves. We are so often ready to share our gifts with other churches and to explain to them how to 'do church properly' (if only everyone else could be like us!). Meanwhile, we keep hidden any aspects of church life that are not fully functioning. Just like those old, chipped cups in the back of the cupboard, when we meet together ecumenically our dysfunctions, sins, or even simply areas of weakness are kept firmly out of sight. Doubtless, every church has within its possession a cupboard with some old, chipped crockery hidden at the back which would benefit from being sifted through. In light of this, receptive ecumenism calls for churches to change their typical way of engaging, since churches are invited to lay out broken and chipped crockery for the other(s) to examine. With its brokenness in sight, one tradition asks another whether God has given to them any gifts which could help heal the brokenness.

Receptive ecumenism as wounded hands receiving healing gifts

Another helpful image is one of a church holding out its hands to receive a gift from another. The core feature of these open hands is that they bear wounds. These wounds, weaknesses or sins may take a number of forms. They might be found in

209

the theology and doctrines of a church, or churches might be struggling with aspects of organization, leadership, culture, or mission and evangelism. Following the way of receptive ecumenism, a church will need to examine itself and ask the Holy Spirit to shine a light on the wounds, sins or dysfunctions in its doctrines and practices. Having done this, and recognizing that it is not yet imaging Christ as fully as it might, each church is called to repent and reach out to others for healing gifts.

Additional resources

A short introductory video introducing receptive ecumenism is available on the Durham University website: https://vimeopro. com/user50612072/receptivity/video/265761120.

Facilitator's job description

- Depending on resources and context, this could be one or two people.
- Encourage people to be respectful of each other's traditions, especially where they might differ radically.
- Think about how to help everyone speak and how you are going to discourage anyone from dominating discussions, if this arises.
- Be sensitive when wounds and challenges are shared, however small they appear to be.
- Encourage a focus on gifts to be received – this will guard against the session becoming overshadowed by challenges, or by moaning about church.
- Remember that some people lean towards focusing on gifts and others towards wounds – aim to facilitate a way through these preferences. Recall that a church is neither wholly bad nor wholly good.
- Keep to time.
- Be kind.
- Listen well and encourage others to do the same.

Appendix 2

Participants' roles

The participants worked in both paid and unpaid roles: academic theologian; catechetical officer; children's worker; choir leader; deacon; eucharistic minister; ecumenical officer; freelance theologian; Holy Orders; hospital lay chaplain; hospitality co-ordinator; lay chaplain; lay minister; lay reader; lead pastor; ordained minister; parish assistant; pastoral worker; prayer representative; presbyter; priest; prison chaplain; school chaplain; social justice worker; theological educator; and youth worker. I have excluded six roles because the participants requested that these remain confidential.

The jargon of receptive ecumenism

When I asked the women what they thought of the phrase 'receptive ecumenism', they responded with comments such as: 'it's jargon, get rid of it'; 'it's unintelligible'; 'I have no idea what it means'; and 'I can't say it, let alone describe it to others'. Only 15 per cent of the participants thought that receptive ecumenism should remain as the principal descriptor for this way of ecumenical engagement. Towards the close of each session, I invited the women to suggest an alternative description, but all agreed that it was difficult to summarize the group's journey in a pithy phrase; so 'receptive ecumenism' remains in use at grass roots as well as in academia, where the phrase is common parlance in ecumenical studies.

FOR THE GOOD OF THE CHURCH

Listening to and with the women's voices

In order that the women's voices come to the fore as much as possible, I employed three phases of listening. First, the topics began to emerge through participant observation in focus groups and interviews; I made notes when matters arose more than once, or when women dwelt upon a particular issue. Second, I listened to recordings of the sessions, read through the transcripts, and tested findings against the notes made during the fieldwork; this practice identified the same themes with further areas emerging. Third, I met with selected participants who read an initial report on the themes. They confirmed that the themes resonated with their experience of the groups; at the same time, they suggested further areas for reflection.

Bibliography

Adams, Nicholas, 'Long-Term Disagreement: Philosophical Models in Scriptural Reasoning and Receptive Ecumenism', *Modern Theology* 29.4 (2013), pp. 154–71.

Aquinas, Thomas, *Summa contra gentiles*: Book 4, translated by Charles J. O'Neil (Notre Dame, IN: University of Notre Dame Press, 1975).

____, *Summa theologiae*, 5 vols (Ottowa: impensis Studii generalis OP, 1941–5).

____, *Summa Theologica*, translated by the Fathers of the English Dominican Province (New York: Benzinger, 1947).

Arterbury, Andrew, *Entertaining Angels* (Sheffield: Sheffield Phoenix Press, 2005).

Avis, Paul, 'Bishops in Communion? The Unity of the Episcopate, the Unity of the Diocese and the Unity of the Church', *Ecclesiology* 13.3 (2017), pp. 299–323.

____, 'Ecclesiology and Ethnography: An Unresolved Relationship', *Ecclesiology* 14.3 (2018), pp. 322–37.

Baptist Union of Great Britain, *Women in Ministry: A Reader Exploring the Story of Women in Leadership and Ministry within the Baptist Union of Great Britain* (Didcot: Baptist Union of Great Britain, 2011).

Barclay, John, *Paul and the Gift* (Grand Rapids, MI: Eerdmans, 2017).

Bauckham, Richard, *The Climax of Prophecy: Studies on the Book of Revelation* (Edinburgh: T&T Clark, 1993).

Beattie, Tina, *New Catholic Feminism: Theology and Theory* (New York: Routledge, 2006).

Beck, Richard, *Unclean: Meditations on Purity, Hospitality and Mortality* (Eugene, OR: Cascade, 2011).

Beeley, Christopher A., *Gregory of Nazianzus on the Trinity and the Knowledge of God: In Your Light We Shall See Light* (Oxford: Oxford University Press, 2008).

Behr-Sigel, Elisabeth, 'Keynote' in Constance J. Tarasar and Irina Kirillova (eds), *Orthodox Women: Their Role and Participation in the Orthodox Church. Report on the Consultation of Orthodox Women, September 11–17, 1976, Agapia, Roumania* (Geneva: World Council of Churches, 1977), pp. 17–29.

_____, *The Ministry of Women in the Church*, translated by Fr Stephen Bigham (Pasadena, CA: Oakwood, 1991).

Bernardi, Jean, *Grégoire de Nazianze: Discours 1–3*. Sources chrétiennes 247 (Paris: Les Éditions du Cerf, 1978).

Bett, Henry, *The Spirit of Methodism* (London: Epworth Press, 1937).

Blount, Brian K., *Revelation: A Commentary* (Louisville, KY: Westminster John Knox Press, 2009).

Boersma, Hans, *Violence, Hospitality, and the Cross: Reappropriating the Atonement Tradition* (Grand Rapids, MI: Baker Academic, 2004).

Bonder, Gloria, *The New Information Technologies and Women: Essential Reflections* (Santiago, Chile: United Nations Publications, 2003).

Borg, Marcus J., *Conflict, Holiness and Politics in the Teachings of Jesus* (Lewiston, NY: Edwin Mellen, 1984).

Bouillard, Henri, *Conversion et grace chez S. Thomas d'Aquin* (Paris: Aubier, 1944).

Bretherton, Luke, *Hospitality as Holiness: Christian Witness Amid Moral Diversity* (New York: Routledge, 2006).

Butler, Judith, *Gender Trouble: Feminism and the Subversion of Identity*, second edition (Abingdon: Routledge Classics, 1999).

_____, *The Psychic Life of Power: Theories in Subjection* (Stanford: Stanford University Press, 1997).

Byrne, Brendan, *The Hospitality of God: A Reading of Luke's Gospel* (Collegeville, MN: Liturgical Press, 2000).

Caesario, Romanus, OP, 'The Theological Virtue of Hope (IIa IIae, qq. 17–22)' in Stephen J. Pope (ed.), *The Ethics of Aquinas* (Washington, DC: Georgetown University Press, 2002), pp. 232–43.

Cahalan, Kathleen A. and Douglas J. Schuurman (eds), *Calling in Today's World: Voices from Eight Faith Perspectives* (Grand Rapids, MI: Eerdmans, 2016).

Calvet-Sebasti, Marie-Ange, *Grégoire de Nazianze. Discours 6–12*. Sources chrétiennes 406 (Paris: Les Éditions du Cerf, 1995).

Campbell-Reed, Eileen R., 'Living Testaments: How Catholic and Baptist Women in Ministry Both Judge and Renew the Church', *Ecclesial Practices* 4.2 (2017), pp. 167–98.

Carnelley, Elizabeth, 'The Future of British Methodism: An Anglican Perspective' in Jane Craske and Clive Marsh (eds), *Methodism and the Future: Facing the Challenge* (London: Cassell, 1999), pp. 161–70.

Caro, Robert A., *The Years of Lyndon Johnson: The Passage of Power* (New York: Alfred A. Knopf, 2012).

Chilcote, Paul W. (ed.), *Her Own Story: Autobiographical Portraits of Early Methodist Women* (Nashville, TN: Kingswood Books, 2001).

Chrysostom, John, 'Homilies on the Gospel of John' in Joel Elowsky (ed.), *Ancient Christian Commentary on Scripture: John 11–21* (Downers Grove, IL: Intervarsity Press, 2007).

Church of England, *The Book of Common Prayer*, 1662 (Cambridge: Cambridge University Press, 1960).

Clutterbuck, Richard, 'Theology as Interaction: Ecumenism and the World Church' in Clive Marsh, Brian Beck, Angela Shier-Jones and Helen Waring (eds), *Unmasking Methodist Theology* (New York and London: Continuum, 2004), pp. 59–69.

Coakley, Sarah, *Powers and Submissions: Spirituality, Philosophy and Gender* (Oxford: Blackwell, 2002).

Coleman, Kate, *7 Deadly Sins of Women in Leadership: Overcome Self-Defeating Behaviour in Work and Ministry* (UK: Next Leadership, 2010).

Cox, Harvey, 'Power' in James F. Childress and John Macquarrie (eds), *The Westminster Dictionary of Christian Ethics* (Philadelphia, PA: Westminster, 1986), pp. 489–91.

Craske, Jane, 'Methodism and Feminism' in James E. Kirby and William J. Abraham (eds), *The Oxford Handbook of Methodist Studies* (Oxford: Oxford University Press, 2011), pp. 664–79.

_____, 'The Threads with which We Weave: Towards a Holy Church' in Jane Craske and Clive Marsh (eds), *Methodism and the Future: Facing the Challenge* (London: Cassell, 1999), pp. 171–86.

Crawford, A. Elaine, 'Womanist Christology and the Wesleyan Tradition', *Black Theology* 2.2 (2004), pp. 213–20.

Cuddeback, Lorraine, 'Becoming Friends: Ethics in Friendship and in Doing Theology', *Journal of Moral Theology* 6.2 (2017), pp. 158–79.

Davies, Brian, *The Thought of Thomas Aquinas* (Oxford: Clarendon Press, 1992).

Davies, Rupert, *Methodism* (London: Epworth Press, 1990).

Day, Abby, *The Religious Lives of Older Laywomen: The Final Active Anglican Generation* (Oxford: Oxford University Press, 2017).

_____, 'Understanding the Work of Women in Religion' in Nicola Slee, Fran Porter and Anne Phillips (eds), *The Faith Lives of Women and Girls: Qualitative Research Perspectives* (London: Routledge, 2013), pp. 39–50.

Dayton, Donald, 'Methodism and Pentecostalism' in James E. Kirby and William J. Abraham (eds), *The Oxford Handbook of Methodist Studies* (Oxford: Oxford University Press, 2011), pp. 172–87.

Derrida, Jacques, 'Hostipitality', *Angelaki: Journal of the Theoretical Humanities* 5.3 (2000), pp. 3–18.

Douglas, Kelly Brown, *What's Faith Got to Do with It? Black Bodies/Christian Souls* (Maryknoll, NY: Orbis Books, 2005).

Drake, Philip, 'Joining the Dots: Methodist Membership and Connectedness' in Clive Marsh, Brian Beck, Angela Shier-Jones and Helen Waring (eds), *Unmasking Methodist Theology* (New York and London: Continuum, 2004), pp. 131–41.

Dreyer, Elizabeth A., 'Spirituality as a Resource for Theology: The Holy

Spirit in Augustine' in Mark S. Burrows and Elizabeth A. Dreyer
(eds), *Minding the Spirit* (Baltimore, MD: Johns Hopkins University
Press, 2005), pp. 179–99.

Dykstra, Craig and Dorothy C. Bass, 'A Theological Understanding
of Christian Practices' in Miroslav Volf and Dorothy C.
Bass (eds), *Practicing Theology: Beliefs and Practices in Christian Life* (Grand
Rapids, MI: Eerdmans, 2002), pp. 13–32.

Elm, Susanna, *Sons of Hellenism, Fathers of the Church: Emperor
Julian, Gregory of Nazianzus, and the Vision of Rome* (Berkeley, CA:
University of California Press, 2012).

Ensign-George, Barry A., *Between Congregation and Church: Denomination and Christian Life Together* (London: Bloomsbury Publishing,
2017).

Evdokimov, Paul, *Women and the Salvation of the World: A Christian
Anthropology on the Charisms of Women*, translated by Anthony P.
Gythiel (Crestwood, NY: St Vladimir's Seminary Press, 1994).

Faith and Order Commission of the Church of England, *The Five
Guiding Principles: A Resource for Study* (London: Church House
Publishing, 2018).

Farrell, Maggie T., 'Thomas Aquinas and Friendship with God', *Irish
Theological Quarterly* 61.3–4 (1995), pp. 212–18.

Finch, Janet, '"It's Great to Have Someone to Talk To": The Ethics of
Interviewing Women – Social Researching' in Colin Bell and Helen
Roberts (eds), *Social Researching: Politics, Problems, Practice* (Lon-
don: Routledge, 1984), pp. 70–87.

FitzGerald, Kyriaki Karidoyanes, *Women Deacons in the Orthodox
Church: Called to Holiness and Ministry* (Brookline, MA: Holy
Cross Orthodox Press, 1999).

Ford, David F., *Christian Wisdom: Desiring God and Learning in Love*
(Cambridge: Cambridge University Press, 2007).

Foucault, Michel, 'The Subject and Power', *Critical Inquiry* 8.4 (1982),
pp. 777–95.

France-Williams, A. D. A., *Ghost Ship: Institutional Racism and the
Church of England* (London: SCM Press, 2020).

Francis, Anne, *Called: Women in Ministry in Ireland 2017*, www.
irishchurches.org/cmsfiles/REPORT-Women-in-Ministry-in-Ireland-
Final.pdf.

Fry, Maddie, 'Women Describe Pitfalls on Path to Priesthood', *Church
Times* (3 July 2020), www.churchtimes.co.uk/articles/2020/3-july/
news/uk/women-describe-pitfalls-on-path-to-priesthood.

Fulford, Ben, 'Gregory of Nazianzus and Biblical Interpretation' in
Christopher A. Beeley (ed.), *Re-Reading Gregory of Nazianzus* (Washington, DC: Catholic University of America Press, 2012), pp. 31–66.

Gallay, Paul and Maurice Jourjon, *Grégoire de Nazianze. Discours
27–31*. Sources chrétiennes 250 (Paris: Les Éditions du Cerf, 1978).

Gehlin, Sara, 'Asymmetry and Mutuality: Feminist Approaches to Receptive Ecumenism', *Studia Theologica: Nordic Journal of Theology* (2020), 197–216.

_____, 'Receptive Ecumenism: A Pedagogical Process' in Vicky Balabanski and Geraldine Hawkes (eds), *Receptive Ecumenism: Listening, Learning and Loving in the Way of Christ. A Forum for Theology in the World*, 5.2 (Adelaide: ATF Press, 2018), pp. 111–22.

Giddens, Anthony, *New Rules of Sociological Method: A Positive Critique of Interpretative Sociologies*, second edition (Stanford, CA: Stanford University Press, 1993).

Gilbert, Peter, *On God and Man: The Theological Poetry of St Gregory of Nazianzus* (Crestwood, NY: St Vladimir's Seminary Press, 2001).

Gouldbourne, Ruth, 'Baptists, Women and Ministry', *Feminist Theology* 26.1 (2017), pp. 59–68.

Gowler, David B., *Host, Guest, Enemy, and Friend: Portraits of the Pharisees in Luke and Acts* (New York: Peter Lang, 1991).

Graham, Elaine, 'Power, Knowledge and Authority in Public Theology', *International Journal of Public Theology* 1 (2007), pp. 42–62.

Gregory of Nazianzus, *Festal Orations*, translated by Nonna Verna Harrison (Crestwood, NY: St Vladimir's Seminary Press, 2008).

Gregory of Nazianzus, *On God and Christ: The Five Theological Orations and Two Letters of Cledonius*, translated by Lionel Wickham and Frederick Williams (Crestwood, NY: St Vladimir's Seminary Press, 2002).

Gregory of Nyssa, *The Lord's Prayer, The Beatitudes*, translated by Hilda C. Graef (Mahwah, NJ: Paulist Press, 1954).

Guest, Mathew, Elizabeth Olson and John Wolffe, 'Christianity: Loss of Monopoly' in Linda Woodhead and Rebecca Catto (eds), *Religion and Change in Modern Britain* (London: Routledge, 2012), pp. 57–78.

Gyarmathy-Amherd, Catherine, 'The Ordination of Women in the Roman Catholic Church' in Ian Jones and Kirsty Thorp (eds), *Women and Ordination in the Christian Churches: International Perspectives* (London: T&T Clark, 2008), pp. 40–53.

Hardy, Daniel W., 'Church' in Ed Hastings (ed.), *The Oxford Companion to Christian Thought* (Oxford: Oxford University Press, 2009), pp. 118–21.

_____, *Finding the Church: The Dynamic Truth of Anglicanism* (London: SCM Press, 2001).

_____, *God's Ways with the World: Thinking and Practising the Christian Faith* (Edinburgh: T&T Clark, 1996).

Haughey, John C., *Revisiting the Idea of Vocation: Theological Explorations* (Washington, DC: Catholic University of America Press, 2004).

Healy, Nicholas, *Church, World, and the Christian Life: Practical–Prophetic Ecclesiology* (Cambridge: Cambridge University Press, 2000).

Hilary of Poitiers, *The Trinity*, translated by Stephen McKenna (Washington, DC: Catholic University of America Press, 2002).

hooks, bell, *ain't I a woman: black women and feminism*, second edition (New York and London: Routledge, 2015).

Hopko, Thomas (ed.), *Women and the Priesthood* (Crestwood, NY: St Vladimir's Seminary Press, 1983).

Jackson, Sue, *Differently Academic? Developing Lifelong Learning for Women in Higher Education* (UK: Springer Publications, 2004).

Jantzen, Grace M., *Becoming Divine: Towards a Feminist Philosophy of Religion* (Manchester: University of Manchester Press, 1998).

Jennings, Willie James, *The Christian Imagination: Theology and the Origins of Race* (New Haven, CT: Yale University Press, 2010).

John Paul II, *Man and Woman He Created Them: A Theology of the Body* (Boston, MA: Pauline Books & Media, 1997).

Johnson, Elizabeth A., *Friends of God and Prophets: A Feminist Theological Reading of the Communion of Saints* (New York: Continuum, 1998).

Jones, Margaret, 'Methodism and Women' in William Gibson, Peter Forsaith and Martin Wellings (eds), *The Ashgate Research Companion to World Methodism* (Surrey: Ashgate), pp. 157–75.

Kasper, Walter, *That They May All Be One: The Call to Unity Today* (New York: Bloomsbury, 2004).

Keller, Catherine, 'Folding Power', paper presented at the Yale Center for Faith and Culture consultation on Good Power – Divine and Human (October 2007).

Kilby, Karen, 'Perichoresis and Projection: Problems with Social Doctrines of the Trinity', *New Blackfriars* 81.956 (2000), pp. 432–45.

_____, 'Second Sex?', *The Tablet* (9 November 2013), pp. 14–17.

_____, 'The Seductions of Kenosis' in Karen Kilby and Rachel Davies (eds), *Suffering and the Christian Life* (London: T&T Clark, 2019), pp. 163–74.

Klapisch-Zuber, Christianne (ed.), *A History of Women in the West: Silences of the Middle Ages* 2 (Cambridge, MA: Belknap Press, 1994).

Knight, Henry H., III, *Anticipating Heaven Below: Optimism of Grace from Wesley to the Pentecostals* (Eugene, OR: Cascade, 2014).

Kobia, Samuel, 'Ecumenism in the 21st Century', *The Ecumenical Review* 70.1 (2018), pp. 21–9.

Koenig, John, *New Testament Hospitality: Partnership with Strangers as Promise and Mission* (Philadelphia, PA: Fortress Press, 1985).

Kosman, L. A., 'Aristotle's Definition of Motion', *Phronesis* 14 (1969), pp. 40–62.

LeClerc, Diane, *Singleness of Heart: Gender, Sin, and Holiness in Historical Perspective* (Lanham, MD and London: Scarecrow Press, 2001).

Lévinas, Emmanuel, 'Responsibility for the Other' in *Ethics and*

Infinity, translated by Richard Cohen (Pittsburgh, PA: Duquesne University Press, 1985).

Lonergan, Bernard J. F., *Grace and Freedom: Operative Grace in the Thought of St Thomas Aquinas*, edited by James Patout Burns (London: Darton, Longman & Todd, 1971).

Lukes, Steven (ed.), *Power* (New York: Red Globe Press, 2005).

MacIntyre, Alasdair, *After Virtue* (London: Duckworth, 1985).

Malan, Gert J., 'Does John 17:11b, 21–23 Refer to Church Unity?', *Theological Studies* 67.1 (2011), pp. 1–10.

Marsh, Clive, 'Appealing to "Experience": What does it Mean?' in Clive Marsh, Brian Beck, Angela Shier-Jones and Helen Waring (eds), *Unmasking Methodist Theology* (New York and London: Continuum, 2004), pp. 118–30.

Martin, John Hilary, 'The Injustice of Not Ordaining Women: A Problem for Medieval Theologians', *Theological Studies* 48 (1987), pp. 303–16.

Mauss, Marcel, *The Gift: The Form and Reason for Exchange in Archaic Societies*, translated by W. D. Halls (London: Routledge, 2007).

McBrien, Richard P. (ed.), *The HarperCollins Encyclopedia of Catholicism* (San Francisco, CA: Harper, 1995).

McCarthy Brown, Karen, 'Writing About "the Other" Revisited' in James V. Spickard, J. Shawn Landres and Meredith B. McGuire (eds), *Personal Knowledge and Beyond: Reshaping the Ethnography of Religion* (New York and London: New York University Press, 2002), pp. 130–3.

McCauley, Leo P. (trans.), *Gregory Nazianzen and Saint Ambrose: Funeral Orations* (Washington, DC: Catholic University of America Press, 1953).

McEwan, Dorothy (ed.), *Women Experiencing Church: A Documentation of Alienation* (Hereford, UK: Fowler Wright Books, 1991).

McGuckin, John A., *St Gregory of Nazianzus: An Intellectual Biography* (Crestwood, NY: St Vladimir's Seminary Press, 2001).

Mercedes, Anna, *Power for Feminism and Christ's Self-Giving* (London: T&T Clark, 2011).

Merikoski, Paula, 'Hospitality, Reciprocity, and Power Relations in the Home Accommodation of Asylum Seekers in Finland' in Synnøve Bendixsen and Trygve Wyller (eds), *Contested Hospitalities in a Time of Migration* (New York: Routledge, 2019), pp. 113–28.

Methodist Church of Great Britain, *The Methodist Worship Book* (Peterborough: Methodist Publishing House, 1999).

Migne, Jacques-Paul, *Patrologia cursus completus, series Graeca*, Vols 35–38 (Paris, 1857–62).

Milbank, John, 'The Gift of Ruling: Secularization and Political Authority', *New Blackfriars* 85 (March 2004), pp. 212–38.

Misch, Georg, *A History of Autobiography in Antiquity* (London: Routledge, 1950).

Moreschini, Claudio, *Grégoire de Nazianze. Discours 32–37*. Sources chrétiennes 318 (Paris: Les Éditions du Cerf, 1985).

——, *Grégoire de Nazianze: Discours 38–41*. Sources chrétiennes 358 (Paris: Les Éditions du Cerf, 1990).

Moreschini, Claudio and Donald Sykes, *Gregory of Nazianzus: Poemata Arcana* (Oxford: Clarendon Press, 1997).

Moschella, Mary Clark, *Ethnography as a Pastoral Practice: An Introduction* (Cleveland, OH: Pilgrim Press, 2008).

Mossay, Justin, *Grégoire de Nazianze. Discours 24–26*. Sources chrétiennes 284 (Paris: Les Éditions du Cerf, 1981).

Murray, Paul D., 'Discerning the Call of the Spirit to Theological–Ecclesial Renewal: Notes on Being Reasonable and Responsible in Receptive Ecumenical Learning' in Virginia Miller, David Moxon and Stephen Pickard (eds), *Leaning into the Spirit: Ecumenical Perspectives on Discernment and Decision-making in the Church* (Cham, Switzerland: Palgrave Macmillan, 2019), pp. 217–34.

——, 'Families of Receptive Theological Learning: Scriptural Reasoning, Comparative Theology, and Receptive Ecumenism', *Modern Theology* 29.4 (2013), pp. 76–92.

——, 'Formal Ecumenism, Receptive Ecumenism, and the Diverse Local Churches of the Global Catholic Communion' in William T. Cavanaugh (ed.), *Gathered in My Name: Ecumenism in the World Church* (Eugene, OR: Wipf and Stock, 2020), pp. 155–73.

——, 'In Search of a Way' in Geoffrey Wainwright and Paul McPartlan (eds), *The Oxford Handbook of Ecumenical Studies* (2017), pp. 1–18.

——, 'Introducing Receptive Ecumenism', *The Ecumenist* 51.2 (2014), pp. 1–7.

——, *Reason, Truth and Theology in Pragmatist Perspective* (Leuven: Peeters, 2004).

——, 'Receptive Ecumenism and Catholic Learning – Establishing the Agenda' in Paul D. Murray (ed.), *Receptive Ecumenism and the Call to Catholic Learning: Exploring a Way for Contemporary Ecumenism* (Oxford: Oxford University Press, 2008), pp. 5–25.

——, 'Receptive Ecumenism and Ecclesial Learning: Receiving Gifts for Our Needs', *Louvain Studies* 33 (2008), pp. 30–45.

—— (ed.), *Receptive Ecumenism and the Call to Catholic Learning: Exploring a Way for Contemporary Ecumenism* (Oxford: Oxford University Press, 2008).

——, 'Searching the Living Truth of the Church in Practice: On the Transformative Task of Systematic Ecclesiology', *Modern Theology* 29.4 (2013), pp. 251–81.

Murray, Paul D. and Andrea L. Murray, 'The Roots, Range and Reach of Receptive Ecumenism' in Clive Barrett (ed.), *Unity in Process: Reflections on Ecumenism* (London: Darton, Longman and Todd, 2012), pp. 79–94.

Newman, Elizabeth, *Untamed Hospitality: Welcoming God and Other Strangers* (Grand Rapids, MI: Brazos Press, 2007).

Neyrey, Jerome H., 'The Social World of Luke-Acts' in Jerome H. Neyrey (ed.), *The Social World of Luke-Acts* (Peabody, MA: Hendrickson Publishers, 1992), pp. 361–88.

Nouwen, Henri, *Reaching Out: The Three Movements of the Spiritual Life* (London: Collins, 1976).

____, *The Wounded Healer: Ministry in Contemporary Society* (New York: Doubleday, 1979).

Nussberger, Danielle, 'Catholic Feminist Theology' in Lewis Ayres and Medi Volpe (eds), *The Oxford Handbook of Catholic Theology* (Oxford: Oxford University Press, 2019).

Oduyoye, Mercy, *Who Will Roll the Stone Away? The Ecumenical Decade of the Churches in Solidarity with Women* (Genève: WCC Publications, 1991).

O'Gara, Margaret, 'Ecumenical Dialogue: The Next Generation' in Margaret O'Gara and Michael Vertin (eds), *No Turning Back: The Future of Ecumenism* (Collegeville, MN: Liturgical Press, 2014), pp. 206–31.

____, *The Ecumenical Gift Exchange* (Collegeville, MN: Liturgical Press, 1998).

Oldersma, Jantine and Kathy Davis, 'Introduction' in Kathy Davis, Monique Leijenaar and Jantine Oldersma (eds), *The Gender of Power* (London: Sage, 1991), pp. 1–18.

Oliver, Simon, *Creation: A Guide for the Perplexed* (London: T&T Clark, 2017).

____, 'The Sweet Delight of Virtue and Grace in Aquinas's Ethics', *International Journal of Systematic Theology* 7.1 (2005), pp. 52–71.

Origen, *On First Principles*, edited and translated by John Behr (Oxford: Oxford University Press, 2017).

Osteen, Mark (ed.), *The Question of the Gift: Essays Across Disciplines* (London: Routledge, 2002).

Palmer, Phoebe, *Promise of the Father* (Boston: Degen, 1859).

Pascoe, David, 'Hospitality Grounded in Humility: A Foundation for Inter-Ecclesial Learning', paper presented at *Receptive Ecumenism and Ecclesial Learning: Learning to be Church Together*, Durham University, UK (January 2009).

Percy, Emma, 'Women, Ordination and the Church of England: An Ambiguous Welcome', *Feminist Theology* 26.1 (2017), pp. 90–100.

Percy, Martyn, *Power and the Church: Ecclesiology in an Age of Transition* (London: Cassell, 1998).

Perera, Sanjee, 'Beyond the Lych-gate; a Strategic Diagnostic of Church

Culture and Practices that Marginalise and Disenfranchise Black, Asian & Minority Ethnic People in the Church of England', https:// anglicanism.org/beyond-the-lych-gate-a-strategic-diagnostic-of-church-culture-and-practices-that-marginalise-and-disenfranchise-black-asian-minority-ethnic-people-in-the-church-of-england.

Perkins, Angela and Verena Wright (eds), *Healing Priesthood: Women's Voices Worldwide* (London: Darton, Longman and Todd, 2003).

Phan, Peter, 'Interreligious and Ecumenical Dialogue at Vatican II: Some Rethinking Required' in *Conversations on Jesuit Higher Education* 42.1 (2012), art. 5, pp. 12–17.

Pizzey, Antonia, 'On the Maturation of Receptive Ecumenism: The Connection between Receptive Ecumenism and Spiritual Ecumenism', *Pacifica* 28.2 (2015), pp. 108–25.

———, *Receptive Ecumenism and the Renewal of the Ecumenical Movement: The Path of Ecclesial Conversion* (Leiden: Brill, 2019).

———, 'The Receptive Ecumenical Spirit: The Role of the Virtues in Guiding Receptive Ecumenical Discernment and Decision-Making', paper presented at the *Fourth International Conference on Receptive Ecumenism: Discernment, Decision Making and Reception*, Canberra, Australia (November 2017), http://arts-ed.csu.edu.au/__data/assets/ pdf_file/0005/2875415/Leaning-into-the-Spirit-Conference-booklet. pdf.

Pohl, Christine, *Making Room: Recovering Hospitality as a Christian Tradition* (Grand Rapids, MI: Eerdmans, 1999).

Polaski, Sandra Hack, *Paul and the Discourse of Power* (Sheffield: Sheffield Academic Press, 1999).

Purvis, Sally, *Power of the Cross: Foundations for a Christian Feminist Ethic of Community* (Nashville, TN: Abingdon Press, 1993).

Putney, Michael, 'A Catholic Understanding of Ecumenical Dialogue' in Elizabeth Delaney, Gerard Kelly and Ormond Rush (eds), *My Ecumenical Journey* (Adelaide: ATF Theology, 2014), pp. 173–90.

Rahner, Karl, *Theological Investigations, Volume IV*, translated by Kevin Smyth (London: Darton, Longman and Todd, 1966).

Reese, Thomas J., SJ, 'Organizational Factors Inhibiting Receptive Catholic Learning' in Paul D. Murray (ed.), *Receptive Ecumenism and the Call to Catholic Learning: Exploring a Way for Contemporary Ecumenism* (Oxford: Oxford University Press, 2008), pp. 346–58.

Rescher, Nicholas, *A System of Pragmatic Idealism*, vols I–III (Princeton, NJ: Princeton University Press, 1992–4).

Reynaert, Machteld, 'A Kenotic Use of Power in Theology: Dangerous or Not?' in Stephen Bullivant, Eric Marcelo O. Genilo, Daniel Franklin Pilario and Agnes M. Brazal (eds), *Theology and Power: International Perspectives* (New York: Paulist Press, 2016), pp. 33–48.

Richard, Lucien, *Living the Hospitality of God* (New York: Paulist Press, 2000).

Richey, Russell E., 'Connection and Connectionalism' in James E. Kirby and William J. Abraham (eds), *The Oxford Handbook of Methodist Studies* (Oxford: Oxford University Press), pp. 211–28.

Rooms, Nigel, 'Missional Gift-Giving: A Practical Theology Investigation into what Happens when Churches Give Away "Free" Gifts for the Sake of Mission', *Practical Theology* 8.2 (2015), pp. 99–111.

_____, *The Faith of the English: Integrating Christ and Culture* (London: SPCK, 2011).

Ross, William D., *Aristotle's Physics* (Oxford: Oxford University Press, 1936).

Rouse, Ruth and Stephen Charles Neill (eds), *The History of the Ecumenical Movement* (London: SPCK, 1954).

Ruether, Rosemary Radford, 'Imago Dei, Christian Tradition and Feminist Hermeneutics' in Kari Elisabeth Børresen (ed.), *The Image of God and Gender Models in Judaeo-Christian Tradition* (Oslo: Solum Forag, 1991), pp. 258–81.

_____, *Sexism and God Talk* (Boston, MA: Beacon Press, 1993).

Rusch, William, 'Impressive Theological Agreement During the So-called "Ecumenical Winter"', *Ecclesiology* 6.2 (2010), pp. 201–6.

Russell, Letty M., *Just Hospitality: God's Welcome in a World of Difference* (Louisville, KY: Westminster John Knox Press, 2009).

Ryan, Gregory A., *Hermeneutics of Doctrine in a Learning Church: The Dynamics of Receptive Integrity* (Leiden and Boston: Brill, 2020).

Ryrie, Alec, 'The Reformation in Anglicanism' in Mark Chapman, Sathianathan Clarke and Martyn Percy (eds), *The Oxford Handbook of Anglican Studies* (Oxford: Oxford University Press, 2018), pp. 1–13.

Saarinen, Risto, *God and the Gift: An Ecumenical Theology of Giving* (Collegeville, MN: Liturgical Press, 2002).

Satlow, Michael L. (ed.), *The Gift in Antiquity* (UK: Wiley-Blackwell, 2013).

Sayers, Dorothy, *Letters to a Diminished Church* (United States: W. Publishing Group, 2004).

Scharen, Christian and Eileen Campbell-Reed, *Learning Pastoral Imagination: A Five-Year Report on How New Ministers Learn Practice* (New York: Auburn Studies 2016).

Schumann, Karina and Michael Ross, 'Why Women Apologize More Than Men: Gender Differences in Thresholds for Perceiving Offensive Behavior', *Psychological Science* 21.11 (2010), pp. 1649–55, https://journals.sagepub.com/doi/abs/10.1177/0956797610384150.

Schussler Fiorenza, Elisabeth, 'Editor's Introduction', *Journal of Feminist Studies in Religion* 1 (2004), p. 1.

Schwartz, Baruch J., David P. Wright, Jeffrey Stackert and Naphtali S. Meshel (eds), *Perspectives on Purity and Purification in the Bible* (London: T&T Clark International, 2008).

Schwartz, Daniel, *Aquinas on Friendship* (Oxford: Oxford University Press, 2007).

Shier-Jones, Angela, *A Work in Progress* (Peterborough: Epworth Press, 2005).

_____, 'Being Methodical: Theology Within Church Structures' in Clive Marsh, Brian Beck, Angela Shier-Jones and Helen Waring (eds), *Unmasking Methodist Theology* (New York and London: Continuum, 2004), pp. 29–40.

Slee, Nicola, 'Feminist Qualitative Research as Spiritual Practice: Reflections on the Process of Doing Qualitative Research' in Nicola Slee, Fran Porter and Anne Phillips (eds), *The Faith Lives of Women and Girls: Qualitative Research Perspectives* (London: Routledge, 2013), pp. 13–24.

_____, *Fragments for Fractured Times: What Feminist Practical Theology Brings to the Table* (London: SCM Press, 2020).

Slee, Nicola, Fran Porter and Anne Phillips (eds), *Researching Female Faith: Qualitative Research Methods* (Abingdon: Routledge, 2018).

Spivak, Gayatri Chakravorty, *Outside in the Teaching Machine* (New York and London: Routledge, 1993).

Sterk, Andrea, *Renouncing the World Yet Leading the Church: The Monk-Bishop in Late Antiquity* (Cambridge, MA: Harvard University Press, 2004).

Stoller, Sylvia, 'Asymmetrical Genders: Phenomenological Reflections on Sexual Difference', *Hypatia* 20.2 (2005), pp. 175–82.

Storin, Bradley L., *Self-Portrait in Three Colors: Gregory of Nazianzus's Epistolary Autobiography* (Oakland, CA: University of California Press, 2019).

Stortz, Martha E., 'Naming and Reclaiming Power' in M. R. A. Kanyoro (ed.), *In Search of a Round Table: Gender, Theology and Church Leadership* (Genève: WCC Publications, 1997), pp. 71–81.

Sutherland, Arthur, *I Was a Stranger: A Christian Theology of Hospitality* (Nashville, TN: Abingdon Press, 2006).

Tanner, Kathryn, *Economy of Grace* (Minneapolis, MN: Augsburg Fortress, 2005).

_____, 'Power of Love', paper presented at the Yale Center for Faith and Culture consultation on Good Power – Divine and Human (October 2007).

Taylor, Charles, *A Secular Age* (Cambridge, MA: Harvard University Press, 2007).

Thomas, Gabrielle, 'A Call for Hospitality: Learning from a Particular Example of Women's Grass Roots Practice of Receptive Ecumenism in the UK', *Exchange* 47.4 (2018), pp. 335–50.

_____, '"Mutual Flourishing" in the Church of England: Learning Receptively from Saint Thomas Aquinas', *Ecclesiology: The Journal of Ministry, Mission and Unity* 15.2 (2019), pp. 302–21.

_____, 'On Being a Priest in Conversation with St. Gregory Nazianzen' in Gabrielle Thomas and Elena Narinskaya (eds), *Women and Ordination in the Orthodox Church: Explorations and Practice* (Eugene, OR: Cascade, 2020), pp. 187–204.

_____, 'Receptive Learning Between Churches' in Larry Miller (ed.), *Proceedings from the Global Christian Forum Gathering, April 2018, Bogotá, Colombia* (forthcoming).

_____, *The Image of God in the Theology of Gregory of Nazianzus* (Cambridge: Cambridge University Press, 2019).

Thomas, Gabrielle and Elena Narinskaya (eds), *Women and Ordination in the Orthodox Church: Explorations in Theology and Practice* (Eugene, OR: Cascade, 2020).

Tjørhom, Ola, 'The Early Stages: Pre-1910' in Geoffrey Wainwright and Paul McPartlan (eds), *The Oxford Handbook of Ecumenical Studies* (2017), pp. 1–12.

Torrell, Jean-Pierre, *Christ and Spirituality in St Thomas Aquinas* (Washington, DC: Catholic University of America Press, 2011).

Trible, Phyllis, 'Adam and Eve: Genesis 2–3 Reread' in Carol Christ and Judith Plaskow (eds), *Womanspirit Rising: A Feminist Reader in Religion* (San Francisco, CA: Harper and Row, 1979), pp. 74–83.

Trisk, Janet, 'Authority, Theology and Power' in Mark D. Chapman, Sathianathan Clarke and Martyn Percy (eds), *Oxford Handbook of Anglican Studies* (Oxford: Oxford University Press, 2015), pp. 608–19.

Van Nieuwenhove, Rik, *An Introduction to Medieval Theology* (Cambridge: Cambridge University Press, 2012).

Vinson, Martha Pollard (trans.), *St Gregory of Nazianzus: Select Orations* (Washington, DC: Catholic University of America Press, 2003).

Volf, Miroslav, *Exclusion and Embrace: A Theological Exploration of Identity, Otherness, and Reconciliation* (Nashville, TN: Abingdon Press, 2006).

_____, *Flourishing: Why We Need Religion in a Globalized World* (New Haven, CT: Yale University Press, 2016).

_____, *Work in the Spirit: Toward a Theology of Work* (Eugene, OR: Wipf and Stock, 2001).

Ward, Kate, 'Jesuit and Feminist Hospitality: Pope Francis' Virtue Response to Inequality', *Religions* 8.71 (2017).

Ward, Pete, 'Is Theology What Really Matters?' in Tone Stangeland Kaufman and Jonas Idestrom (eds), *What Really Matters: Scandinavian Perspectives on Ecclesiology and Ethnography*. Church of Sweden Research (Eugene, OR: Pickwick Publications, 2018), pp. 157–72.

Ward, Rosie, 'Doing Leadership Differently? Women and Senior Leadership in the Church of England' in Ian Jones, Kirsty Thorpe and Janet Wootton (eds), *Women and Ordination in the Christian*

Churches: International Perspectives (London: Bloomsbury, 2008), pp. 76–86.

Ware, Kallistos and Colin Davey (eds), *Anglican–Orthodox Dialogue: The Moscow Statement* (London: SPCK, 1977).

Watkins, Clare, *Disclosing Church: An Ecclesiology Learned from Conversations in Practice* (Abingdon: Routledge, 2020).

Wawrykow, Joseph, 'The Theological Virtues' in Rik Van Nieuwenhove and Joseph Wawrykow (eds), *The Theology of Thomas Aquinas* (Notre Dame, IN: University of Notre Dame Press, 2005), pp. 287–307.

Wesley, Charles, *Methodist Church: Hymns & Psalms*, No. 4 (London: Methodist Publishing House, 1983).

Wexler, Celia Viggo, *Catholic Women Confront their Church* (Lanham, MD: Rowman & Littlefield, 2016).

Williams, A. N., 'The Future of the Past: The Contemporary Significance of the Nouvelle Theologie', *International Journal of Systematic Theology* 7 (2005), pp. 347–61.

Williams, Delores S., *Sisters in the Wilderness: The Challenge of Womanist God-Talk* (New York: Orbis Books, 1993).

_____, 'Theological Integrity', *Cross Currents* 45.3 (1995), pp. 312–25.

Wilson, Sarah Hinlicky, 'Elisabeth Behr-Sigel's Trinitarian Case for the Ordination of Women' in Gabrielle Thomas and Elena Narinskaya (eds), *Women and Ordination in the Orthodox Church: Explorations in Theology and Practice* (Eugene, OR: Cascade, 2020), pp. 99–113.

_____, *Woman, Women, and the Priesthood in the Trinitarian Theology of Elisabeth Behr-Sigel* (London: Bloomsbury, 2013).

Woodhead, Linda, 'A Woman's Place', *The Tablet* (1 December 2012), p. 20.

World Council of Churches, *The Nature and Mission of the Church: A Stage on the Way to a Common Statement*. Faith and Order Paper 198 (Geneva: World Council of Churches, 2005).

Yrigoyen, Charles, Jr (ed.), *T&T Clark Companion to Methodism* (London and New York: T&T Clark, 2010).

Zahl, Simeon, 'Tradition and its "Use": The Ethics of Theological Retrieval', *Scottish Journal of Theology* 71.3 (2018), pp. 308–23.

Index of Names and Subjects

and reciprocity 27–8, 32, 47,
49, 133, 194
self-giving 191n67
vocation as gift 118–21, 132
Global Christian Forum (Bogotá,
2018) 19
God
as giver of good gifts 15, 23,
26–7, 31, 108, 116, 181, 182,
183, 194, 195, 197
divine action 149
and 'Good Shepherd' metaphor
179–80, 181, 182, 185,
see also priests, priesthood,
shepherd metaphor
and happiness 152
hospitality of 95–6, 97, 98, 101
image of 129, 131
knowledge of 122–4
participation in 149
and power 178, 179–80, 185
as Trinity 123, 127, 182, 184,
191n69
union with 23, 24–5
Gouldbourne, Ruth 170
grace 140, 147, 148–54, 156,
157, 158, 162n31, 175
auxilium 148, 149
habitual grace 148, 149
Graham, Elaine 7
Great Schism (1054) 13
Gregory of Nazianzus 2, 95–6,
101, 116, 118–19, 122–4,
126–7, 128, 129, 130–3,
135n10
Gregory of Nyssa 125

habit 154–5, 157–8
Hardy, Daniel 13
healing 3, 12, 45, 47, 59, 64, 84,
90, 91, 96, 105, 123, 126–7,
129, 130, 137n41, 140, 193,
see also priest as healer
and reconciliation 126
Healy, Nicholas 12–13, 21
Hilary of Poitiers 27–8

holiness 104–6, 191n64
Holy Spirit 12, 15, 20, 30, 64,
97, 99, 101, 104, 106, 108,
120, 123–4, 132, 135n10, 150,
157, 165, 173, 174, 176, 179,
181–2, 184, 185, 186, 190n59,
192, 194, 195
communication of 23, 25–6,
31–2, 194
divinity of 118, 123
filioque 21–2
as gift 26–7
honesty 3, 12
hooks, bell 79
hope 29, 30–1, 32, 64, 193
hospitality 6, 29, 30, 32, 58,
59, 63, 64–6, 85n8, 89–108,
109n9, 110n17, 164
as 'Christian' 96–7, 103
definition of 95–8
and 'entertaining' 96
of God 95–6, 97, 98, 101
and refreshments 65, 89, 96,
97, 98, 99, 100–1, 108
and welcoming strangers 96–7,
98
humility 26, 29, 30, 32, 64, 193,
194

identity 109n9, 132
integrity 12, 118, 124, 125, 131,
132, 133

Jantzen, Grace 3
Jesus Christ 23–4, 25, 26,
30, 31, 90, 92, 104–6, 108,
113n51, 122, 123, 127, 130,
151–2, 174, 177, 192, 193–4
as gift 26, 31, 194
incarnation 96, 127, 147, 148,
151–2, 156
John Chrysostom 24–5
Johnson, Elizabeth 97
joy 119
Judaism 25

1

Ecumenical and Interfaith
Group (EIG) 98, 103
networking 82
Nouwen, Henri 110n17, 126

Oduyoye, Mercy Amba 2,
175–6, 182
O'Gara, Margaret 12
ordination services 145, 157
organizing 11, 99
Origen of Alexandria 24

Palmer, Phoebe 181
pastors 16, 42, 118, 123
patriarchy 40, 49, 188n23
Paul the Apostle 119, 127, 152,
187n10
Percy, Emma 142, 160n16
personhood 117
Pizzey, Antonia 29, 30, 32, 98,
109n1, 112n38
planning 83
pluralism 20
pneumatology, see Holy Spirit
Pohl, Christine 30, 96–7
Pope Francis 15
Pope John Paul II 15, 85n4, 90,
92–5, 107, 109n8, 117
Pope Paul VI 15, 16, 34n21
Porvoo Declaration (1995) 16
power 6, 7, 29, 58, 59, 63, 65,
72, 74–7, 83, 84, 89, 97, 100,
102, 108, 111n27, 147, 156,
164–86, 189n48, 191n64,
191n68, 194, 195
and authority 167, 168, 169,
176, 178–9, 185
characterizations of 86n17,
165–7, 186n2
and gender 75–7, 166, 189n48
and God 178, 179–80, 185
and leadership 76–7, 167–70,
184, 191n69
and Methodist theology 165,
177–80, 184, 185, 186
pragmatism 20, 22

prayer 23–4, 30, 31, 42, 50–1,
99, 101, 104, 108, 113n51,
118, 122, 125–6, 129, 131,
133, 158, 192, 193–4, 195–6
daily offices 125, 158
World Day of Prayer 98,
111n24
preaching 63, 70–1, 83, 85n13,
91–2, 106, 107, 114, 120, 123,
167, 174, 184, 191n64
priests, priesthood 53, 69, 107,
116, 117, 119, 121, 134,
139, 140, 142, 143, 145–6,
147, 154, 157, 159, 161n21,
161n23, 176
clericalism 70, 115
as healer 116, 126–30, 133
as leader 116, 130–3
shepherd metaphor 123,
136n24, see also God and
'Good Shepherd' metaphor
as theologian 116, 121–6, 133
prophecy 25–6, 90, 108, 194
Protestant Reformation 13–14
privilege 7–8, 85n13, 97, 125
public theology 7
publishing 83
purity 104–6

racism 51–2, 64, 79–80, 81, 171,
193, 197
Rahner, Karl 182–3
reasoning 20
receptive ecumenism
afternoon tea metaphor 2–3,
8n2, 11, 44, 193, 209
conferences 17, 19, 35n28,
39–40, 90, 95, 96, 98–104,
106, 107–8, 111n23
definition of 2, 211
journey metaphor 5, 11, 29, 84,
100, 133, 193–6
models for gatherings 198–210
mosaic metaphor 12
open/wounded hands metaphor
11, 44–5, 209–10